Laura McKenzie's

Travel Guides

ROME

LAURA MCKENZIE'S TRAVEL GUIDE SERIES

HAWAII

LONDON

LOS ANGELES AND
SOUTHERN CALIFORNIA

ORLANDO

PARIS

ROME

Laura McKenzie's

Travel Guides
ROME

BORU BOOKS

Library of Congress Catalog Card Number: 95-081126

ISBN 1-887161-05-8

Published in the United States by
Boru Publishing, Inc.
12004-B Commonwealth Way
Austin, TX 78759

Distributed to the trade by
National Book Network
4720-A Boston Way
Lanham, MD 20706

Books are available in quantity for promotional use.
Write to Director of Special Sales, Boru Publishing, Inc.,
12004-B Commonwealth Way, Austin, TX 78759
for information on discounts and terms.

Manufactured in the United States of America.

Cover design by Eyetooth Design, Inc.
Cover photograph of St. Peter's Basilica by
Vladimir Pcholkin/FPG International Corp.
Interior design by Marysarah Quinn/Mark Garofalo

5 4 3 2 1

DEDICATION

To my husband who knows all the special meanings that Rome has for us and the love we share. A love that has been a great passion in our lives for eighteen years, and has done nothing but grow as the years have passed.

Laura McKenzie

DISCLAIMER

Readers are advised that prices fluctuate in the course of time, and travel information changes under the impact of the varied and volatile factors that affect industry. Although every effort has been made to ensure the correctness of the information in this book, the publisher and author do not assume, and hereby disclaim, any liability to any party for any loss or damage caused by errors, omissions, misleading information or any potential travel problem caused by information in this guide, even if such errors or omissions are a result of negligence, accident, or any other cause.

CONTENTS

Part 3: Turning In

Part 4: Taste of the Town

PART 6: OUT OF TOWN

INTRODUCTION

by Laura McKenzie

I grew up in St. Louis, traveling during every school break. Since then I've worked and traveled all over the world, experiencing all price ranges and budgets. I've traveled poor and I've traveled flush—and I've learned a lot of tricks and tips along the way.

My books are different from the others on the shelf. I strongly voice what I like and don't like. Maybe it's because I know that there's a lot to choose from out there. Maybe it's because I've made mistakes, been "taken" a few times, and learned a few good lessons from it. Or maybe it's because I've learned that no matter how much you're paying or what you're buying, you can always find a better value if you know what to look for.

I remember years ago, when I first started my home video series, a friend in the television business gave me some valuable advice. She said: "Face it. People who really travel don't want to see pretty sights and fluff—they want to know what to wear, where to go to have a good time, where to find a good restaurant, and where to stay that's a decent value. If something's overrated or not worth it, say so." So ever since, I've taken that advice. I've given my honest opinion, whether it agreed with anyone else's or not.

For years, I've been advising travelers on how to get the best value for their travel money and time through TV, radio, newsletter, and home video. But when it came to travel books, I was out there just like you, trying to find one book that had all the information I needed. When I would find a book that offered good hotel reviews, the maps were bad. If there were good food and sightseeing tips, they were hard to read. So I ended up buying three or four books just to cover the basics. It's hard to get good personal tips and honest advice on what's overrated or not worth the time.

So I decided it was time to write a travel guide book series based not only on my experience, but on what I wanted in a good travel guide! I wanted solid travel information—where to go, what to see, what to avoid, and suggested itineraries to plan my vacation day by day. I wanted each destination to feature current hotels and restaurants in all price ranges. So when I wrote my travel guides I included all of this, then I added my personal opinions. I took the same approach I've used in my home videos and TV programs: I tell you what I really think!

Since you want to know the best way to get around, I give you all the options—from walking tours to car rentals—with tips on how to save time as well as money (even ways to have fun while you're doing it). Plus, I include suggestions on where to go at night when you want to have fun. There's something for all ages, lifestyles, and tastes.

Each destination features lots of shopping and money tips—where to go, what to buy, how to pay for it, and how to get it home. Then, for those with an adventurous spirit, I also include my favorite "adventures"—what's available, and where to find it. From hot air ballooning to river rafting to tandem skydiving, you discover what's out there, and whether the equipment will be provided by the outfitter.

Many want recommendations on romantic hotels and restaurants, and tips on where to go to fall in love all over again. My suggestions and special coding system for that special evening or weekend make these options easy to find, so you can spend less time searching and more time romancing. I've identified these special places with a ❤. I've used a ✔ to mark those places that I believe stand out.

The books also have a "before you travel" section, that includes packing tips, budget planning ideas, a before-you-leave-the-house checklist, and tips on securing your home so you don't come back to a break-in.

When you ask a friend or relative about their trip, they tell you exactly what they think. That is what I've done and why my books are different. I want value—not only for the money, but for the limited amount of free time I have. So I made sure the maps and information are good and easy to read. Most important, I made sure it's the only book you're going to need. And that saves you money on your very next trip!

QUICK HISTORY OF ROME

Rome was founded more than 2,700 years ago, and it's impact on the world cannot be underestimated. Rome served as the capital of the Roman empire, and later as the capital of the Catholic empire. Many aspects of city life throughout the world have been patterned after Rome, including language, politics, and architecture.

Rome was built during the Iron Age, in the middle of the eighth century B.C. At that time it was a mere village of huts. The tribespeople of the area were shepherds, and many farming communities had been established.

Around 800 B.C., the Etruscans arrived on the eastern coast of Umbria. By 600 B.C., they had seized Rome. While in this position of power, the Etruscans introduced many art forms to the Latin tribes. Roma (an Etruscan name) became the capital of all Latium. Roma grew at a tremendous rate.

Around 600 B.C., the Gauls invaded the northern part of the Etruscan territory. In 509 B.C., the Etruscans were pushed back to their homelands when the Romans revolted and regained control, resulting in their own republic. The rest of Italy was soon to fall under the Romans' control, as did Spain, North Africa, England, and Greece. As Rome grew through its conquests, Roman allies and newly conquered peoples were granted partial or full Roman citizenship, with the stipulation that they would serve in the military. By 49 B.C., Rome had control of all the Mediterranean world. This quick expansion of the empire made democracy eventually impossible. Dictatorships took over, and Augustus became the first emperor. It was during his reign that Christians believe Jesus Christ was born. Although the empire persecuted Christians for four centuries, Christianity gained momentum, and Rome became the Christian capital. Never before had Rome been in control of so much, and yet the Romans became more dissatisfied with a government that seemed interested only in business abroad. Corruption spread, and Constantine effectively assured the death of Rome when he moved the capital to Constantinople (later Istanbul). Rome was left as nothing more than a regional capital, with few defenses against invasion.

In 395 A.D., there was a split between the eastern and western parts of the empire, leaving each side without the defense benefit it had once received from its other side. In 410 A.D., Alaric laid damage to Rome. Forty years later, Attila the Hun had his turn, followed by Gaiseric the Vandal five years later. In 476 A.D., the ravaging of the empire finally ended, leaving it in tatters.

In an effort to help calm the chaos, the popes began to assume more of the emperor's powers. In 731 A.D., Pope Gregory II declared that Rome was no longer spiritually dependent upon Constantinople. In 800 A.D., Pope Leo III crowned Charlemagne as the Holy Roman Emperor. In the meantime, Italy continued to dissolve, putting its power in the hands of feuding landowning families.

Rome experienced a decline during the Middle Ages, and then an almost miraculous rebirth in the middle of the fifteenth century. It was here that the Italian Renaissance took hold, unleashing a spirit of creativity unparalleled in history. In 1861, Rome became the official capital of this newly-unified Italy. Rome was absorbed into the new nation, erasing the borders of the papal states. As a result, relations between the pope and the government of Italy remained unstable until 1929. It was at this point that Mussolini divided the Vatican and Italy, making the Vatican politically and fiscally autonomous, although this concordat was annulled in 1984.

World War II closely linked Mussolini and his support of the fascists with the Nazis in Germany. In April 1945, Italian partisans captured Mussolini as he was fleeing to Switzerland. He was shot along with his mistress and several other loyal supporters.

Politics in Italy, and specifically Rome, have continued in this unsteady tradition. During the 1960s, Rome survived a powerful socialist campaign by Aldo Moro, who was later assassinated by terrorists. At that time, Rome was also struggling with an unprecedented number of bankruptcies that continued into the 1970s. Then terrorism raged on through the 1970s and 1980s, and in the early 1990s around 6,000 politicians and businesspeople were involved in a government graft scandal. Today, the so-called Mafia and its underground economy continue as serious rivals to the legitimate Italian government.

But for all this, you have only to look at the rich history of Rome, the architecture, culture, and the art to know that Rome will survive and prosper. It has proven itself as truly the "Eternal City."

PART 1

Before Your Trip

VISITOR INFORMATION

Planning is the key to a successful trip. That's why it's a good idea to do a little research before you travel. You might even save some money in the process. This section provides the telephone numbers of information sources you can contact prior to your trip.

Contact the Italian Government Travel Office as soon as you have decided to visit Rome and ask for information, promotions, and discount books.

ITALIAN GOVERNMENT TRAVEL OFFICES

In the U.S.

500 North Michigan Ave., Suite 1046, Chicago, IL 60611. Tel. (312) 644-0990, fax (312) 644-3019.

12400 Wilshire Blvd., Suite 550, Los Angeles, CA 90025. Tel. (310) 820-0098, fax (310) 820-6357.

630 Fifth Ave., Suite 1565, New York, NY 10111. Tel. (212) 245-4822, fax (212) 568-9249.

In Canada

One Place Ville Marie, Montréal, QB H3B 3M9. Tel. (514) 866-7667.

In the U.K.

One Princes Street, London W1R 8AY, England. Tel. (171) 408-1254.

ITALIAN CONSULATES

12400 Wilshire Blvd., Suite 300, Los Angeles, CA 90025. Tel. (310) 820-0622, fax (310) 820-0727.

2590 Webster St., San Francisco, CA 94115. Tel. (415) 931-4924, fax (415) 931-7205.

1200 Brickell Ave., Eighth Floor, Miami, FL 33131. Tel. (305) 374-6322, fax (305) 374-7945.

500 N. Michigan Ave., Suite 1850, Chicago, IL 60611. Tel. (312) 467-1550/1/2/3, fax (312) 467-1335.

630 Camp Street, New Orleans, LA 70130. Tel. (504) 524-1557, fax (504) 581-4590.

100 Boylston Street, Suite 900, Boston, MA 02116. Tel. (617) 542-0483/4, fax (617) 542-3998.

535 Griswold Street, Suite 1840, Detriot, MI 48226. Tel. (313) 963-8560, fax (313) 963-8180.

690 Park Ave., New York, NY 10021. Tel. (212) 737-9100, fax (212) 249-4945.

1026 Public Ledger Building, 100 South Sixth Street, Philadelphia, PA 19106. Tel. (215) 592-7329, fax (215) 592-9808.

1300 Post Oak Blvd., Suite 660, Houston, TX 77056. Tel. (713) 850-7520, fax (713) 850-9113.

ITALIAN EMBASSY. 1601 Fuller St. NW, Washington, DC 20009. Tel. (202) 328-5500.

OVERSEAS CITIZENS EMERGENCY CENTER

Room 4811, Washington, DC 20520 (include S.A.S.E.). Tel. (202) 647-5225, fax (202) 647-3000.

This office provides consular information sheets that have all the entry requirements, currency regulations, embassy locations, as well as the latest on the political situation, crime, security, and health risks.

MEDICAL ASSISTANCE FOR TRAVELERS

For a list of English-speaking doctors in Italy, contact the **International Association for Medical Assistance to Travelers (IAMAT).**

U.S.: 417 Center St., Lewiston, NY 14092. Tel. (716) 754-4883.

Canada: 40 Regal St., Guelph, ON N1K1B5. Tel. (519) 836-0102.

BEST TIME TO VISIT

DECIDING WHAT TIME OF YEAR TO VISIT

The peak tourist season in Rome is from mid-April to mid-September. Traveling to the Eternal City during the month of August can be a little tricky. This is when most Italians close their businesses and take off for their vacations, creating many congested highways and crowded resorts. It's a very common tradition. You may arrive to find yourself in an area where half of the shops are closed. Those that stay open will be crowded with local vacationers. At the end of March, bus loads of kids out of school pour into the city. The off-season is the best time to travel so that you can enjoy lower rates and fewer crowds of tourists. The off-season is generally from November to Easter. The shoulder months, those immediately before and after the peak seasons, offer good deals and usually good weather. The time that best combines fewer crowds and good weather is May and early June.

Climate is certainly something to consider. There are basically two climatic regions in Italy: the northern plains and Po Valley typified by Venice, and the rest of the country, typified by Rome. Rome is known for its generally temperate climate, but some seasons do see the occasional extreme. Although Italy brings to mind images of a sunny country, Rome does get a good deal of rain overall, especially from October to December.

In the spring, the weather is pleasant and not too hot.

In the fall, the weather has cooled off a little and becomes more bearable.

In the winter, the weather can get very harsh, with overcast skies for days. A raincoat with a lining is a good idea.

In the summer, the temperatures can be scorchingly hot–driving out many Italians, but attracting droves of tourists. Note that there are many facilities in Rome that do *not* have air conditioning.

Average Low/Hi Temperatures and Rain (inches) for Rome

Jan.	41°F-52°F (3.6)	**July**	68°F-87°F (0.2)
Feb.	42°F-55°F (3.2)	**Aug.**	67°F-86°F (0.7)
Mar.	45°F-59°F (2.9)	**Sept.**	62°F-79°F (3.0)
Apr.	50°F-66°F (2.2)	**Oct.**	56°F-72°F (4.0)
May	55°F-74°F (1.4)	**Nov.**	49°F-61°F (3.9)
June	63°F-82°F (0.7)	**Dec.**	44°F-55°F (2.8)

ENTRY REQUIREMENTS

PASSPORT AND VISAS

U.S. CITIZENS

When traveling to Rome as a U.S. citizen, you will need to have a U.S. passport to enter Italy. This is true even for infants. Generally, this is the only document required, although immigration officers in Italy may ask for proof of sufficient funds for your trip, or ask to see a round-trip ticket. Visitors from EC (European Community) countries and Americans are not required to have a visa, but visitors from other countries should contact the Italian Consulate, or their travel agency, for additional information. As a general rule, a passport allows a tourist to stay in Italy, without working, for up to ninety days. If you have a passport, it can be renewed by mail or in person. You will need a completed passport renewal application, form DSP-82; driver's license or photo ID; two recent, identical 2x2 inch pictures of yourself; your current passport; and a check, cash, or a money order for $65.

> **The State Department assesses a $30 rush charge for people who wait until the last minute to get a passport. That extra fee can raise the cost of a new passport or a renewal to $95. Then you have to add the cost of photo charges. The busiest months to get a passport are March, April, and May.**

If you haven't applied for a passport before, you need to apply in person at least five weeks before your planned departure. Passports can be obtained from U.S. Passport

Agencies or often from your local county courthouse, probate courts, and even some post offices. You will be required to:

- Complete a passport application, form DSP-11.
- Provide proof of your citizenship. A certificate of birth issued by your birth state's Hall of Records, or naturalization papers will work for this.
- Provide proof of identity. You will need identification that is valid and has your photo and signature on it, such as a driver's license, military ID, or student ID card.
- Provide two recent pictures of yourself. These can be black and white, or in color, but they must be identical and measure two square inches each.
- Pay a fee of $65 for a ten-year passport, or if you're under eighteen, $40 for a five-year passport. This can be paid by check, money order, or cash in exact change.

Passports are usually mailed within four weeks, but during the peak travel season, spring through the summer, it may take five weeks. Once you have a passport, you can renew it in person, or by mail. For additional information, call the **Department of State Office of Passport Services** information line, *tel. (202) 647-0518*. It is located at *1425 K St. NW, Washington, DC 20522*. There are also thirteen regional passport offices:

Boston	(617) 565-6998
Chicago	(312) 341-6020
Honolulu	(808) 522-8283
Houston	(713) 209-3153
Los Angeles	(310) 235-7070
Miami	(900) 225-5674
New Orleans	(504) 589-6728
New York	(212) 399-5290
Philadelphia	(215) 597-7480

San Francisco	(415) 744-4444
Seattle	(206) 220-7777
Stamford, CT	(203) 325-4401
Washington	(202) 647-0518

LOST PASSPORT
If your passport is lost or stolen while abroad, go immediately to the nearest American embassy or consulate, where you can start the process of getting a new passport. (This is when you will need a photocopy of your passport. You should carry a photocopy in your luggage, and leave one at home, in case a friend needs to fax you a copy.) You should also have it reported to the local police.

CANADIAN CITIZENS

Canadian citizens will also be required to have a valid passport to enter Italy for stays of up to ninety days. Passports are valid for five years and are usually mailed within two weeks of your application. Children under the age of sixteen may be included on a parent's passport if they will be traveling with the parent. However, if they will be traveling without their parents, they must have their own passport. Passports and renewals must be applied for in person. There are twenty-three regional passport offices and travel agencies that provide passport services. Applications can also be found at post offices. For additional information in French or English, call the **passport office.** *Tel. (514) 283-2153 or (800) 567-6868*.

CUSTOMS

When traveling abroad, there's one thing you can't avoid: customs. Depending on your residency, the list of acceptable items that you may take in and out of the visiting country will vary.

ITALIAN CUSTOMS

Personal tax-paid (not duty-free) items that are obviously for your own personal use, and not for sale, can be imported into Italy in any quantity. These can include such things as your bicycle and/or car.

Below is a chart indicating the items that may be taken into Italy, if your resident country is outside the European Community.

YOU CAN TAKE INTO ITALY, DUTY-FREE:

ITEM	USA/OTHER COUNTRY OUTSIDE EC
One of the following:	
Cigarettes	200 or
Cigarillos	100 or
Cigars	50 or
Tobacco	250 grams
PLUS:	
Wine	2 liters Plus
One of the following:	
Spirits *(over 22% volume)*	1 liter or
Spirits *(under 22% volume)*	2 liters or
Wine	2 liters
PLUS:	
Perfume	50 milliliters
Toilet Water	250 milliliters
Coffee	200 grams
Tea	100 grams

Exceed these limits, and you'll be taxed going into Italy and again in your home country.

If you are on medication and plan to travel to a foreign country, pack only the required amount of medication for the time abroad. If you show up at customs with an unusually large amount of medication, customs may detain you. Keep the medication in the prescribed bottle instead of a pill box.

FROM WITHIN THE EC

There is no longer any limit or customs tariff imposed on goods carried within the EC countries. As long as you have paid duty on the items, you can transport quantities of alcohol and tobacco from one EC country to another. You're allowed 800 cigarettes, 90 liters of wine, 110 liters of beer, 20 liters of alcohol less than 22% proof, and 10 liters of alcohol over 22% proof. Travelers within the European Community will continue to be eligible to make duty-free and tax-free purchases until the end of June 1999. For duty-free goods, you're allowed to carry 200 cigarettes or 50 cigars, one liter of alcohol over 22% proof or 2 liters of alcohol under 22% proof or 2 liters of wine.

RETURNING TO THE U.S.

If you have been out of the country for more than twenty-four hours and haven't made an international trip in the past thirty days, you are allowed $400 in foreign acquisitions, duty-free. This includes one carton of cigarettes (200), 100 cigars (not Cuban), and one liter of liquor or wine (if over twenty-one years). Then you pay a flat 10% duty on the next $1,000 worth of goods.

FORBIDDEN IMPORTS

U.S. regulations prohibit certain items from being brought into the United States. These include fresh fruits, vegetables, most meat products (except certain canned goods), dairy products (except fully cured cheeses), and articles made from plants or animals on the endangered species list.

Above $1,400, the rates vary depending on the type of goods. If you are traveling with your family, you can make a joint customs declaration, meaning your exemptions may be pooled so that one of you can bring in more if another brings in less.

For a free copy of *Know Before You Go*, contact the **U.S. Customs Service.** *Box 7407, Washington, DC 20044. Tel. (202) 927-6724.* This brochure details what you may and may not bring back into the United States, and also covers rates of duty and other tips.

> **You're required by U.S. law to declare all items acquired in other countries. That includes repairs to items you took with you and any gifts you may have received. You'll fill out a customs declaration form when re-entering the United States. Keep a record of what you acquire abroad, and keep your receipts. Take the necessary time to register any foreign-made jewelry or electronic equipment at the customs office before you leave, to prove you didn't buy them on the trip. Appraisals, receipts, insurance policies, and permanently affixed numbers are proof of prior ownership. If you fail to register these items, you may be required to pay a duty on them when you return home. The most important thing you can do is be informed. *Believe me—this is one situation where honesty is definitely the best policy!***

RETURNING TO CANADA

You may bring in, duty-free, C$500 worth of goods once every calendar year, if you're away for more than seven days. If you've been gone less than this, but more than forty-eight hours, you can then bring in C$100 duty-free, but this can be claimed an unlimited number of times. For absences of twenty-four hours or more, a C$20 duty-free exemption can be claimed an unlimited number of times. None of these exemptions can be combined, pooled with family members, or divided out over time. Goods claimed under the C$500 duty-free exemption may follow you home by mail, but goods claimed under any lesser exemption must come back with you.

Alcohol and tobacco can only be claimed under the C$500 and C$100 exemptions, and they must accompany you on your way home. You may bring in, duty-free, if you meet the age restrictions of the particular province you're coming in from, 1.14 liters of wine or liquor, or two dozen 12-ounce cans or bottles of beer or ale. You may also bring in, duty-free, if sixteen or older, 200 cigarettes, 50 cigars or cigarillos, and 400 tobacco sticks or 400 grams of manufactured tobacco.

For more information and a free brochure called *I Declare/Je Déclare* including more about duties on items that exceed your duty-free limit, contact the **Revue Canada Customs and Excise Department** at *2265 St. Laurent Blvd. S., Ottawa, Ontario KIG 4K3. Tel. (613) 993-0534.*

YOU CAN TAKE OUT OF ITALY, DUTY-FREE:

Item	Into US	Into Canada
One of the following:		
Cigarettes	200 or	200 or
Cigars	100 or	50 or
Tobacco	250 grams	400 grams
PLUS:		
One of the following:		
Spirits *(over 22% volume)*	1 liter	1.14 liters or
Wine *(under 22% volume)*	1 liter	1.14 liters or
		two dozen 12-ounce cans or bottles of beer or ale

Antiques that are at least one-hundred years old, as well as drawings, artwork, crafts, or paintings (if done entirely by hand), are duty-free.

Gifts under $50 may be mailed duty-free to stateside friends or relatives. But you can mail only one package per day, per addressee.

RECLAIMING SALES TAX

As a visitor who resides outside the European Community, you have the right to reclaim the sales tax (VAT, or Value Added Tax) you paid on Italian goods. However, it's estimated that over 65% of Americans don't get their VAT refunded. The larger shops will usually provide you with tax forms and help you fill them out. If not, ask the store for one of the forms. Then, as you leave the country, or EC, file the forms with customs, who will then send the forms back to the shop where you bought the goods. It may take a little while, but the shop should eventually send you the tax refund.

Some of the larger airports will refund your money immediately at the VAT desk, although the paperwork can be extensive and may take a lot of time. A lot of countries, however, try to make this process difficult.

As soon as you arrive at the airport, go straight to the VAT desk. You will be required to present your purchases with the receipts and have your tax form stamped. Because this desk is on the inside of the passport control area, you have to carry the goods on the plane with you to get the refund.

Stores are not required to participate in this program. If your store doesn't, it still may be possible to get a refund, but it's a very complicated process. Ask the store for the special forms required. These must then be stamped by Italian customs at the airport. The best policy? *Ask before you buy!*

Duty-free shops are usually located in airports. They can provide bargain prices on goods imported to Italy from other countries. However, be cautious. Not all of the foreign goods are automatically less expensive.

Unless you know the regular price asked for the item, you may be better off making your purchase at home. Buying at one of these duty-free stores may save you a duty fee at Italian customs, but it won't help you with the U.S. import duty when you return to the States.

GETTING THERE

If you're in Europe, there are many traveling options to get to Rome. You can travel by plane, train, automobile, and ship. If you enjoy driving, this can be a convenient way to travel, and you have the continued use of the car after arriving at your destination. If you like last-minute side trips, then driving is almost a must to avoid ticket hassles. However, most travelers don't have much time for their trip, and prefer to travel by plane for its convenience. Direct flights are available from all European capitals, and most main cities in the States.

TRAVELING BY PLANE

Air fares. To locate the best deal for air fare or travel packages, you'll have to start with some of your own research, then locate a good travel agent.

Begin your research by making a few calls, and spot check the newspaper for sales. Here are a few tips:

- Make your airline reservations well in advance.
- Check low-fare regional and discount airlines for their prices. These don't always show up on a travel agent's computer.
- Check your local newspaper, the Sunday *New York Times*, and *USA Today* travel sections for advertised low rates.
- Try to pick your travel time during the off-season of your destination. Rates will be cheaper, and if you can travel during the week, rates will be even

lower. Usually, the cheapest air fares are on Tuesday or Wednesday, mid-day and late-night flights. The highest priced flights are on Mondays and Fridays. On international flights, the fares for children operate a little differently. For infants under two not occupying a seat, the fare is usually 10% of the adult fare, or free, whereas children between two and eleven years usually pay half or two-thirds of the adult fare.

- Remember to check with your credit card companies for award points that can be converted into frequent flyer miles for free trips or discounts. If you plan to use your award points for summer travel, book your flight at least six months in advance.
- When calling an airline, ask for the lowest available fare.
- If at all possible, book your flight at least thirty days in advance for the best price, then keep checking to see if the price drops. If the ticket price drops after you buy it, but before you use it, many airlines will reimburse you for the difference, *if you ask*.
- If you belong to travel clubs such as AAA, AARP, or American Express, check with them for travel deals.

Once you find a discount package that you are interested in, be sure you are familiar with the company. If you're not, contact the Better Business Bureau, or your local State Consumer Protection Bureau to find out whether any complaints have been registered against the company. It's a good idea to pay with a credit card if possible, and consider trip cancellation and default insurance.

Dealing with the Airlines

Most travelers don't realize that once you agree to make a connection at a hub airport, you've agreed to give up control over the remainder of your trip. You're at the mercy of connecting times, delayed flights, misdirected luggage, and cancellations. *However*, there is a way to foresee and prevent some of these problems. The best way is to schedule yourself on a non-stop flight. If this is not possible, take a "direct flight," which means it stops, but you don't have to change planes. If you *have* to make a connection, don't schedule flights close together, in case the first one is delayed. It also helps if you can connect "interline," which means within the same airline.

If you get "bumped" from an overbooked, confirmed flight, you may be entitled to more than you think. The Supreme Court has ruled that passengers can now sue the airline for damages. This is especially good news for business travelers who may have missed a meeting, lost an account, or even lost their job because they were involuntarily refused passage on a confirmed flight.

With canceled flights, airlines are *supposed* to pay for a hotel room and meals if they don't reschedule you that same day. Otherwise, how do you deal with a canceled flight? The only rule that applies is—every person for himself! There are a lot more passengers for the next flight than there are seats, especially if you're flying first class. So, as soon as you hear the bad news, if you're not the first in line to buy a new ticket, make a beeline for a phone. Call the airline and tell them you're at the airport. Then give them the canceled flight number and reserve a seat on the next available flight. You can worry about transferring your luggage *after* you've gotten a seat.

Travel Agents. The benefit of a good travel agent should not be underestimated. A good travel agency will have the latest information to make your trip easier, cheaper, and more enjoyable—but that knowledge is only as good as the agent who accesses it. Find an agent who puts your interests before a commission, and who will let you know if a lower air fare becomes available between the time of your ticket purchase and your flight. Until recently, passengers were not charged a fee for low-priced tickets, even though the cost to a travel agent is about $25. But with the airlines capping travel agents' commissions on domestic tickets, the agents are passing this cost onto the consumer. So, do your research, then call your agent.

TIPS FOR AIR TRAVEL

- When you pick up your ticket, check to see that all the information is correct. Be sure your name is spelled correctly, and that you have a coupon for each flight. Your ticket must match the name on your passport.
- Write down the ticket number, date, and place of purchase. Keep this information in your wallet or other safe place.
- If you do lose your ticket, immediately call the airline's refund department. Have the ticket number, date, and place of purchase ready.
- Special dietary arrangements should be made at least twenty-four hours before departure, but preferably at the same time as your reservation.
- Confirm your flight departure before leaving for the airport.
- Take all unnecessary tags off your luggage. All you need on the outside of your bag is an ID and the flight tags for this trip. Make sure you do not list your home address on your luggage tags. Use a P. O. Box or an office address to thwart would-be burglars who

cruise the airport reading "departing flight" tags.

- It's important to board a flight as soon as you are allowed. This will give you the pick of overhead storage space for your carry-on luggage.

- If it's been longer than six months since your last dental visit, you should make an appointment for a check-up before you leave. A minor toothache at sea level can become a major pain at 30,000 feet. If you experience tooth pain during your flight, check with your dentist when you return home. You may have a cavity or bad root canal, and the rapid depressurization in the cabin can cause the tooth cavity to expand painfully.

  For tooth pain relief during your trip, use oil of cloves (a natural anesthetic). If you've lost a filling, rinse your mouth with warm saltwater to help disinfect the exposed area.

  To make the solution, dissolve one teaspoon of salt in eight ounces of warm water. Then go to the local pharmacy and purchase "DenTemp," a putty-like substance that acts as a temporary filling. For swelling, again use a saltwater rinse. Don't use crushed aspirin, Super Glue, or a file on broken teeth. If the pain is severe, call the American consulate for an American-trained, English-speaking dentist.
- If your ears begin to hurt in flight, try the Valsalva maneuver. Hold your nose and squeeze your diaphragm to exert air pressure to open the passageway between your mouth and ears. You can also try yawning or chewing gum.
- If you're having problems with allergies, take an antihistamine prior to your flight to avoid head and ear discomfort.

- If you suffer from breathing problems, headaches, and sore throats while flying (and after), try eating fruits and vegetables high in vitamins C and E, and even taking an extra vitamin supplement. Vitamins C and E play a vital role in safeguarding against high ozone and nitrous oxide levels that are commonplace in airline cabins (due to high altitudes and recirculated air).
- If you accidentally leave something behind on the plane, immediately call the airline's 800 or local number, and give them your flight number and a detailed description of the lost item. Airlines typically hold an item for five days or so, and then forward the item to the airline's central baggage office, where it's typically held for ninety days.

Seating. With some planning, it's possible to get a better seat. Seating varies, depending on the airline and aircraft, but you can often get the seat you want if you get your boarding pass when you buy your ticket. Aisle seats are most popular, so they usually go first. Emergency exit rows have more leg room, but can be colder in temperature. These rows also have restrictions and are saved until a ticket agent assesses your ability to handle the exit doors. Aisle seats near the over-wing emergency exits are said to be safer. These seats are commonly in the mid-section of the plane, accessible to several exits. Try to avoid seats in front of an exit, or on the very last row because those seats don't recline. When traveling in pairs, always request an aisle and window seat, leaving the center seat open. Center seats in back are the last to be booked, and they often go empty. If someone should book the center seat between you and your companion, they are usually happy to exchange the center seat with you for an aisle or window seat.

PLANE ETIQUETTE

Believe it or not, there is an unwritten code of polite behavior for sharing tight airplane space. We all know there are more elbows than armrests—so whose space is it? The aisle seat gets the outer one, and the window seat gets the one under the window. That leaves the middle passenger, who gets his choice of one or both! Let him choose, then claim the leftovers. As far as storage space goes—you are entitled to the space under the seat in *front* of you, not *under* you. Storage bins above the seats are unofficially open storage for whoever gets there first.

TIPS FOR CARRY-ON LUGGAGE

I've discovered you can get by with a lot if you read the rules carefully. They say that in addition to the two carry-ons, you can bring one purse, a briefcase, a coat, an umbrella, camera equipment, a reasonable amount of reading material, and a baby seat. The rules say that all carry-on luggage must fit in the overhead bins or under the seat. This shouldn't be a problem if you get there early to claim enough overhead space. Be careful, though. You may get past the door, but the flight attendant has veto power over everything brought on board.

Airline Food. One of the most common complaints made by passengers concerns the airline food. In an effort to change this, several airlines are introducing new menus. Northwest Airlines has introduced "À La Carte" menus that are probably the closest thing to a "restaurant in the sky." United Airlines offers the "Golden Arches" on its flights, and Continental Airlines is now dishing up some competition by offering Subway sandwiches on selected flights. To special order meals that include low calorie, kosher, vegetarian, and more, call the reservation line at least twenty-four hours in advance. These meals are usually the freshest.

Plane safety
Once on board the plane, count and memorize the number of rows to the nearest exit. In case of an emergency, it's probable that you'll *feel* your way to an exit. The safest clothing in a fire is made of natural fibers like wool or cotton, and avoid panty hose (it's flammable), and high heels. If the cabin fills with smoke, stay as low as possible, even if that means crawling. Toxic smoke is what kills. Until airlines provide portable smoke hoods for all passengers, many experts advise bringing your own. The extra minute it provides could save your life.

Flying into Rome. Rome has two main airports, Leonardo da Vinci Airport, otherwise referred to as Fiumicino Airport, and a military airport called Ciampino. Leonardo da Vinci, Rome's principal airport, has two terminals, one for domestic flights and the other for the international arrivals. These two terminals are only a short walk away from each other. Ciampino is much smaller, and handles mostly charter travel, although the occasional international flight arrives there.

Leonardo da Vinci (Fiumicino) Airport

Airport Information	6/ 65 951 or 6/ 60 121 or 6/ 65 95 4252

Ciampino Airport

Airport Information	6/ 794 941

Airlines Serving Rome

Air France	(800) 237-2747
Air India	(800) 223-7776
Air New Zealand	(800) 262-1234
Alitalia	(800) 223-5730
American	(800) 433-7300
British Airways	(800) 247-9297
British Midland	(800) 788-0555

Canadian Airlines	(800) 426-7000
Continental	(800) 231-0856
Delta	(800) 241-4141
Lufthansa	(800) 645-3880
Northwest	(800) 225-2525
Qantas	(800) 227-4500
TWA	(800) 892-4141
United	(800) 538-2929
USAir	(800) 428-4322

Airport Distances from Downtown Rome

Leonardo da Vinci	19 miles
Ciampino	9 miles

Tips for a Comfortable Overseas Flight

- To make the most of cramped coach seating, travel in light, loose clothing, and bring a sweater or jacket. There are blankets on board, but usually only one per passenger, and the cabins can get chilly.
- If there are any extra blankets or pillows, get them immediately.
- You may find that your feet tend to swell, so wear sneakers or well-worn, loose shoes.
- Avoid too much carry-on luggage, as space on the aircraft is limited.
- Board the plane as soon as possible to put your carry-on in the overhead bin, as having to stow your luggage at your feet will lessen your leg space and comfort.
- Bring an inflatable neck pillow, ear plugs, and eye shades. Sometimes eye shades and ear plugs are provided, but it's safer to bring your own.
- Eat lightly and choose a high-carbohydrate/low-protein meal if you want to sleep.
- Ask your doctor for a sleeping pill for the flight if you're flying at night, and, if possible,

try to schedule a flight that arrives in the afternoon or evening so you don't have to force yourself to stay awake all day once you get there.

TRANSPORTATION FROM THE AIRPORT TO ROME

FROM LEONARDO DA VINCI (FIUMICINO)

An urban railway line now links this airport to the Porta San Paolo metro station, not far from the center of Rome. It is open from 5:35 A.M. until 1:30 A.M. Trains leave every 15 to 20 minutes for the 22 minute trip. For more information, call **rail air terminal, Piazzale Ostiense,** *tel. 6/ 59 15 551*. There is another rail service with two trains that drop off at Trastevere, Ostiense, Tuscolana, and Tiburtina. Ask someone which train drops off closer to your hotel. The trains run daily from the airport between 6:55 A.M. and 10:55 P.M., and from Rome between 6:00 A.M. and 10:00 P.M., leaving about every ten minutes. The trip takes about 40 minutes, and the fare is L7,000. Tickets can be purchased from the automatic ticket machines, a tobacco shop, or from the ticket office.

A bus also drops off at the bus air terminal next to Termini Station. From the airport the bus departs every 15 minutes between 7:00 A.M. and 12:45 A.M., otherwise every hour. From the bus air terminal, the departures are from 7:00 A.M. to midnight. You should be prepared for the trip to take an hour if you're traveling at a peak time. For more information, contact the **bus air terminal, Via Giolitti,** *tel. 6/ 464 613*.

Taxis from either airport are very expensive (around $50 to $60). From Leonardo da Vinci, you must add in a L10,000 surcharge. This surcharge increases to L15,000 when the trip is from the airport to the city center. This doesn't include the charges for each piece of luggage. All told, expect to pay around L60,000 for the thirty to forty minute trip.

Tip: Use only the white or yellow officially-licensed cabs, and make sure the meter is set on zero before you start the trip.

FROM CIAMPINO AIRPORT

There's the COTRAL bus that leaves from 6:15 A.M. to 10:20 P.M. about every 15 minutes and drops off at the Anagnina metro station. From here you can go by metro to the city center. To get to the airport from the city center, allow about an hour, as traffic can slow things down considerably. Tickets can be purchased from the automatic ticket machines or from the newspaper stand.

DRIVER'S LICENSE

If you have a valid driver's license and are over the age of eighteen, you can drive while in Italy. You do not need an international driver's license.

TRAVELING BY CAR

When you take a road trip in Italy, the gasoline buying process is a little different from what North Americans are used to. Most service stations are not self-service, and Italian gas stations close for lunch, just like other businesses. Plan accordingly! Gasoline, or *benzina,* is sold by the liter, and filling up a medium-sized car can be quite expensive, upwards of $35!

Driving Rules in Italy. The first rule is to stay within the speed limits, because when you get caught speeding the fines are very large. Toll highways, *autostrade*, have a 110 km.p.h. limit (68 m.p.h.) for little cars, 130 km.p.h. (81 m.p.h.) for cars with engines more powerful than 1100 cc. On the toll-free highways, 110 km.p.h. (68 m.p.h.) for all cars, 90 km.p.h. on secondary roads (56 m.p.h.). Speeds of at least 100 m.p.h. are not unusual, and neither is tailgating at these speeds. So the best advice is to let these people pass when they want to, as Italy has one of the highest accident rates in all of Europe. Gasoline stations on the autostrade stay open twenty-four hours a day, although other stations are only open until 6:30 or 7:30 P.M. For more information about traveling conditions as you drive through Italy, contact **Autostrade Information** at 6/ *4363 2121* for information in English.

Packing the Car for Safety. Aside from taking enough maps, it's a good idea to prepare for emergencies. These items can help:

- Car rental and insurance information
- Identification and medical information for everyone traveling
- First aid kit
- Blanket and sheet
- Flashlight or lantern
- Small tool kit that includes two screwdrivers, regular and Phillips
- Jug of water
- Battery jumper cables, heavy duty jack, and lug wrench (be sure it works)
- Paper towels and small plastic trash bags. A container of pre-moistened towels (i.e., "wet wipes")

Packing the Car for a More Pleasurable Trip. Road trips are great, but there are a few things you can pack to make your trip more pleasant. When traveling on a country road, or in the mountains, even all that beautiful scenery can get a little dull. Listening to the radio in a foreign country is a good idea so you can get a feel for the music and spirit of the area. The kids can bring along their "walkman" radios, headsets, and favorite tapes. You can also pop in one of the latest forms in audio entertainment, books on tape. There are topics for everyone, from business to children's titles. Tapes are for sale at your local book or video store. Prices range from $2 to $20. It's an inexpensive way to turn a boring car trip into an exciting, or even productive one.

TO AVOID FATIGUE AND BACK STRAIN
Take a rest every 100 miles; change your posture and seat position often, and don't unload heavy luggage right after a long day of driving.

TRAVELING BY TRAIN

This is a convenient and economical way to travel, with or without a **Eurailpass,** which offers special train benefits (more details later). If you will be traveling just inside Italy, a Eurailpass really is not needed. You should get one only if you plan to visit other countries. There are special passes available for just the **Italian State Railways.** All of these offer unlimited travel during a pre-set period of time. A bonus is that once you use your pass for the first time, you no longer have to stand in the ticket lines. For more information, contact **Rail Europe** at *(800) 438-7245* in the U.S.

If you're coming in from another country, there are many rail options. There are, in addition to the standard trains, special *rapido*, or fast, trains available. The fast train from London to Paris via the Channel Tunnel takes three hours, and from Paris it's only five-and-a-half hours to Milan. There's also a fast train that makes the trip from Milan to Rome in just under four hours. As the standard trains from England involve ferry crossings of the Channel, the trips take longer.

The most luxurious train available is the **Venice**

Simplon Orient Express. This train goes from London to Venice in 32 hours, with stops in Paris, Zurich, Innsbruck, and Verona. For more information, contact the **Orient Express** at *One World Trade Center, Suite 1235, New York, NY 10048.*

The Italian State Railways is one of the cheapest ways to travel by train. It offers standard trains, as well as the fast trains. The services provided on the trains vary greatly. Some offer first- and second-class travel with a separate dining car, and others only have meal trays for the seats. Contact **Rail Europe** for more information, *tel. (800) 438-7245* in the U.S.

Almost all of the long-distance trains arrive at the Stazione Termini. This is at the center of the metro and the bus networks.

> The pickpockets and thieves in Rome have gained much notoriety, and with good reason. Purse snatchers work on motorscooters, so stay away from the curb. Gypsy children are also notorious for surrounding you and picking your pocket, hiding their score under an outstretched newspaper. If a group of kids approaches you, put your hand on your wallet and yell for them to get away. Be very careful with purses and wallets! Always keep your luggage in sight, especially in crowded stations and terminals. Be especially careful in crowds and never carry large amounts of cash or all of your credit cards. It's not unheard of for people arriving in Rome to get everything stolen without even having left the airport.

THE FIVE TRAIN STATIONS OF ROME

Stazione Ostiense 6/ 57 50 7320

Near the Porta San Paolo station. Trains available to the airport. On the main lines from Pisa and Genoa, Naples, and Nettuno.

Stazione di Piazzale Flaminio
(Roma Nord) 6/ 36 10 441

Close to Villa Borghese, good to get to the COTRAL bus station at Saxa Ruba, provides service to the north side of Rome.

StazioneTermini 6/ 48 19 885

The main terminal in Rome, handles most of the national and international lines.

Stazione Tiburtina 6/ 44 24 5104

The second-major station. Handles many of the main lines, and becomes the main station when Termini is closed.

Stazione Trastevere 6/ 58 16 076

Good for catching the local and airport trains on the Roma-Genoa-Pisa line.

If you are traveling throughout Europe for at least 15 days, it might be in your best economic interest to purchase a **Eurailpass**. The standard Eurailpass allows for unlimited travel anywhere in Europe except for the British Isles, but it is good in Ireland. The pass can only be sold outside of Europe and North Africa, to people who aren't citizens of these places. A 15-day pass (the shortest time available), runs $498, 21-days costs $648. A one-month pass costs $798, two months $1,098, and three months for $1,398. Rail Europe also offers a **Eurail Flexipass** for unlimited travel during a certain number of days in a two-month period. Choose from five days of travel for $348, ten days for $560, or 15 for $740. For those touring Europe in groups of at least three during April 1 through September 30, or at least in pairs at any time, Rail Europe offers a **Eurail Saverpass**. You get unlimited travel for either 15 days for $430 per person, 21 days for $550 per person, or one month for $678 per person. For younger passengers who will be under twenty-six on the first day of their travel, an option is the **Eurail Youthpass**. This pass entitles the youth to unlimited travel for 15 days for $398, one month for $578, or two months for $768. There's even a **Eurail Youth Flexipass** for travel for the two-month period and either five days for $255, ten days for $398, or 15 days for $540. These youth passengers must also be under twenty-six on the first day of their travel. For all except the youth passes, children from four to eleven travel at half price, and children under four travel for free. Any Eurailpass also entitles you to many discounts, especially on ferries, etc., which will be needed if you cross the Lombardy Lakes to places like Capri and Sardinia. Ferries provide the only non-air route to Sicily, and they also link Italy with Greece. For more information and advance-purchase rail passes in the U.S., call **Rail Europe** at *(800) 848-7245*, *fax (800) 432-1329.*

TRAVELING BY BUS

Traveling by bus may not be the most comfortable way to travel, but it does save money. However, fellow passengers may be a little scary. With **Eurolines**, there are more than 3,000 destinations around Europe, but common trips are to and from London, Rome, Stockholm, and Frankfurt, with fares ranging from $70 to $250. The buses come equipped with toilets and stop every four hours or so for stretching and refreshments. For more information, contact the Paris office, *6/ 40 38 9393*.

Another bus line that goes all over Italy, as well as the rest of Europe is **Europabus.** Here the fare includes not only transportation, but also a tour with hotel, meals, and guides.

COTRAL is a bus company that connects Rome with the outlying areas and cities of the Lazio region. For more information call *6/ 59 15 551*.

TRAVELING BY SHIP

Crossing the Atlantic movie-star style for vacations in Europe has lost popularity. Currently there is only one way to make a transatlantic crossing by sea, the *Queen Elizabeth 2*. The ship has everything you can imagine: pools, spas, saunas, boutiques, tennis, restaurants, and even a movie theater. With all these amenities, it's a very expensive travel option, but many U.S. travelers like returning home on the ship from the continent, as the relaxing pace allows time to unwind from the trip. The eastbound trips are scheduled mainly for England, but many more of these return west directly from Le Harre, which isn't that far from Rome. For more information, call *(212) 880-7500* or *(800) 221-4770*.

TRIP PLANNING CHECKLIST

Everyone would like to arrive at their destination with everything they needed. Then you'd never have that last minute panic attack when you reach for your very important item, only to discover it's not there. After years of traveling, I've developed a checklist to help with planning and packing for a trip.

Here are a few suggestions:

- Place a box next to the kitchen door. Every time you think of a special toy for one of the kids, or something you want to be sure to take with you, put it in the box. If you would like to continue using this item prior to your trip, put a note reminding you of the item in the box. Then, when you pack, check this box and you'll know what to take.
- Re-confirm travel and hotel reservations a few days before your departure date. Gather together confirmation numbers, locator numbers, the agent's name you spoke with, and the date of your call. Pack this information in an area that is easy to get to when you check in at your hotel.
- Contact the Italian government travel offices to request information (allow four weeks).
- Remember to make necessary ground transportation reservations such as car rentals and local public transit passes.
- Purchase traveler's checks, and exchange enough money for lire to get you through taxis and tips upon arrival.

- If you plan to send postcards, etc., make a list of addresses to take.
- Gather guide books, magazines, maps, etc., to take along on your trip.
- Prepare a medical travel kit to take along. Be sure to include any prescription medications you are taking, and medications for stomachache, earache, pain, and diarrhea. You should also carry a copy of your eyeglass or contact lens prescription, and an extra pair of both.
- Be sure to make arrangements to have your mail and newspaper deliveries stopped, or picked up by someone. If you have plants or pets, make arrangements for someone to take care of them. Set up light timers, and let your neighbors know you're taking a trip.
- Leave your travel plans with a relative or neighbor in case of an emergency.
- Consider purchasing insurance for travel, health, trip cancellation and interruption, auto, baggage and personal effects, life, or default/bankruptcy insurance (see the "Insurance" section for additional information).
- Make two copies of your passport. Leave one copy with a neighbor or relative who can be reached twenty-four hours a day while you are away. Pack the second copy.
- Check all your documents thoroughly before you leave the house for the airport, and have them readily available in your carry-on bag.
- Decide what luggage you will be taking. Check to be sure the zippers and locks are in good shape. Use carry-on luggage to hold your valuables.
- Put identification tags on your luggage. Be sure to use only your first initial, last name, office address, and phone number.

If you would like to leave someone a special message, such as a happy birthday wish, or saying goodnight to your kids, but you're going to be 30,000 feet in the air, use a phone-in message service. Major telephone companies such as MCI, Sprint, and AT&T have phone-in message services that let you record a one-minute message from any domestic phone. For less than $2, the phone company will then ring the designated number, according to your instructions, every fifteen minutes to an hour until someone answers. When the phone is answered, your message will be played. You can also program the message so that it won't ring the number until a designated time. Sprint will let the recipient record a one-minute response, which can later be retrieved from an 800 number. Call your phone company for details.

PLANNING YOUR ITINERARY

The amount of time you have for your trip will help you to determine your itinerary. You'll want to give yourself enough time to see the major attractions and sample the restaurants. Begin by figuring your arrival and departure travel time. Then review the "Sights To See" chapter and make a list of places you would like to visit. Use this list as a guideline to approximate your needed vacation time. Remember to add additional time for day trips. If you allow sufficient time, you'll enjoy a more relaxing trip.

If you'd like to see other area sights, look over the "Day Trips and Excursions" section. Once you've determined what you'd like to see, you can fill out the itinerary worksheet and schedule your reservations.

SUGGESTED ITINERARY

Below I've listed an itinerary based on my experience and personal suggestions.

ARRIVAL DAY

Morning: Hotel check in. (Inform your hotel in advance if you need an early arrival check-in.)

Afternoon: Take a half day sightseeing tour by bus or private car to get an overview of the city. Get as much sunlight as possible to help you overcome jet lag.

Evening: Have an early dinner and try to stay awake until a normal bedtime without napping.

DAY TWO

Morning: Sightsee "Ancient Imperial Rome" with visits to the Colosseum, the Roman Forum, and Circus Maximus.

Afternoon: Lunch at Piazza Navona, with shopping or museums in the afternoon. Sunset on the Spanish Steps.

Evening: Cabaret dinner in Trastevere.

DAY THREE

Morning: Sightsee "Papal Rome" with a visit to St. Peter's Square and the Sistine Chapel.

Afternoon: Continue with visits to the Vatican Museums and Castel Sant Angelo.

Evening: Dinner with a view of the city at Les Etoilles (on the roof of the Atlante Star Hotel) or the Roof Restaurant (at the Hotel Hassler.)

DAY FOUR

Morning: Visit the Baths of Caracalla (also great to see at night during an opera performance.)

Afternoon: The Appian Way and Catacombs.

Evening: The Campidoglio Sound and Light Summer Spectacular.

IF YOU'RE THERE ON A SUNDAY

Morning: Get up early...what's open in the morning, closes in the afternoon. The Flea Market of Rome is open from 7 A.M. until 1 P.M. Almost two miles of bargains galore, between Porta Portese and the Trastevere Rail Station. Museums are also open on Sundays from about 9 A.M. to 1 P.M.

Afternoon: Take one of the recommended day trips, as most shops and museums in Rome are closed on Sundays. Attractions in Tivoli and Ostia Antica are open until sunset.

Itinerary Worksheet

Traveling to Rome

Departure: Date ________ Time ________
Airline, Flight #: ________
Arrival: Date ________ Time ________
Rental Car Agency: ________
Confirmation #: ________
Accommodations: ________ Number ________
Confirmation #: ________
Dinner Reservations: ________ Time ________

While in Rome—Day 1

Accommodations: ________
Sights to See: ________

Dinner Reservations: ________ Time ________

While in Rome—Day 2

Accommodations: ________
Sights to See: ________

Dinner Reservations: ________ Time ________

While in Rome—Day 3

Accommodations: ________
Sights to See: ________

Dinner Reservations: Time

While in Rome—Day 4

Accommodations:
Sights to See:

Dinner Reservations: Time

While in Rome—Day 5

Accommodations:
Sights to See:

Dinner Reservations: Time

While in Rome—Day 6

Accommodations:
Sights to See:

Dinner Reservations: Time

Leaving Rome

Departure: Date Time
Airline, Flight #:
Arrival: Date Time

PLANNING YOUR TRIP BUDGET

Travel and vacation expenses in Rome will depend on how long you stay, and what you'd like to do during your visit. It also depends on whether it's a family vacation or a singles' retreat. When you take your children on a summer vacation, you're creating memories that will last a lifetime. But, with a family of four, if you're not careful, you'll go through several thousand dollars. To give you an idea of what to expect when you arrive in Rome, here's a list of some average prices. Keep in mind that the exchange rate changes just about every day, so these prices are estimates.

Economize your food money. If you prefer to eat out for breakfast, ask the concierge or front desk for the nearest bakery or sidewalk café. Avoid ordering expensive room service. Another idea is to pack a small toaster, or have cereal in the room. Bring an immersion heater for coffee and hot chocolate (don't forget the voltage adapter), and why not keep a cooler full of soft drinks or snacks? If the weather is nice, you might want to enjoy it with a picnic.

General	
Soft drink	$ 1.30
Glass of wine	$ 2.00
Pint of beer	$ 3.75
Local telephone call/pay phone	$ 0.12
Food	
Continental breakfast at a café	$ 3
Budget lunch for one, no wine	$ 14

Moderate lunch for one, no wine	$ 27
Budget dinner for one, no wine	$ 23
Moderate dinner for one, no wine	$ 32
Expensive dinner for one, no wine	$ 75
Transportation	
Taxi fare from the central train station to Piazza di Spagna	$ 43
Unlimited subway fare or public bus from anywhere to anywhere in Rome (one-month pass)	$ 38

TRIP BUDGET FORM

To prepare your trip budget, begin by estimating the major expenses of your travel plans. Use the provided space to figure a few trial budgets. Disregard the areas that do not apply to your trip. For example, if you're flying to Europe and won't be renting a car, then you won't have to take into account fuel or rental costs.

EXPENSE CATEGORIES /	TRIAL BUDGETS		FINAL
Pre-Trip Expenses			
Automobile preparation (if already in Europe)			
Travel (cancellation) ins.			
Passport/visa fees			
Travel supplies: film, clothing prep, etc.			
Transportation			
Air fare, or train/ship/bus fare if already in Europe			
Car fuel (total round trip)			
Overnight stops (total, more for car/train trips within Europe)			
Meals on the road (for car and train trips)			
Sightseeing/side trip			
Emergency fund in route			
Expenses in Rome			
Accommodations			
Meals (total cost)			
Snacks and refreshments			
Car rental			
Car fuel			
Entertainment/Recreation			
Shopping and Souvenirs			

EXPENSE CATEGORIES / TRIAL BUDGETS			FINAL
Emergency fund			
Side trips			
Other			
Total Estimated Expenses			
Your Funds $			
Amount Over/Under $			

1. Fill in your Total Vacation Funds in all three columns.
2. Fill in all areas for which you have a firm price.
3. Fill in your estimated expenses in the categories that apply to your plans.
4. Add all of your figures, then subtract your Total Estimated Expenses from your Total Funds.
5. If your trial budget exceeds your funds available, gather more information about your trip, adjust your plans, then go to the next trial column and recalculate.

WORK SHEET

Total meals:

_______x_______x_______x $_______ = $_________

(no. of people) x *(meals per day)* x *(number of days)* x *(average meal cost)* = *(total meal cost)*

INSURANCE

Today you can find insurance to cover just about anything. Some of the most popular types cover accidents, medical expenses, trip cancellation, loss or theft of personal property, and airline bankruptcy. Travel insurance can be beneficial as it covers stolen, and sometimes even lost, valuables such as cameras or money. Some travel insurance will also cover health and medical expenses. Talk to your travel agent for more information.

When traveling with valuables, purchase additional insurance. If your luggage is lost, collecting on insurance will be much easier if you have receipts for the missing items.

Automobile insurance provides you with collision, theft, property damage, and personal liability protection while driving.

Baggage and personal effects insurance can be purchased to cover your luggage and contents in case of damage or theft during your trip.

Bankruptcy and/or default insurance can be purchased to provide coverage if the airline, tour company, or travel company should default and/or go bankrupt.

Flight insurance covers accidental injury or death while flying.

Personal accident and sickness insurance covers cases of illness, injury, or death in an accident while traveling.

Trip cancellation insurance and interruption insurance will cover you if trip cancellation is necessary, and in some cases, will even reimburse you for other travel expenses that are required to return home early.

Excess-valuation insurance can be purchased directly at the airline check-in counter. This insurance will cover valuables the airline insurance will not cover. The airlines' liability insurance will cover up to $1,250 per passenger, excluding valuables that are listed in the fine print on your ticket, in the event of loss, damage, or theft on domestic flights. Some homeowner's policies cover these additional valuables, or off-premises theft, but you should check with your insurance company.

Here are some companies that carry health, accident, trip cancellation, and lost luggage insurance:

Travel Guard International. 1145 Clark St., Stevens Point, WI 54481. Tel. (715) 345-0505 or (800) 826-1300.

Wallach and Company. 107 W. Federal St., Middleburg, VA 22117-0480. Tel. (540) 687-3166 or (800) 237-6615.

Travelers Insurance Co. One Tower Square, Hartford, CT 06183-5040. Tel. (860) 277-0111 or (800) 243-3174.

Mutual of Omaha. Mutual of Omaha Plaza, Omaha, NE 68175. Tel. (800) 228-9792.

CAR RENTALS

Renting a car while in Rome is not advisable. In the city, there's plenty of public transportation available at very reasonable rates. It is virtually impossible to drive around the city, especially if you're not used to the Italian style of driving. Renting a car is only a feasible consideration if you're planning many excursions outside Rome.

If you decide to rent a car, remember to allow yourself enough time when leaving and returning to the airport. Take a minute to have the rental agent mark a map for you before you leave the airport. Most car rental agencies provide maps at no charge. Even if you've been to the airport before, there's a chance construction may be under way, so ask. This can save you time and grief.

Most rental agencies will pick up your rental car at your hotel. This saves a lot of time. It can also save some considerable money, because the rental time clock stops when the concierge calls to tell the agency that you're ready. Ask if there's a fee for this service.

If you are on a budget, tell your travel agent you would like a budget-priced car. Sometimes they can find rentals at off-airport companies. If that's an option, the company will make arrangements to pick you up from the airport and take you to your rental car. However, those companies often have long lines, so allow extra time on arrival or return. Overseas budget and moderate cars usually have a manual transmission and come with no air conditioning.

Car rental reservations should be made prior to your trip. Some rental companies have started "months in advance" or "purchase in advance" rental plans. This will guarantee that a car will be available when you need it, and most international companies will cut their standard rates by 15% to 30% with reservations made at least twenty-four hours in advance, and pre-payment of your rental a minimum of three days prior.

When looking for the best rates, don't overlook packages that include air fare, accommodations, and a rental car with unlimited mileage. Some airlines also run promotions with car rental agencies that offer air mileage with the car rental. Organizations, including AARP and AAA, offer discounts for their members.

These are the usual requirements for renting a car in Italy: a major credit or charge card, a valid driver's license, a valid passport, and be between the ages of twenty-one (or in some cases twenty-five) and seventy. Some companies will rent to younger people, but there is a surcharge. An International Driver's Permit, available from the American Automobile Association, is a good idea.

If your plans are to pay for your car rental with a credit card, check to see if the card offers a collision damage waiver and, if so, what are the restrictions and exemptions. Diner's Club, *tel. (800) 234-6377*, provides primary coverage in the United States and worldwide. Most others provide secondary coverage, which means you have to try to collect from your home or personal insurance first.

Insurance. Inquire about insurance, and check to see that it is included with the rental price, as insurance is compulsory in Italy.

I recommend renting from a well-known car agency and taking the collision damage waiver. Even though your credit card benefits often include rental insurance, it's usually secondary insurance—not worth the time and paperwork.

Finding a major rental car agency in Italy won't be difficult. Rental car agencies represented are:

Auto Europe	(800) 223-5555
Avis	(800) 331-1084
Budget	(800) 472-3325
Dollar	(800) 800-6000
Europe by Car	(800) 223-1516
European Car Reservations	(800) 535-3303
Foremost Euro-Car	(800) 272-3299
Hertz	(800) 654-3001
Maggiore	(800) 935-5000
National	(800) 227-7368

Most offer unlimited mileage rates that will vary among the agencies.

Statistics show that most rental car accidents occur as drivers are trying to figure out how to leave the airport. Before leaving the car rental counter, ask the rental agent to mark a map with directions to your destination.

A Few Tips

- Before you rent a car from a company, be sure it offers twenty-four-hour roadside assistance.
- Ask for instructions to follow if your rental car should break down.
- Give your rental car a good once-over before you leave the lot. Check to see that the headlights, windshield wipers, and brakes are working correctly. The fuel tank should be full and, if it isn't, make a note on the rental contract and have the rental agent initial it before you leave.
- Many rental cars have a giveaway letter in their license plate that can make travelers a potential victim. Most agencies have made an effort to change these, but you should insist on a nondescript license plate.

JET LAG

When traveling across time zones you may begin to feel the physical symptoms of jet lag. These can include dehydration, headaches, insomnia, and just general fatigue. To minimize these symptoms try the following:

- If you're going to travel through several time zones, try to leave in the morning to arrive in the evening. If you will be arriving at an overseas destination early in the day, get several hours of sunlight, and stay awake until a normal bedtime, without napping.
- Get plenty of rest before your flight.
- During your flight eat lightly and drink plenty of water—avoid alcohol, caffeine, and carbonated beverages.
- Upon departure, immediately set your watch to the time of your destination and avoid thinking about what time it is at home. If you adjust your mind to the new time zone, your body will adjust more quickly.
- When flying from east to west, eat a low-calorie breakfast with coffee. Eat high-calorie meals at destination time blocks. Once you arrive, eat normal meals, and get on a destination-time sleep routine. The day that you arrive try to get at least five hours of sunlight.
- When flying from west to the east, eat low-calorie meals and have an early dinner. It is recommended that you don't drink coffee in the evening and try to get to bed around 11:00 P.M. After you arrive,

eat normal meals, go to sleep at the normal time at your destination, and *don't nap*!

- When flying west, it helps to travel as early as possible because the day is lengthening and adjustments can be made more easily.
- Avoid dehydration by taking along a water bottle and some fruit or other healthy snacks. Try to snack and drink lightly every hour.

Italy follows Central European Time. It has its own version of Daylight Savings Time, and from the last Sunday in March to the last Sunday in September, the clocks are put ahead one hour.

Time Differences. The chart below shows the different times when it is 12:00 noon in Los Angeles when Los Angeles is not on Daylight Savings Time. During Daylight Savings Time, Los Angeles is three hours ahead of Hawaii.

USING DAYLIGHT SAVINGS TIME

Los Angeles	Hawaii	Orlando	London	Rome
12:00 noon	10 A.M.	3 P.M.	8 P.M.	9 P.M.

USING STANDARD TIME

Los Angeles	Hawaii	Orlando	London	Rome
12:00 noon	9 A.M.	3 P.M.	8 P.M.	9 P.M.

For more information on how to handle jet lag, physicians involved in circadian or twenty-four-hour research have published a book, *How to Beat Jet Lag: A Practical Guide for Air Travelers*.

HOTEL RESERVATIONS

When selecting a hotel (or any accommodation), there are many things to take into consideration. Location, type, size, and time of season are important factors that will affect the rates. During the year, rates will vary according to the seasons. Rates generally begin with the price for one person, and increase with each additional person.

Hotels are rated using a star system to indicate quality. A four-star rating is for a luxury accommodation, three-star for deluxe, two-star for an average quality tourist type accommodation, and one-star for a budget accommodation. In the lower end accommodations, there may be no private bathroom, or the bathroom may be down the hall. Fortunately most hotels today have central heating, although the rooms are usually kept cooler than most Americans are accustomed to. This is supposed to be better for our health.

Chain Hotels. For those on a budget or who plan to spend more time out and about than in the room, chain hotels are a good idea. They are pretty simple, but offer a clean room. Here are some of the major hotel chains:

Choice Chain (Clarion, Comfort, Econo Lodge, Friendship, Quality, Sleep Inn)	(800) 424-6423
Forte Hotels	(800) 223-5672
Holiday Inns	(800) 465-4329
Ramada Inns, Ramada Limited	(800) 228-3838
Sheraton Corporation	(800) 325-3535

Anyone who travels a lot knows it can be hard to get a good night's sleep in a noisy or unfamiliar room. Some people have had success with sound tapes, but I find them annoying. Tapes of the "ocean waves" going in and out just don't put me to sleep. What does work for me is a *travel sound conditioner.* You plug it in and it runs all night. There is a volume control and a rain-to-waterfall adjustment. The sound is constant so you don't have to worry about its stopping just as you fall asleep. It's made by Marsona and sold at Hammacher Schlemmer, or through most airline catalogues, for around $100. There's a dual voltage travel version, and it also works well at home for masking the noise of barking dogs.

HOTEL ALTERNATIVES

If you would like to avoid staying in a hotel altogether, try a bed and breakfast, villa, apartment, or even a home.

Bed and Breakfasts. These are pretty common in Rome; however, many of them do not have private bathrooms. They range from one to several rooms and may be located in a mansion or a private home. Many of them include a breakfast with the cost of your stay, but rarely have air conditioning.

Apartments, Condos, Homes, and Villas. If you're looking for more room, or plan to spend a week or more in Rome, try renting an apartment, home, or villa for your vacation. The cleaning and cooking are left up to you. There are several agencies that offer this special service with locations worldwide:

Barclay International Group	(800) 845-6636
British Travel Associates	(800) 327-6097

Hideaways International* (800) 843-4433
Rent-a-Home International (800) 488-7368
Vacation Home Rentals (800) 633-3284

*This is a travel club with a yearly membership fee of $99. Membership entitles you to an in-house travel agency.

Hostels are alternative low-cost accommodations at rates of about $15 per person, per night for non-members. If you pay the $25 annual adult membership fee ($10 under eighteen, or $15 if over fifty-four), you can get even lower rates or discounts on other travel services. For locations and information, contact **Hostelling International/American Youth Hostels.** *Tel. (202) 783-6161.*

HOTEL INFORMATION

Hotel Lobby Convenience. Many hotels are adding travel and business centers, or kiosks, to their lobbies for the use of their guests. Some hotels are installing automated teller machines in their lobbies. Other hotel lobbies are adding CD-ROM touch-screen machines to give detailed information on restaurants and local attractions in several different languages. Walk-in business centers with copiers, printers, fax machines, and free coffee are also becoming popular.

Faxes. Today the fax machine is a popular form of communication. They can be useful for business, but also for keeping in touch with the family. Most hotels in Rome now have a fax machine, but will charge both incoming and outgoing pages. To call or fax Rome, precede the fax number with 011 39 (country code), 6 (city code), so if the fax or phone number is 64 79 52, dial 011 39 6/ 64 79 52.

HOTEL FAXES

When sending or receiving faxes, omit the cover page to save on the fax fees. Hotels usually charge by the page.

Concierge. Finding a hotel with a good concierge is getting harder all the time. Today, *if* the hotel has a concierge, it's hard to tell what their experience is. Hotels are increasingly substituting a novice employee, or worse yet, allowing a tour group employee to dress up as a hotel staff member and act as a concierge to save money. Fortunately, there are still a few hotels that recognize their value. A good concierge has to be ready for just about any request. They have to have good connections and know everything about the city. From theater tickets to babysitting, they should be able to steer you in the right direction in the shortest amount of time possible. This is particularly important when you have a medical problem, forget certain clothing items, or just run into some old friends and need dinner reservations for six instead of two at a booked restaurant!

To find out if a hotel has a professional concierge, simply ask if it belongs to "Les Clefs dOr." This is an international organization of professional concierges who know exactly what their job is and how to do it well. A good rule of thumb is that the better the hotel, the better and more experienced the concierge will be.

The first thing you should do when you check in is find out what amenities the suites offer that the standard rooms don't (usually a bathrobe, slippers, upgraded toiletries, etc.). Then when you get to your standard size room, if it doesn't have a bathrobe, call housekeeping and ask to "borrow" one. They'll send one right up. Other items that are available from housekeeping include iron and ironing board, hypoallergenic or down pillows, extra towels, soap and shampoo, hair dryers, shoe polish, extra blankets, sometimes a toothbrush and toothpaste, and sewing kits. If your room has twin beds, you can usually have them pushed together and re-made into a king.

Hotel tipping. Although tipping in the United States has become a way of life, it is still a voluntary act. In

Rome, the tourists are expected to tip even though the locals themselves rarely do. While staying at a hotel, the usual tipping procedure is to tip the door attendant L1,000 if he hails a cab. If a bellhop takes your luggage to your room, give him L1,000 to L2,000 per bag. Check your room-service bill carefully. Often, service charges have already been added on. A good rule to follow, if you are pleased with your hotel room's cleanliness is to leave L1,000 to L3,000 for each day you've stayed. Put it in an envelope marked "housekeeping," and leave it in the hotel room when you check out.

If you find yourself with a laundry problem while traveling, you can run into the problem of inflated laundry costs in hotels. Although some hotel laundry services are cheaper than others, the average cost of having a jacket dry cleaned while staying at an American hotel is $10. Having the same jacket cleaned in Europe could double or triple the cost. Try to find a dry cleaner with good prices and fast service that is close to the hotel. Ask at the front desk or use a local phone book. Most drycleaners have a same-day service if you get it there before 10:00 A.M.

Once you've decided on a hotel, here are a few tips for making reservations:

- Ask if the hotel is offering any family or promotional packages. Most hotels offer a "frequent guest program," with their own 800 numbers for members to check their balances, awards, etc., twenty-four hours a day.
- When booking a double occupancy room, ask what type of beds are in the room. The term "double" usually refers to one bed, a "twin" is two narrow beds, a "double-double" is two double or queen beds, and a "king" is a king. In some overseas hotels, it's not uncommon to find two twin

beds, or a simple double bed. If you want a king, ask for a king or a "twin" and push the two beds together.

- Ask if the bathroom is located in your room, and if it is a complete bathroom. This is not necessary when dealing with the more expensive hotels. There are instances of private bathrooms being located outside your room, although you have a private key. You may also find there is a sink in your room, but the other facilities are down the hall.
- Ask for a confirmation number. (If you're booking far enough ahead, ask for written confirmation.)
- Once the clerk books your reservation, repeat the reservation date, number of people in your party, type of room, and price to avoid misunderstandings. Ask the clerk for their name before hanging up the phone. This information could come in handy if you arrive at the hotel and your reservation is not as you booked it.
- A credit card number usually will hold your room until 12:00 noon the next day. Popular hotels frequently overbook and plan on cancellations. Consequently, you may find yourself without a room upon your arrival. To avoid this, authorize the person taking your reservation to charge your room to your credit card, but ask for the cancellation policy (usually twenty-four to seventy-two hours before arrival), otherwise you'll be charged for one night.
- Ask if the hotel is under any remodeling or construction. If it is, it is better to make another selection for your stay. Vacation time is not when you want to be disturbed by the sound of construction, or arrive to find the pool closed.
- If you have any doubt, ask if each room has its own temperature control for heating and air conditioning.

- If your overseas flight arrives in the morning, advise the hotel you'd like an early check-in if possible. If the room isn't ready, they may have a holding room you can relax in.

Your travel agent is the best person for overseas hotel information, unless you call an international hotel chain's 800 number, such as Hilton International or Sheraton International.

Getting the best rate on a hotel room means playing 20 questions. When you call for a hotel rate, they will quote you the "rack rate," which is the standard price. The hotel person is not going to volunteer the discounted prices. You have to ask for them. Begin by asking if they have a military, senior citizen, or AAA discount. Ask for weekend or weekday promotions. Then when you arrive to check in, ask again. Sometimes, if the occupancy is low, they'll release some rooms at a discounted price. And always ask for an upgrade to a better room. All they can say is no.

If you need to make a reservation or if you're looking for a cheaper rate, but all you're hearing is, "Sorry those dates are booked up," try a **hotel consolidator.** Currently there are four top hotel consolidators that offer hotels in all categories for far less than if you were to call the hotel directly. The way they accomplish this is by striking deals with various hotels and buying a block of rooms in advance at a greatly reduced rate. Then they re-sell them to the public at 30% to 40% off the standard price. While these consolidators can save you money, there is one flaw. The majority of them require you to pay for the room in advance with a credit card, making payment non-refundable and non-changeable. For more information call the **Hotel Reservations Network**, *tel. (800) 846-7000* or **RMC Travel**, *tel. (800) 245-5738.*

If you are traveling and something happens to your dissatisfaction, address it immediately. Remain calm and polite at first. Ask to speak to a manager or supervisor and see if they will help you. Explain your problem as specifically as possible. If you feel that you are getting nowhere, then change your tone from calm and polite to frustrated and firm. Remember to make it clear to the person you are speaking with that it is not "personally" their fault, but their company's. If you strike out with them, then make a point to write "the powers that be" of the organization, and inform them of your plight. You'll find that letters get a better response than phone calls. Send *copies* of any documentation you may have (i.e., photographs, receipts, contracts, notes, etc.). It is important to keep the originals.

WHAT TO PACK

When it comes to packing, no one does it exactly the same way, and frankly, that's the way it should be. There are no absolute rules for the right or wrong way to put your possessions into a suitcase. However, there are a few points to consider before you decide what to pack. In Rome, the locals dress anywhere from casual to dressy. *Where* you are going seems to dictate the dress. The young crowd tends to dress more casually than the middle-aged, upscale restaurant or theater patron, where they dress *very* nice. Shoes should be comfortable and with a thicker type of sole to walk the cobblestone streets. (Between the cobblestone streets and gravel walkways, you can really ruin a pair of nice shoes, and thin soles will kill your feet.) If you plan to visit the cathedrals, there is a strict dress code. Women are expected to cover bare shoulders and arms, so pack a light shawl or shirt. Some cathedrals may also require a head covering. It is unacceptable for men and women to wear shorts while visiting the churches. Most of the nicer establishments prefer that you don't wear shorts or jogging outfits. Remember to pack a sweater for the possible sudden change in weather, and regardless of the time of year, be on the safe side and pack a raincoat and umbrella.

When traveling and walking a lot, take along shoes preferably a half size larger to allow for swelling. I usually put pads in my shoes that can be removed after my feet begin to swell.

When it comes to buying new luggage, there's always the question of whether it should be soft- or hardsided. Although softsided luggage has to be fully packed to gain some degree of sturdiness, it is lighter, flexible for packing, and stores easier. Hard case luggage on the other hand doesn't need to be filled to be durable. The hard case protects the contents better, and often comes with built-in locks. Surprisingly, soft luggage tends to last longer, especially if it's made from canvas or high-tech nylon. Hard cases that take a beating often get their hinges and frames bent, while soft cases tend to roll with the punches. Whatever you decide to buy, save the pricey designer bags for your carry-on. Expensive suitcases just beg to be stolen.

Before you start packing, prepare a list, taking into consideration the climate and your travel plans. Don't forget to pack your medication in your carry-on bag instead of in your checked luggage.

PACKING FOR YOUR TRIP:

- an inflatable neck pillow for the trip
- voltage converters and adapter plugs (available at most luggage stores). Rome uses 220 volts, 50 cycles AC.
- an extension cord (outlets are invariably inconvenient)
- travel coffee pot or an immersion heater for packages of instant coffee, soups, and hot chocolate
- simple comfortable clothing that is nice but doesn't scream "wealthy tourist"
- medication such as regular prescriptions, and something for pain (Tylenol or Advil), motion sickness, diarrhea and constipation treatments, antihistamine tablets (for allergies), and cortisone cream (for itching and insect bites)
- travel alarm

- language translator (one that converts phrases or a book of Italian/English)
- currency calculator (not absolutely necessary, but nice)
- suntan lotion SPF 15 or higher
- insect repellent
- sunglasses
- extra pair of glasses or contact lenses
- sewing kit
- swimsuits
- a shawl or light, long-sleeved shirt if you plan to visit the churches
- raincoat and folding umbrella
- recreational equipment
- tennis shoes
- walking shoes
- toiletries (pack these in kitchen, resealable freezer bags that can be reused, and will keep your shampoo, etc., from leaking)
- hair dryer
- stationery and address book
- cash and traveler's checks
- checkbook
- camera and extra film (it costs considerably less at home)
- belts
- travel sound conditioner (see tip in "Hotel Reservations")
- a lightweight book bag for shopping or lunches
- a duffel-type bag that can be folded for packing and can be used for the new purchases on your return trip
- plastic, resealable bags for laundry, wet swimsuits, and snacks

Notes

BEFORE YOU LEAVE THE HOUSE-CHECKLIST

As your trip gets closer, there are a few important things to remember and prepare for. Below is a checklist to assist you.

- Leave a car parked in your driveway.
- Set the automatic timer for the lights in your house. Use two or three timers to control the lights in different areas.
- Give your neighbor a key to your house to be used in the event of an emergency.
- Leave a list of emergency telephone numbers that includes someone for plumbing and AC/heater repair.
- Check your pantry and refrigerator for anything that will spoil during your absence.
- Set the thermostat at a low or high temperature (depending on the time of year). In the winter the thermostat should be left at 50 degrees so the pipes won't freeze.
- Unplug televisions, computers, washers, and other appliances.
- Turn off the garage door opening system.
- Be sure to leave copies of your itinerary, tickets, passport, credit cards, traveler's checks, and medical prescriptions with someone you can reach, day or night, just in case the originals are lost or stolen.
- Don't change the message on your answering machine; however, if you receive a lot of calls, have someone pick them up, or forward your calls

to an answering service. Otherwise, your machine may overload.

- Pack the following in your carry-on luggage:
  - -hotel confirmations
  - -tickets and other transportation information
  - -camera/film
  - -medication
  - -necessary credit cards (leave unnecessary ones at home)
  - -wallet
  - -cash/traveler's checks
  - -folding umbrella
  - -passport
  - -inflatable neck pillow, eye shades, and ear plugs
  - -reading material
  - -jewelry or valuables

ABOUT MONEY/ CREDIT CARDS/ATMs

While vacationing, it's not unusual to find yourself needing more money from home, whether it's for the great buy you've found or sudden excursion you've just decided to take. When you're traveling, the last problem you need is a shortage of ready cash. Generally, it's not that difficult to access your money if you have the right identification. In fact, with the popularity of ATMs and credit cards, the use of traveler's checks is dwindling.

Note: Exchange rates fluctuate. Check with your bank for the current rate.

Currency in Rome

The currency unit in Rome is the lira, (L) or lire when plural. Coins are: L5, L10, (neither are commonly used), L50, L100, and L200, and L500. Bills/notes are in denominations of L1,000, L2,000, L5,000, L10,000, L50,000, and L100,000. You may hear Italians quote prices as "L5" instead of L5,000, because they sometimes drop the last three zeros. The Italian currency you will need to take with you for tips, taxis, metro, etc. when you arrive are the L1,000, L2,000, and L5,000 notes.

If you have memorized your PIN number as a word or letters, re-memorize it as numbers. The key pad in Rome shows no letters, only numbers.

ATMs and Cash Machines

Automated-teller machines, commonly called ATMs, can let you access money from your account, or get an advance from a credit card account with a PIN, or personal identification number. In Italy, the bank ATMs are labeled "Bancomat 3." Check with your bank or credit card company before you travel, as some accounts have limits on withdrawals and cash advances. They may also require you to reprogram your PIN number for the area you will be visiting. Usually four-digit PINs are used overseas. Fees for the use of the ATM machines are usually higher when accessing them overseas, but Cirrus and Plus systems use the same wholesale rates as major banks. You may find that many of the ATM machines in Rome are in operation only during normal banking hours. For **Cirrus** ATM locations in the Rome area, call *(800) 424-7787*. For the foreign Plus locations consult your local bank.

Credit Cards and Exchange Rates

The price you think you pay overseas is rarely what shows up on your credit card bill, due to the exchange rate. The exchange rate at the time and day of your purchase is rarely the same exchange rate your credit card company uses to calculate your bill. Most companies use the exchange rate on the day your charge clears, not the day of your purchase. The amount of time it takes for the charge to clear depends on the card issuer and the location of the purchase. This could work against you, depending on the value of the dollar. It's been rumored that some credit card companies delay charges if the dollar is fluctuating. You won't know the rate used until you get your bill, and there's no central source. Some companies will use the rate indicated in the *Wall Street Journal*. Some will use two different bank rates, then average the two. All use a service fee to calculate the exchange. The only way to really know what you pay for a purchase is to pay with cash or traveler's checks.

Credit Cards

The use of credit cards is still the easiest and safest way to handle your finances when you travel. You can use them for purchases or to draw cash advances. You should only carry the credit cards that you will need for the day. Spread them out over a few pockets, put some in the hotel safe deposit box, and leave the department store cards at home. That way, if you lose something, it's not a total loss. The most commonly used credit cards are American Express (AE), Carte Blanche (CB), Diners Club (DC), MasterCard (MC) (EuroCard in Europe-EC, Access in Britain, Chargex in Canada), and Visa (V) (Barclaycard in Britain, in France it's Carte Bleue). (Discover is only accepted in the United States.) I've used the above credit card abbreviations in this guide. You should note that not all hotels, restaurants, etc., accept credit cards.

Overseas Credit Card Purchases

If you use a credit card for a purchase or service overseas, keep your receipts and double check your bill. There are thousands of mistakes on international credit card purchases, but unfortunately there's little recourse. One common problem is receiving defective merchandise that has been shipped. The law only protects you if it was shipped within your home state, or you live within one hundred miles of the mailing address. Therefore, don't ship without good insurance. Then what about the merchant who adds zeros, or moves the decimal point to increase the charge? Or adds charges to the rental car invoice after you've left? This happens all the time. You need to notify your card company immediately in writing within sixty days, with copies to the appropriate federal agencies, and, believe it or not, the Director of Tourism of the offending country. Often the promise of bad publicity from an American tourist can nudge the merchant to withdraw.

Traveler's Checks

When using traveler's checks, treat them as if they were personal checks. Keep a log and don't expect them to be accepted everywhere. Traveler's checks used to be thought of "just like cash," but not anymore. Now, they're more like a personal check. Merchants don't have to accept them, and often, they don't. In Rome, U.S. traveler's checks are accepted at most places, and can be cashed at banks or check issuing offices. It used to be that signing them on the top line in front of the merchant would identify you as the legal bearer. As long as your signature matched the one on the bottom line, you could make your purchase and leave with the merchandise. This worked especially well for people who didn't use credit cards. Now, you have to show identification, sometimes even a credit card, as security. Often a manager's permission is needed for acceptance and if it's not a *major* brand of checks—forget it. They can still be valuable as insurance if you lose them or get robbed—that is, as long as you have the check numbers put away safely. But if you haven't kept a log of what check numbers you've already used, you'll have a lot of trouble trying to get a refund. The most widely used traveler's checks are American Express, Citicorp, Diners Club, Thomas Cook, and Visa. These can all be purchased at larger banks. Usually the bank will charge a fee of up to 3% of the face value of the check, but 1% is normal.

When cashing traveler's checks at foreign banks, you may be charged as much as 20% of the face value. You are more likely to find the lowest fee by cashing your traveler's checks at a bank that also sells the same brand.

Wiring Money

The most recognized way to wire money is through **Western Union.** You can send a wire in person using cash, a cashier's check, MasterCard, or Visa. Your other option is to place the order over the phone and charge the money you'd like to have sent to your MasterCard or

Visa. When you send money from the United States or Canada, the money will be available for pick up at any of hundreds of locations in Italy within minutes. For locations, or to make a wire over the phone using MasterCard or Visa, call *(800) 325-6000*.

American Express also offers a wire service, and you don't have to be a card holder to use it. You can send or receive up to $10,000 using a Money Gram® agent, located at convenience stores and American Express travel offices. You can charge up to $1,000 on your credit card; but above that, you must pay with cash. Once you place the order, you are allowed one long distance call to give your recipient the transaction code. Then all the recipient has to do is present identification and the transaction reference number at the nearest MoneyGram® agent to pick up the money. Fees range anywhere from 3% to 10%, depending on the amount and type of payment used. For more information and locations call *(800) 926-9400*. For money transfers call *(800) 866-8800*. The Rome branch is located at *Piazza di Spagna, 38. Tel. 6/ 67 64 1*.

Currency Exchange

To make a currency exchange, you can use the currency exchange booths called "Cambio," (located in airports, stores, hotels, and transportation stations), or privately operated exchange firms or banks. You will often get a better rate of exchange at the banks. Even if you plan to primarily use traveler's checks and credit cards, some foreign currency will be needed. For additional foreign currency exchanges, contact agencies such as **Thomas Cook Currency Services,** *630 5th Ave., New York, NY 10111, tel. (609) 987-7300*, in New York City (call collect); *(212) 757-6915*, for offices in major U.S. cities and abroad; *(609) 987-7300 or (800) 223-7373* for lost or stolen traveler's checks; *(800) 223-9920* for MasterCard traveler's checks; Rome's location, *Piazza della Republica, 62. Tel. 6/ 48 64 95*. **American Express,** *tel. (800) 221-7282*. Rome location, *Piazza di Spagna. Tel. 6/ 67 64 1*.

The currency exchange rate fluctuates about 1% daily. The chart below is based on $1 = approximately 1,500 lire. When you're ready to take your trip, check with your bank for the current exchange rate. The table below is provided to give you general currency exchanges.

Lire	U.S.$	U.K.£
50	.03	0.02
100	.07	0.04
300	.20	0.12
500	.33	0.20
700	.46	0.28
1,000	.66	0.40
1,500	.99	0.60
2,000	1.32	0.80
3,000	1.98	1.20
4,000	2.64	1.60
5,000	3.30	2.00
6,000	3.96	2.40
7,500	4.94	3.00
10,000	6.60	4.00
15,000	9.90	6.00
20,000	13.20	8.00
25,000	16.50	10.00
30,000	19.80	12.00
35,000	23.10	14.00
40,000	26.40	16.00
45,000	29.70	18.00
50,000	33.00	20.00
100,000	66.00	40.00
125,000	82.50	50.00
150,000	99.00	60.00
200,000	132.00	80.00
250,000	150.00	100.00
500,000	300.00	200.00

CAMCORDERS/ CAMERAS/LAPTOPS

When you're out of town and having a great time with family or friends, you want to capture the moment on film. Long after the trip is over, the memories are easily recalled when you pull out pictures or videos. With some precaution and preparation, you'll be able to enjoy these memories for a long time.

Cameras. Before your trip, decide what camera you are going to take with you on vacation. If you plan to use your own camera and have been using it, change the batteries. If you haven't used your camera recently, take a few pictures and have them developed. It is better to spend a little extra time before your trip than to discover that your camera was taking terrible pictures when you've returned home. Usually airport security X-rays won't damage your film, but to be on the safe side, put your film in a clear plastic bag and ask the security guard for a hand inspection. If you carry the film in your clothing as you pass through the metal detector, your film will be fine, but it will set off the alarm. The central information center at **Kodak** can provide you with further information. *Tel. (800) 242-2424*.

If you find yourself out of town and needing a camera, don't overlook disposable cameras. You can buy them almost anywhere. They're pocket size and can even go under water. They also come with or without a flash.

Videotape. Your safest bet is to ask for a hand check. The security X-rays shouldn't damage the tape, but if you carry it through the security walk-through detector, the magnetic field will. The airport security guards may ask you to turn your camcorder on, so make sure you have a fully-charged battery. Remember to pack blank video tapes. (They're hard to find overseas and when you can find them, they'll be exorbitantly expensive.)

Laptops. If you travel with a laptop computer, you know how invaluable it can be on the road. However, going on the road with your PC can be risky. The best way to prevent mishaps is to be prepared. Always pack the essential accessories—phone wires, connectors, cables, AC adapter, blank disks, miniature tool kit, and an extra battery. Lost disks or a crashed hard drive can create serious problems. Or what if your laptop is stolen while you are distracted at airport security? If you're on a business trip, the backup information at the office won't help you if you need the information immediately. Before your trip, make two backup disks with all the information. Pack one of the disks, leave the other at home. If your rolodex and calendar are on the laptop, pack a copy.

If you're only using the word processing system, strip your computer system down to the basics to get more RAM and battery life. If you haven't found the perfect portable printer, one way to get a hard copy is through the hotel fax system. Using your modem, fax to the hotel business center. Make sure you bring phone connectors for the Italian phone system.

Airport X-rays and laptops may create problems. It's natural to worry about the hard drive on your laptop when going through airport security. As far as the hard drive is concerned, there's no conclusive evidence of damage or safety. I'm a bit skeptical, so I still request a hand check for my laptop. I can remember when they said X-rays wouldn't harm film, and I came home with unexplainable foggy pictures. I know it's time-consuming, but unless you have all your files backed up, you may want to ask for a hand check with the laptop.

CHILDREN AND TRAVELING

Children and traveling don't always go hand in hand. However, with some tricks of the trade, planning, and involvement, traveling can be a pleasant experience for the whole family. It can really help if you get the kids involved with planning the trip. During this process, you'll learn what it is the kids are interested in seeing during the trip.

Here are a few items to pack:

- Wet wipes, or pre-moistened towels
- A small travel bag with an extra change of clothes. If you are traveling by car and planning to spend the night before you reach your final destination, you won't want to unpack everyone's suitcase for one night.
- Games, headsets, music tapes
- Small plastic trash bags
- Paper towels (car)
- Granola bars, instant soup, cocoa mix, favorite snacks. Even when traveling by plane, these can save the day.
- Be sure to keep common medications packed where you can get to them easily.

Traveling by Air

Many airlines offer discounts for children when they fly with an adult. On domestic flights, children under the age of two can travel free if they don't occupy a seat. This means you hope the flight won't be full, or you will be holding the child for the duration of the flight, which is unrealistic unless you have an infant. No child will sit on your lap for longer than thirty minutes without becoming uncomfortable and irritated. Children over the age of two can usually travel for the lowest available adult rate. Even "lap" children will be charged a fee on an international flight. Be realistic when thinking about flying overseas with someone in your lap, as international flights are usually full. Safety seats are recommended by the Federal Aviation Administration (FAA) during flight. However, airline policies vary, and you would have to purchase a ticket for the seat used by the infant carrier. Only approved models are allowed to be used.

For more information, write the **Federal Aviation Administration,** *APA-200, 800 Independence Ave. SW, Washington, DC 20591. Tel. (202) 267-3479. Information Hotline (800) 322-7873.*

When you're traveling with a baby, remember to bring several more diapers on board than you think you'll need in case of delays or layovers. Also bring a change of clothes in case of an accident.

TRAVELING BY CAR

Children enjoy moving around and are usually full of energy. Sitting in a car for countless hours is not something they usually enjoy. To limit their boredom, have them bring along games and headsets with their favorite music. Try to schedule stops along the way. Roadside parks are a great place for the kids to stretch their legs. You may even want to pack a lunch. Encourage the kids to run to their hearts' content.

SUGGESTIONS FOR THE PHYSICALLY CHALLENGED

Today, those who are physically challenged can travel with more comfort and ease than ever before. There are still a few obstacles, but most of them can be worked around with some planning.

> **There's a directory called "Travelin' Talk" that helps to alleviate some problems of the physically challenged traveler by connecting them to a network of real people in more than 800 different destinations. You will be connected with local people in your destination area who are willing to share their knowledge of the area, and sometimes provide services to physically challenged visitors. Directories cost $35. For more information, call (615) 552-6670.**

Here are some suggestions:

- Allow yourself plenty of time to pack and prepare for your trip. Pack everything you need to accommodate your needs.
- Airlines exempt wheelchairs as baggage, so you can go right up to the door of the plane.
- Trains can accommodate wheelchairs.
- Newer hotels are more likely to be well-equipped than historic inns.
- Although the world is becoming more "user friendly" for the physically challenged person, it's still a good idea to travel with a friend or relative.
- Ask your travel agent about tours for physically

challenged travelers that follow the same agenda as those for non-physically challenged.

- When making reservations, be sure to make your specific needs clear. Specify not only seating and bedroom arrangements, but be sure the bathroom, pool, and lounge are accessible.
- Request to have a hotel room on the lowest floor where accessible services are offered.
- Guests with hearing impairments should contact hotels in advance about devices to alert them visually to the ring of the telephone.
- If you are flying, pack your medication in two separate bags, one in your carry-on, and an extra set in your checked luggage in case one is lost or stolen.
- Diabetics should carry extra vials and store them in different places in case one breaks. Carry food to snack on, and be sure you are wearing your medical emergency ID bracelet.
- If you plan to take your wheelchair, make sure to bring extra nuts, bolts, and specialized tools in case you have to dismantle the chair. Remember to pack an extra fuse.
- If possible, try to plan your trip during the cooler months of your destination. During these times the humidity is usually lower.

Rome Information

Rome's streets, restaurants, hotels, and sights are becoming more aware of physically challenged visitors, but ramps are still the exception rather than the standard. For information about facilities available for physically challenged travelers, contact the **Information Center for Individuals with Disabilities**, *Fort Point Pl., 27-43 Wormwood St., Boston, MA. 02210. Tel. (617) 727-5540* or *(800) 462-5015*. **MossRehab**, information to telephone callers. *Tel. (215) 456-9603*.

For information about tours: **Society for the Advancement of Travel for the Handicapped**, *347 Fifth Ave., Suite 610, New York, NY 10016. Tel. (212) 447-7284* (yearly membership runs $25 seniors/students and $45 others).

Air Transportation and wheelchair accessibility in Rome. For general information about flying: *Air Transportation of Handicapped Persons*, (a free circular, by the U.S. Department of Transportation). Write to *Free Advisory Circular No. AC12032, Distribution Unit, U.S. Department of Transportation, Publications Division, M-4332, Washington, DC 20590.* Visitors from the U.K. can contact the **Royal Association for Disability and Rehabilitation, (RADAR)** *12 City Forum, 250 City Rd., London, EC1V 8AF. Tel. (171) 250-3222, fax (171) 250-0212.*

SUGGESTIONS FOR SENIOR CITIZENS

Today's senior citizens are healthier and more active than ever. With retirement, there is more time for traveling. Many places provide discounts for their senior customers. Here are a few preparations and precautions that can be taken to ensure a safe and enjoyable trip:

- Always keep a valid photo ID to qualify for your senior discount.
- Call in advance and ask for seniors' special rates and features.
- Contact your insurance carrier to see what it's able to cover if you become sick or injured while traveling.
- For traveling protection, it's wise to have proper forms of medical ID. Most pharmacies offer simple ID bracelets and necklaces for allergies and other medical problems. If you have a problem finding these, you can call **Health Enterprises** at *tel. (800) MEDIC-ID*.
- Always check with your physician before scheduling a trip.
- Even if you are traveling where you are not required to have additional immunizations, you may want to take the precaution. Your physician has access to publications issued by the Center for Disease Control and the quarterly publication *Travel Medicine International*. For more information contact: **Immunization Alert, Kenneth Dardick, MD,** *PO Box 406, Storrs, CT 06268. Tel. (203) 487-0422.*

- If you need special services or medical attention, call before you travel. You or your travel agent should contact the airline or hotel.
- Airports will transport you from terminal to terminal on a people-mover vehicle, or via wheelchair so you can move through the crowds more easily.
- Take an ample amount of prescription medicine in case you extend your trip.
- Take a list of generic names of medicines you are taking, since some name brands may be different at your travel destination.
- Have a brief summary of your medical history, including important information about anything you are currently being treated for.
- Bring a list of your physician's colleagues in the area you are planning to travel to.

Tips for Sightseeing

- Begin your day early when there are fewer people and it's cooler.
- Plan what you want to see before you start your day.
- Join a tour specifically designed for older travelers.
- Protect yourself from the sun by wearing a hat, and use sunscreen.
- Don't get overheated. Rest in the shade during the mid-afternoon, and have a small snack in an air-conditioned room. Drink plenty of water.
- Eat early or late to avoid mealtime crowds. Find an air-conditioned restaurant to take a break.
- When it comes to your food, don't try to pinch pennies. Traveling takes a lot of energy and only good food can replenish the supply.
- Becoming overheated is very dangerous. Try to avoid the big attractions or sights during the mid-afternoon hours to keep out of the sun.

For information on additional discounts and programs available for seniors, contact the **American Association of Retired Persons (AARP),** *601 E St. NW, Washington, DC 20049. Tel. (202) 434-2277.* If you are fifty or older, you can join for an $8 membership fee.

CRIME/SAFETY/HEALTH

As the date of travel departure nears, it's easy to become so preoccupied with trip preparations that travel precautions are overlooked. Unfortunately, crime and health problems are no strangers to vacations. Whether traveling for business or pleasure, precautions should be taken. Listed below are a few things to take into consideration before you travel.

CRIME

Traveler's Checks. Try to avoid carrying large sums of cash when you're traveling. Purchase a major brand of traveler's checks instead. Try to avoid obscure brands that are hard to cash or collect on. Sign them right away and keep a record of the serial numbers in a safe place. When you use them, keep a checkbook-style log. You will need this if your traveler's checks are lost or stolen.

Credit Cards. Leave the credit cards that you won't be using at home. There is no reason to take extra cards. You only risk their being stolen. As you are traveling around a city, take only a couple of cards with you. Leave the others in your hotel safe deposit box. Cover the numbers on the phone when using telephone credit card numbers, and be aware that thieves also use binoculars.

> **Divide your money and credit cards. Use a fanny pack or travel wallet. *Never* put your wallet in your back pocket. If someone bumps into you or tries to distract you, it could be to pick your pocket. Leave the good jewelry at home.**

Pickpockets. Italy is famous for pickpockets, and there are two types to watch for: "Thieves on motorscooters," who drive by and snatch your purse off your shoulder; and "gypsy" children, who surround you begging for money while another picks your pocket, opens your purse, or reaches into your packages. A popular trick they use, is to hold out a newspaper to shield your pants pockets, purse, or package from your view. If you see a group of kids coming toward you, hold onto your wallet and yell for them to get away. Loud yelling will draw attention, and they'll leave you alone. They are very bold.

Passports. Make photocopies of your passport and leave one set with a neighbor or family member who can be contacted twenty-four hours a day. Carry a copy with you, and pack a copy in your suitcase. Keep a close eye on your passport. On the black market, passports sell for thousands of dollars.

Packing and Luggage. Don't pack your valuables in your checked luggage, just in case it gets stolen or lost. Don't write your home address on your luggage identification tags. Many thieves read luggage tags at the departure terminal to see who won't be home for a while. Use a post office box or office address. Put good locks on your luggage; don't rely on the inexpensive ones that come with the suitcase. Criminals who rifle contents usually avoid luggage that's not easy to open. Avoid checking expensive luggage at the airport. To a thief, this could be an indication that the contents are expensive. If you check a designer bag, the whole bag may be stolen. Never leave your luggage unattended at a hotel. Doormen and bellmen are notorious for putting your bags on a cart or stacking them on the curb and walking away. Make sure the bags are taken inside the hotel before you walk away, and preferably watch them leave the public area or lobby. And whoever you entrust your luggage to—*get a name*. If you can't point a finger, you really don't have a leg to stand on.

When the doorman leaves my baggage cart sitting in the middle of the lobby (and I'm traveling with someone who can keep an eye on the

cart), I pick up a small bag from the cart and proceed to my room, as a test. When the cart arrives, I ask the bellman where that small bag is. They never know, and they're never responsible for the loss. I witnessed an expensively dressed woman picketing a famous five-star Denver hotel. It turns out that she left her bags with the doorman at the curb and walked off. Apparently, so did her luggage, *and the hotel refused responsibility.*

At the Airport. The airport is where 85% of crimes take place during trips. Be aware of what is going on around you. I've had a bag snatched right from my feet at Los Angeles Airport. Before you notice it's gone, they've passed it twice to accomplices. Don't walk away from your carry-on bags to pick up a suitcase from the carousel. If you're traveling with a companion, one person should not only watch the bags at a major airport, but also keep a hand *on* them. Never leave your luggage unattended at the airport, coming or going. That includes when you turn your bags over to a skycap. Make sure the skycap tags the bags and wheels them away before you walk off. Remember that the pros look for unattended bags, whether they're sitting tagged at the curbside or at the carousel. Security checkpoints are hot spots for stealing briefcases and purses. Thieves often work in pairs or threesomes. One holds up the line by carrying keys or change in their pockets to set off the alarm as they pass through the security door. While this is distracting everyone, the second thief will grab your purse or briefcase from the belt before it even goes through the X-ray. If you travel in pairs, send one person through security to watch the bags come through from the other side, and don't walk through security until you watch your bags go through. Be sure not to let yourself be distracted for a second.

WHEN IN ROME

- Certain areas of the city are worse than others. Pickpockets are particularly known for hanging around bus route number 64. The bus runs between Stazione Termini and the popular Vatican area.
- Often while walking down the street, gangs of gypsy children will swarm you and pick your pockets. Another technique they use is the deaf-card begging approach. They pretend to be deaf and show you a card asking for money. While you are distracted, they pick your pockets. They often carry knives and chains. If you see them coming, run the other way!

SAFETY

- Blend in. Be inconspicuous. Avoid looking like a tourist. The "Rome" T-shirt and camera around your neck are a dead giveaway.
- Don't walk around with your nose in a map or guidebook. Do your homework *before* you go out. Tear the pages you need for the day out of the guidebook, fold them up, and carry them in your pocket. Then you can sneak an occasional peek. Guidebooks are usually outdated before the next trip, so destroying the book is no big deal. But walking around with your nose in a book looking like a prime target is asking for trouble.
- Don't rely on the in-room safes. I don't trust them, and hotels claim no responsibility for any losses.
- Unless your room key is the computer-card type that is changed for every guest, just figure that someone else will have a key, and therefore access to the room. If keys are computer cards, then a thief will have to wait until the maid is working on your room to rummage through it.
- Don't flash a roll of cash when you're making a purchase.
- Walk far from the curb to keep shoulder bags and purses from moped-riding snatchers.

- Be alert to potential pickpockets. Some of their favorite places are tourist-related areas such as museums, street markets, subways, buses, elevators, and crowds. Avoid groups of children who will crowd you and pickpocket as a team.
- Don't leave your purse on the back of your chair, or under it, in a restaurant. I like to wrap the strap of my fanny pack a few times around the arm rest or chair leg, so I always feel it next to me, and a snatcher would have to unwind it to get it.
- Ladies, if you want to go back to your hotel room at night alone, *make sure no one follows you*. Don't leave the door unlocked for your husband or roommate. Double lock and deadbolt the door from the inside, even if it means you'll have to get up to open the door. In many assaults, the assailant counted on the fact that the women didn't deadbolt the door.
- When driving, keep windows up and doors locked. At stoplights, allow room between you and the car in front of you in case you need a fast getaway. A popular ploy used by a robber or carjacker is to bump your car and wait for you to pull over to assess the damage. Another is to pull alongside of you, pointing at your car like something's wrong. If that happens, look for a service station, police station, or crowded area before pulling over.
- If you are confronted by someone demanding your money, car, or passport, *give it up without an argument*. Avoid direct eye contact with the robber. It could be taken as a challenge or a threat.
- When checking into your hotel, if by some chance the front desk clerk announces your room number aloud for everyone to hear, ask for a different room with the number written down.
- When visiting a new area, always ask someone at the hotel desk or concierge about the safety of the area you plan to walk or travel to.

When you put your valuables in a hotel safe, put your credit cards in a sealed and signed envelope so you know whether they've been used when you get them back.

- Hotel thieves are getting more brazen. One alarming technique they use is to strike up a conversation with their victim in the hotel elevator, then step off at the same floor and pretend to be occupied. When the victim has opened the door, the robber pushes in behind them. If you return to your room late at night, be aware of who's around you, and who's in the elevator with you.
- First-class airline passengers are favorite targets of the pickpocket. While a passenger sleeps, goes to the lavatory, or watches the movie, the thief reaches under the seat to take cash and credit cards out of a purse or briefcase. Most of the time you won't miss them until you are off the plane.
- Don't answer the door in a hotel without verifying who it is. If a person claims to be an employee, call the front desk and ask if someone is supposed to be at your room, and for what purpose.

If you're worried someone might enter your room at night, pack a rubber door wedge. When you're in your room, wedge it against or under the door.

- If you're staying at a budget hotel, check for unblocked fire exits. Avoid rooms near the stairs, or on the first floor where thieves have an easy exit.

HEALTH

- If you have allergies and are planning to travel to another city, call ahead to either a local hospital or the chamber of commerce to find out what the local pollen count is.
- Airplane flights are tough on the sinuses, so keep a sinus pain medication and saline nasal spray in your carry-on bag.

- Prepare yourself mentally for an upcoming vacation. That could mean being organized and unhurried when making trip preparations. Pack over a period of several days rather than at the last minute.

Aromatherapy remedies can perk you up in a matter of seconds. Use scents to manipulate your emotions. Some doctors feel treatments with fragrance can relax and rejuvenate you, lower stress, and even relieve pain. In three seconds, a chilled mineral water facial spray with herbal extracts will perk you up. Mint and citrus will give you a burst of energy; while honey and vanilla will comfort you.

When Traveling Overseas

- Check your health insurance. Many policies won't cover you once you leave the U.S. If you need insurance, there are a number of companies that offer travel coverage plans including American Express, International SOS Assistance, Medex, and Health Care Abroad.

Notes

TRAVELING WITH PETS

Pets bring joy and companionship into the lives of their owners. If you plan to travel with your pet, or find it necessary to transport your pet, there are some preparations that will make traveling less stressful.

QUARANTINE INFORMATION

You will need to obtain a current certificate of health for your pet before your trip. To do this you'll need to call your veterinarian. Most larger veterinarian practices will be familiar with the quarantine procedure required. They will need to contact the local United States Department of Agriculture and Veterinary Services (USDA) and request the telephone number for the nearest Italian consulate's office. The Italian consulate's office will provide the forms and health certificate that must be completed by the veterinarian, stamped by the USDA office, and returned to you before your trip. For the telephone number of the nearest USDA Veterinarian Services office, contact the Federal Information Center at (800) 688-9889. From the telephone menu, select #9 if you are calling from a touch-tone phone.

PACKING FOR YOUR PET

- A copy of your certificate of immunizations and vaccinations
- An extra collar and leash
- A long line of rope can be very useful!
- A blanket to cover the back seat of your car

- Chew toys, balls, frisbees, etc.
- Room deodorizer
- If you plan to go hiking with your dog, pack large resealable bags. They make great water bowls.
- Food, bowls
- Pooper scooper

To Make Your Pet's Vacation More Enjoyable

- Don't feed or water your pet for two hours prior to your planned departure.
- Exercise your pet before you leave. A tired pet travels and adapts more easily.

When Flying

- Find out the pet policies of the airline your pet is flying.
- Be sure to reserve a place—you want the cargo area to be pressurized, lighted, and temperature-controlled.
- Check with your veterinarian for a check-up and sedative if necessary.
- Allow your pet to become familiar with the flight-approved travel case.

For more information contact: **Do It, Bud Brownhill,** *2147 Avon Circle, Anaheim,* CA *92804*. This is a support organization that deals with problems and questions with the airline industry.

Leaving your Pet

An option to consider when it comes time to leave your pet, is a caretaker. They offer a foster home for the small animals while you travel. After a computer match, you will be given a compatible caretaker's name in your area. For more information contact: **Pets Are Inn,** *27 North Fourth Street, Suite 500, Minneapolis,* MN *55401. Tel. (800) 248-PETS.*

PART 2

While in Rome

TRANSPORTATION

In Rome, you'll find that the traffic is congested nearly all of the time. Most of the streets are narrow, and you'll find yourself barely squeezing through with only inches to spare. So, if you can, it's best to avoid driving in the city area. Most of the city between the river, Piazza del Popplo, Piazza di Spagna, and Piazza Venezia is closed to private cars throughout the day. If you happen to be staying at a hotel in this area, you will have access by special permit. Traveling by any aboveground transportation will be slow due to the traffic. Your best options are to walk or use the underground metro.

PUBLIC TRANSPORTATION

The cost of public transportation in the Rome area is inexpensive, compared to other European cities. There are three companies that make up Rome's public transportation system. The ATAC transit authority operates buses and trams throughout the city. A company called COTRAL operates regional and suburban bus services, as well as Rome's two metro lines. Then there are the state railways, FS, that operate the rail lines in the Rome suburban area, from Termini, Porta San Paolo (Ostiense), and Roma Nord. Overall, the public transportation system is safe in Rome. Just remember to keep an eye on your valuables. Pickpockets are notorious and you're an easy target in a crowd.

THE METROPOLITANA (METRO)/ UNDERGROUND

This is the fastest way to cross the city, or to reach a few of the main sights. The Metro is a subway system that stretches across Rome with two rail lines (A and B). *Linea* A (red) runs in an east to west direction, while *Linea* B (blue) runs north to south by means of underground and surface railroad. The two lines cross and meet each other at the Termini Station.

Linea A begins at Ottaviano next to the Vatican and travels southwest of the city area to Anagnina with several stops in between. You can catch a bus that goes to Ciampino airport. This line operates between 5:30 A.M. and 12:00 P.M.

Linea B runs from Rebibbia, connecting the northeast part of the city with EUR in the southwest area. Here, you can connect with buses leaving for the coast. This line operates between 5:30 A.M. and 9:00 P.M. Monday through Friday.

Stations aren't difficult to find if you look for the metro logo. There's a sign displayed with a red background and large printed "M."

Metro Fares

Fares run L1,200 or L6,000 for a booklet of 10 tickets. You can purchase them from vending machines found in all the stations. The machines accept the following coins: 50 lira, 100 lira, and 200 lira. Booklets can be purchased at tobacco stores *(tabacchi)* located in the stations. If you plan to take the metro more than four or five times a day, consider buying a BIG ticket. With this you can travel on buses, trams, and metros.

Buses and Trams

Traveling by bus or tram is one of the most reasonable forms of transportation, but they are overcrowded, hot, and a pickpocket's paradise. The buses are operated by the organization **ATAC**. There are numerous orange buses and trams operating from about 6:30 A.M. until 12:00 midnight. During the month of August, bus drivers are off on vacations, and service drops dramatically with fewer buses available. Buses are not allowed through the historic areas of Rome, but have stops very close to historic sights. Some of the most popular route stops are at Largo Argentina and Piazza del Risorgimento. For more information call 6/ 46 95 4444.

Bus and Tram Fares

You need to purchase your tickets before you plan to travel. There are ticket booths at the metro stations, but they are often closed or swamped. The ticket machines only take coins and don't give change. That is *when* they are working. Tickets are also available at newsstands and bars. It's a good idea to purchase more than one ticket when you find them. If you board a bus without a ticket, be prepared for a *steep* fine. Bus and tram tickets are valid for ninety minutes so you can change buses or get on and off the bus or tram as many times as you want to during this time. If you plan to be in Rome for longer than a week, the weekly tourist passes are a little less expensive and can save you the time of looking for a place to purchase tickets.

If you are using a regular ticket to board the bus during the day, use the back door to enter. Then, have your ticket time-stamped at the orange machine. If you are using a bus pass or have used your ticket within the last ninety minutes, you can enter the bus through the front. But, be prepared for the surge of riders leaving the bus.

TAXIS

The official cabs are yellow and have a "taxi" sign on their roof. They are found in front of hotels, at large stations, and generally all the usual places you find them in the U.S. Unlike in the U.S., they are *not* supposed to stop on the street to pick you up. You'll find that the drivers are generally accommodating, but fares are not cheap. This is not the way to get around Rome, unless you have luggage or want to go somewhere that is nearby or difficult to find.

TAXI FARES

Fares can really mount up as the meter ticks and traffic is sitting still. You'll be charged extra for luggage, trips on a holiday or Sunday, and trips made after 10:00 P.M. and before 7:30 A.M. The first nine minutes or three kilometers (1.8 miles) you'll be charged the minimum rate fare. After that, the fare jumps a lot. You'll also be expected to give a 10% tip.

If you are approached by anyone offering taxi services, never accept. They usually charge as much as 400% more than a legitimate cab. And even in a legitimate cab, remember to look at the meter when you get in. It should be set at the minimum fare for the first three kilometers (1.8 miles).

Scooters and mopeds. With the heavy traffic problems in Rome, scooters and mopeds have picked up popularity. But, be prepared for some less than friendly driving practices from drivers sharing the road who think these are a nuisance. If riding a motorcycle, helmets are required by law. Moped riders don't have to wear them if they are over eighteen, but I'd suggest it. They are available for rent at several places in the old city center. Here's a few rental centers: **Scoot-a-long,** *302 Via Cavour, tel. 6/ 67 80 206.* **Scooters for Rent,** *66 Via della Purificazione*, next to Piazza Barberini, *tel. 6/ 48 85 485.* **St. Peter Motor and Scooter,** *43 Via Porta Castello*, next to the Basilica di San Pietro, *tel. 6/ 68 75 714.*

Horse-drawn carriages. Horse-drawn *carrozzelles* are nice for a tour of the historic district. They hold up to five people and are available for hire in most city squares. Trips are expensive and can last anywhere from a half hour to a day. The longer the trip, the more it will cost. Before you ride, get the price confirmed and ask if the price is per person, or for the whole carriage. You can hire them at Piazza San Pietro, di Spagna, Venezia; and Novona city squares, in front of the Colosseum, next to the Fontana di Trevi, on Via Veneto, or in Villa Borghese.

Boat. If weather and water levels are good, you can take a round-trip, half-day river cruise to Ostia Antica with up to three hundred other passengers, on the *Tiber II*. For information on reservations call **Tourvisa** at *6/ 44 50 284*. For boat rentals call **Acquario** at *6/ 50 10 360*. **Axa-Riga Yachts** has charters available, *tel. 6/ 50 90 222, fax 6/ 50 91 7530*.

GETTING ACQUAINTED WITH ROME

BUSINESS HOURS

Bank business hours are Monday through Friday from 8:30 A.M. to 1:20 P.M. Some of the larger banks will re-open from 3:00 to 4:30 P.M. Banks are closed on week-ends and holidays.

Shops. Merchants generally open from 9:00 A.M. to 1:00 P.M., then re-open 4:00 to 7:30 P.M. They are closed on Sundays, Monday mornings, and Saturday afternoons during summer months.

Street markets are usually open Monday through Saturday from 6:00 A.M. to 2:00 P.M.

Grocery stores operate from 8:00 A.M. to 1:30 P.M., and re-open from 5:00 to 7:30 P.M. They are closed on Thursday afternoons in the winter and on Saturday afternoons during the summer.

Exchange offices operate from 9:00 A.M. to 1:30 P.M., then re-open from 4:30 till 8:00 P.M. They are closed on Sundays.

Pharmacies operate from 8:30 A.M. to 1:00 P.M. and re-open from 4:30 to 8:00 P.M. They are closed on Saturday afternoons and on Sundays. If you have an emergency see, "While in Rome-Emergency Telephone Numbers."

ELECTRICITY

The electric current in Rome is 220 volts AC cycle, as opposed to the 115-120 volts AC cycle used in the United States. The prongs are two-pin round. You will need an adapter or converter to be able to plug the flat pins of your appliance plugs into outlets in Rome. It's best to bring your own adapters; however, some hotels do furnish them.

ETIQUETTE

The Roman people are generally friendly and don't like to be rushed. They expect common considerations. Most of the time they won't mind your English and will attempt to understand it. Becoming drunk, loud, or rude is frowned upon. Romans usually drink at meals.

MAIL

You'll probably be back in the States before the letters you mail from Rome arrive. The postal system is extremely slow, and even slower during August when workers are taking off for vacation. Postage is very expensive. Stamps are sold at the tobacco stores where they display a black-and-white "T" sign or at post offices. There are twenty-four-hour post offices at Piazza San Silvestro, Termini, and the airport.

RESTROOMS

These aren't the easiest to find. In fact, they are pretty scarce and when you do find one, there's usually no paper. Be prepared and carry tissue with you. If you find yourself in a predicament, most cafés will let you use theirs. You will also find a public toilet in St. Peter's Square.

SMOKING

Smoking is allowed in restaurants and clubs, but it is not allowed on public transportation.

TELEPHONE

Telephone booths are scattered throughout Rome. They are a little difficult to find. You can usually find one in a bar, but look for the telephone symbol hanging outside. You needn't feel obligated to buy something when you use the phone. This is a very common occurrence. Some of the phones will be at the counter and you pay after the call is made. Recently, they've introduced a new style of telephone box. You can use 500, 200, and 100 lire coins, or a phone card. Phone cards are sold at newsstands, bars, and vending machines. You will be charged a minimum of 200 lire for a call.

To make a direct international call, look for the telephones marked "*teleselezione*."

WATER

Drinking the local water is considered to be safe. However, anytime you travel to a different area, you may find that the water doesn't agree with you. I usually stick with bottled water. If you plan on traveling to areas outside Rome, especially those to the south, drink *only* bottled water.

EMERGENCY TELEPHONE NUMBERS

EMERGENCY INFORMATION

In Rome, for police, fire, or an ambulance, dial 113.

AUTOMOBILE BREAKDOWN

If you have car trouble, call 116 for help and the Automobile Club (ACI) will tow the car. ACI has emergency phones every few miles.

DENTISTS

For twenty-four-hour dental service, contact **Instituto George Eastman**, *Viale Regina Margherita, 287A*, at *6/ 44 53 887.*

DOCTORS

For a list of English-speaking doctors in Italy, contact the **International Association for Medical Assistance to Travelers (IAMAT).**

U.S.: 417 Center St., Lewiston, NY 14092.
Tel. (716) 754-4883.
Canada: 40 Regal St., Guelph, ON N1K1B5.
Tel. (519) 836-0102.

DRUGSTORES

Italian drugstores may not be open all night, but a pharmacist is always on call and can fill a prescription at any time of the day or night. Drugstores are identified with a red cross or a caduceus (a professional medical symbol of a staff with one or two serpents wrapped around it) in the front of the store. To get a hold of the pharmacist, call the operator or the police. Major pharmacies include **Farmacia Internazionale,** *Piazza Barberini, 49. Tel. 6/ 48 25 456;* **Farmacia Internazionale Copranica,** *Piazza Corpranica, 96. Tel. 6/ 67 94 680;* and **Cola de Rienzo,** *Via Cola di Rienzo, 213. Tel. 6/ 32 43 130.*

HOSPITALS

There are both public and private hospitals in Rome. In an emergency the patient is taken to a public hospital for treatment. If the patient is in stable condition, they may transfer to a private hospital. Hospitals include the **Rome American Hospital,** *Via Longoni, 67. Tel. 6/ 22 551;* **Casa di Cura Privata Salvator Mundi,** *Viale delle Mura Gianicolensi, 67. Tel. 6/ 58 89 61;* and **Policlinico Umberto I** *Viale Policlinico. Tel. 6/ 49 97 1.*

OTHER TELEPHONE NUMBERS

AA	6/ 67 80 320
Airport Limousine	6/ 67 98 207
American Lawyer	6/ 48 20 147
Current Time	161
Emergency Assistance	113
Emergency Room	6/ 44 62 341
Morning Wakeup Service	114
News Briefs	190
Poison Treatment Center	6/ 49 06 63
Postal Information	160
Red Cross Ambulance	5510
Road Report	1941
Taxi	570, 4994, 88177
Tourist First Aid Service	6/ 44 53 887
Train Information	4775
U.S. Embassy	46741
U.S. Embassy Health Unit	6/ 46 74 2150
Weather Report	1911

PART 3

Turning In

ACCOMMODATIONS

One of the most difficult and important decisions to make for your trip is where to stay. This is always difficult because you usually know very little about the city areas. Some areas may suit your travel plans better than others. This, of course, will depend on where your interests lie. Another factor to consider is that not all the hotels come equipped with bathroom facilities within the hotel room. You may discover that you have to share your bathroom with other guests. The hotels that do offer a private bath in their rooms have either a tub or a shower, although some contain both. Another point to consider is that air conditioning is not provided at most accommodations. So if you would like to stay somewhere other than what I have listed, ask about the air conditioning before you book a room. Naturally you want your stay in Rome to be a pleasant one, so choose a hotel that meets as many of your standards as possible.

AVENTINE/PALATINE

The Aventine is the southernmost hill in Rome. Once the home of rich merchants, it remains a fashionable and affluent neighborhood. The Palatine is the grandest hill in Rome, and became the home of many of Rome's influential citizens and emperors. The hotels here generally will offer you a good value for the money, although, locationwise, it's not the best. It may not be as close to Rome's good shopping and restaurant districts as you would like.

CAMPO DE'FIORI

The piazza here is now a food market. The Palazzo Farnese, the Galleria, Palazzo Spada, and Galleria Spada are located here. Several trendy shops are in this area, along with the kind of scenery and atmosphere that Rome is famous for. The people who live in this area range from those of the young chic scene to those of lower incomes benefiting from rent control programs. This area offers mostly budget to mid-range accommodations.

CAPITOL/FORUM/COLOSSEUM

This is where you can find the Capitol, the Forum, and the Colosseum areas. The Roman Forum area has many temples for all kinds of divinities, as well as a treasure-trove of statues and ruins to be admired. The hotels here are more on the expensive side. It is pretty noisy during the day, but at night it quietens down, as there aren't many bars or clubs nearby.

PANTHEON

This awe-inspiring building is the tomb for both kings and painters alike. Near the Pantheon area are the Piazza Minerva and Santa Maria sopra Minerva, the only truly Gothic church in Rome. The restaurants and clubs outnumber the hotels and shops, which results in a busier and noisier atmosphere. The hotels are generally nice. There exists a wide range of price levels, depending on the location and the amenities in the rooms.

PIAZZA DI SPAGNA

This international area located in the heart of Rome offers some of the best shopping that you'll find in Rome. This is where you'll find the famous Spanish Steps, named because of the nearby Spanish Embassy. If you like exclusive shopping, visit the Via Condotti. The Piazza del Popolo is also to be found here. All of the hotels in this area offer an excellent location so the price variations between the hotels are based on the quality of the hotel and the amenities each offers. To stay at a hotel that offers all the amenities that come standard in a U.S. hotel room, prices will be in the very expensive range in this area. But if you're willing to do without some of the frills for the location, then the price goes down to mid-range and even some budget.

PIAZZA NAVONA

Here is where you can find the famous Fountain of the four Rivers. There are many palazzos and piazzas here. Although it's a relatively quiet area, the rooms don't offer much, and what you pay for is the excellent location. If you plan to spend most of your time out and about, and don't want to spend much on transportation, this can be a good area to stay in, as some of the hotel prices are reasonable.

THE QUIRINALE

The Quirinale is the tallest of Rome's seven hills. Here you will find the presidential palace, along with countless examples of baroque art and architecture. The hotels here are equally grand, as are their prices.

STAZIONE TERMINI

There are plenty of restaurants and bars in this area, but very few that are worth frequenting. Although the churches and art in the area are some of the most breathtaking in Rome, the area is dirty, noisy, and in a state of a perpetual traffic jam. It's because of this that it's one of the most inexpensive areas to stay in Rome.

TRASTEVERE

Since ancient times, this has been the area of the working-class sector located across the river from Rome. Recently, however, it's turning into a chic place to live. It has been an artist's corner for centuries. Now, streets are full of clubs and shops, as well as several good restaurants. Unfortunately, the hotel scene has yet to catch up. Although they're all clean, very few have en suite facilities, even though you really can't beat the prices.

THE VATICAN

The Vatican is a sovereign state, independent of Rome. In fact, it's the smallest state in the world. You won't find many trendy bars or clubs in this area, but the hotels are grand, and many are converted residences. It's because of their grandeur that many of the hotels are very expensive here, although there are better prices if you reserve ahead.

VIA VENETO/PIAZZA BARBERINI

The nearby Via Veneto is the street that was the playground of the jet set, immortalized in Fellini's *La Dolce Vita*. There are still plenty of classy hotels and bars left over from that era of *La Dolce Vita*, but it isn't quite as fashionable as it used to be. However, due to the famous reputation of the area and excellent location, many of the hotels' prices are outrageous. This is definitely not the area for mid-range and budget travelers.

VILLA BORGHESE

Villa Borghese is without a doubt the most stunning park area in Rome. Not only does it feature gardens with fountains and lakes, it also has museums and galleries filled with exceptional collections of art. It's also the home of Rome's zoo. Most of the hotels here are in the higher price ranges, although the location isn't very convenient to the popular shops, sights, or restaurants. But the views of the lavish gardens might well make it worth it.

OUTER ROME

The area surrounding Rome features mostly resort-style accommodations, usually fifteen to twenty minutes away from Rome's center. There are very few, if any, budget accommodations out here, so when you consider this area be sure to budget in an expensive room rate and transportation to and from Rome.

EXPENSE CHART

CATEGORY	COST*
Expensive	L250,000 and over
Moderate	L120,000-L250,000
Inexpensive	L120,000 and under

*for a standard double room

AVENTINE/PALATINE

MODERATE

L180,000–L250,000 DOMUS AVENTINA. *Via S. Prisca 11B, 00153. Tel. 6/ 57 46 135.* Within walking distance to many of ancient Rome's attractions, this former convent sits at the foot of Aventine Hill. The rooms are large and simply decorated in pastels, some with their own balconies. Each room offers a private bath with tub and shower, direct-dial private phone with 24-hour switchboard service, color TV with CNN and the Sky Channel, and air conditioning. *Facilities: 26 rooms (18 with balcony), on-site bar, business facilities.* Accepts all major credit cards.

L179,000–L315,000 PALAZZO AL VELABRO RESIDENCE. *Via del Velabro 16. Tel. 6/ 67 92 758 or 6/ 67 93 450, fax 6/ 67 93 790.* Located just up the street from the Arch of Janus, this apartment-hotel was built from an old palace. You must stay a minimum of one week, although there's no maximum. Each of the two- and three-bedroom apartments has a kitchenette, full bath with tub and shower, satellite TV with CNN, air conditioning except in October, and telephone with 24-hour switchboard service. Great for families. *Facilities: Sofa-bed, bathroom, double bed room, polite staff.* Accepts all major credit cards.

L140,000–L300,000 VILLA SAN PIO. *Via Sant'Anselmo 19, 00153. Tel. 6/ 57 43 214 or 6/ 57 43 547, fax 6/ 57 83 604.* This villa hotel is situated in the middle of a garden and still keeps an air of the eighteenth century. There's velvet and brocade galore, in both the rooms and the public areas. The rooms are simple, but some are more elaborately decorated than others, with doors that open onto the garden. *Facilities: 59 rooms, 24-hour room service available, business facilities, pets allowed, on-site bar.* Accepts all major credit cards.

INEXPENSIVE

L75,000–L110,000 AVENTINO. *Via S. Domenico 10, 00153. Tel. 6/ 57 45 232, fax 6/ 57 83 604.* This villa hotel is a little out-of-the-way. Not exactly stylish, however, it does offer large, comfortable rooms, each with its own full bathroom, some with tubs and others with showers, private telephone with 24-hour switchboard service and direct dial, and no air conditioning. The archaeological zone is nearby, and the villa is surrounded by a beautiful garden. *Facilities: 23 rooms, on-site bar, 24-hour room service available, babysitting, business facilities, nearby pay-extra car park, fax, laundry, multi-lingual staff.* AE, MC, V.

L75,000–L96,000 CASA KOLBE. *Via di San Teodora 44. Tel. 6/ 67 94 974.* Located close to the Roman Forum, this reasonably priced little hotel has a lovely garden. However, you might want to note that there is no TV or air conditioning. Guest rooms include a private bath with shower and tub, and a direct-dial private phone with 24-hour switchboard service. *Facilities: 60 rooms.* No credit cards.

L70,000–L180,000 SANT'ANSELMO. *Piazza Sant'Anselmo 2, 00153. Tel. 6/ 57 45 174, fax 6/ 57 83 604.* Although not in the center of Rome, this is a good choice for those who want to be slightly away from the city. Within walking distance to the Colosseum, this villa hotel has pretty rooms for a bargain, some with lovely antiques, and most with private full bath with tub and shower, telephone with direct dial and 24-hour switchboard service, and no air conditioning. There's also a garden, as well as rooms for the disabled. *Facilities: 46 rooms (43 with private bathrooms), on-site bar, babysitting, currency exchange, fax, laundry, multi-lingual staff, room service, TV on request.* Accepts all major credit cards.

CAMPO DE'FIORI

MODERATE

L140,000–L229,000 CARDINAL HOTEL. *Via Giulia 62, 00186. Tel. 6/ 68 80 2719 or 6/ 68 80 5175, fax 6/ 67 86 376.* This building was converted into a hotel in the 1970s, but there are several ancient touches. The hotel almost seems to have an opulent feel to it. All the rooms feature a private bath with tub or shower, direct-dial private phone with 24-hour switchboard service, color TV with CNN and the Sky Channel, and air conditioning until September. On the fifth floor, most of the rooms have a balcony. Breakfast is included in the price of the room. *Facilities: 74 rooms.* AE, DC, V.

L145,000–L190,000 PONTE SISTO. *Via dei Pettinari 64, 00186. Tel. 6/ 68 68 843, fax 6/ 68 30 8822.* This hotel, the largest in this area, offers decent-sized rooms which include a full bathroom with tub and shower, telephone with direct dial, and no air conditioning. The public areas are friendly and informal, and include a terrace in the courtyard of the hotel. Close to restaurants and bars in the areas. *Facilities: 130 rooms, wheelchair accessible, on-site restaurant, 24-hour on-site bar, fax, laundry, car park, multi-lingual staff.* Accepts all major credit cards.

L105,000–L180,000 SMERALDO. *Vicolo dei Chiodaroli 11, 00186. Tel. 6/ 68 75 929, fax 6/ 65 45 495.* This small hotel offers rooms with air conditioning, and some, not all, with a private bathroom. The rooms themselves are neat and uncomplicated. *Facilities: 35 rooms (18 with bathrooms), on-site bar, pets allowed.* AE, MC, V.

L180,000–L300,000 TIZIANO HOTEL. *110 Corso Vittorio Emanuele II, 00816. Tel. 6/ 68 65 019, fax 6/ 68 65 019.* This hotel is set literally in the middle of a palazzo. There can be a lot of noise coming from the Corso Vittorio. Unless you plan to join in the carousing, you may have a little trouble sleeping, so request a room in the back. The rooms are centrally heated and air-conditioned, each with bathroom, mini-bar, TV with CNN and the Sky Channel, and telephone. Within walking distance of the Roman Forum and Colosseum. Rates include breakfast. *Facilities: 46 rooms, 4 suites, on-site bar, on-site restaurant, nearby pay-extra car park, limousine service, weekend packages available*. AE, CB, DC, MC.

INEXPENSIVE

L77,000–L160,000 ALBERGO CAMPO DE'FIORI. *Via del Biscione 6, 00186. Tel. 6/ 68 80 6865, fax 6/ 68 76 003*. This wonderful budget hotel has recently refurbished several of its rooms, the best of which are on the first floor, except for the wonderful honeymoon suite on the sixth floor. The rest of the rooms are on the more-than-small side. The rooms include full bath with tub and shower, telephone with 24-hour switchboard service and direct dial, and no air conditioning. The villa hotel is situated in the historical center of Rome, and in a market area that the roof garden overlooks. Breakfast is included in the price of a room. *Facilities: 27 rooms (9 with showers)*. MC, V.

L59,000–L83,000 ARENULA. *Via Santa Maria dei Cadlerari 47 (Ghetto, Rome). Tel. 6/ 68 79 454*. This is a hotel that offers a relaxed atmosphere and a pretty good location. Rooms include a shower only, telephone with direct dial, and satellite TV with CNN. *Facilities: 45 rooms*. MC, V.

L97,000–L145,000 RINASCIMENTO. *Via del Pellegrino 122. Tel. 6/ 68 74 813, fax 6/ 68 33 518*. The rooms in this converted palazzo tend to look a little run-down, but they all offer air conditioning, TV with CNN, telephone with 24-hour switchboard service and direct dial, mini-bar, and bathroom with tub and shower. Breakfast is included in the price of a room. *Facilities: 13 rooms, on-site bar*. AE, MC, V.

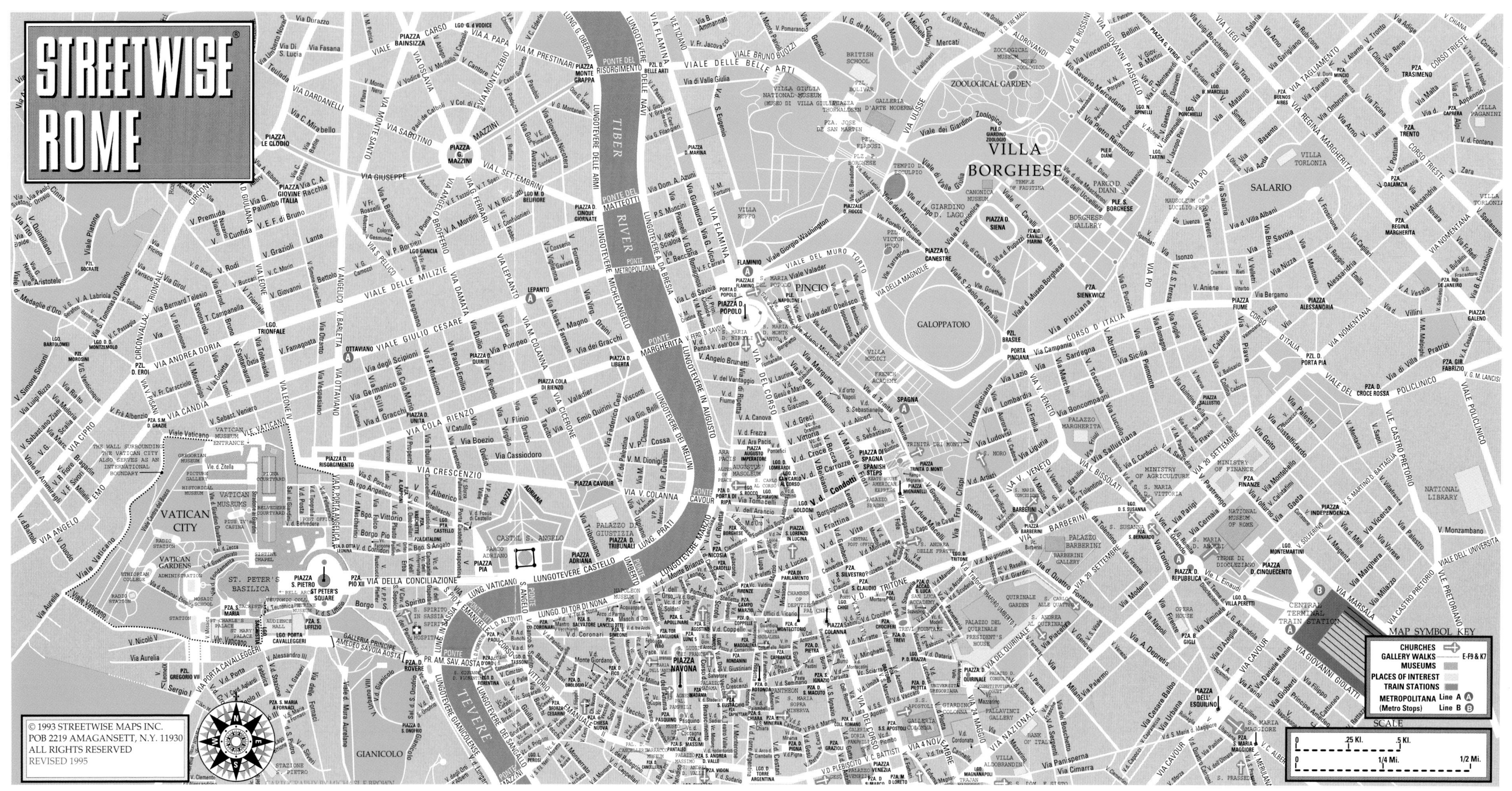

STREETWISE®
ROME
TIBER RIVER
TEVERE
VATICAN CITY
VATICAN MUSEUMS
VATICAN GARDENS
ST. PETER'S BASILICA
ST PETER'S SQUARE
CASTEL S. ANGELO
VIA DELLA CONCILIAZIONE
VILLA BORGHESE
ZOOLOGICAL GARDEN
GALOPPATOIO
PINCIO
PIAZZA D. POPOLO
SPANISH STEPS
PIAZZA NAVONA
PANTHEON
TREVI FOUNTAIN
QUIRINALE GARDEN
PALAZZO DEL QUIRINALE PRESIDENT'S HOUSE
PALAZZO BARBERINI
NATIONAL MUSEUM OF ROME
CENTRAL TERMINAL TRAIN STATION
NATIONAL LIBRARY
VILLA TORLONIA
SALARIO
GIANICOLO
THE WALL SURROUNDING THE VATICAN CITY ALSO SERVES AS AN INTERNATIONAL BOUNDARY
MAP SYMBOL KEY
CHURCHES
GALLERY WALKS E-F9 & K7
MUSEUMS
PLACES OF INTEREST
TRAIN STATIONS
METROPOLITANA (Metro Stops) Line A Line B
SCALE
0 .25 Kl. .5 Kl.
0 1/4 Mi. 1/2 Mi.

L65,000–L110,000 SOLE. *Via del Biscione 76, 00186. Tel. 6/ 68 80 6873, fax 6/ 68 93 787.* Conceivably the oldest hotel in Rome, the Sole has its own garage and garden, and has been a favorite for many years for guests from college back-packers to seniors. About half of the rooms have private baths. The rooms have lots of character, and there's a terrace with a snack machine. *Facilities: 62 rooms (31 with bathrooms), 24-hour room service available, business facilities, pets allowed, garden.* Accepts all major credit cards.

L75,000–L110,000 TEATRO DI POMPEO. *Largo del Pallaro 8, 00186. Tel. 6/ 68 72 566, fax 6/ 68 80 5531.* This unique hotel has the distinction of being built on the ruins of the Theater of Pompey, where Julius Caesar was rumored to have said his final words, "Et tu Brute?" This small hotel has wood-beamed rooms with air conditioning available (you may have to pay a little extra), as well as mini-bar, hair dryer (on request), TV, radio, and telephone. You can eat your breakfast in the remains of the theater. *Facilities: 12 rooms, room service, on-site bar, babysitting, fax, laundry, multi-lingual staff.* Accepts all major credit cards.

CAPITOL/FORUM/COLOSSEUM

EXPENSIVE

L300,000–L450,000 HOTEL FORUM. *25 Via Tor de Conti, 00184. Tel. 6/ 67 92 446, fax 6/ 67 86 479.* Highly recommended, this converted convent is a few feet away from the Roman Forum and Piazza Venezia. The rooms here are a good size and most offer amazing views. If not, you can always eat at the rooftop restaurant, or in the rooftop garden. The rooms themselves are elegantly decorated, and include hair dryer, minibar, TV, radio, and safe. Guest rooms feature private bath with tub and shower, direct-dial in-room phone with 24-hour switchboard service, color TV with CNN and Sky Channel, and air conditioning. *Facilities: 76* *rooms, 24-hour room service, on-site restaurant, on-site bar, babysitting, fax, laundry, multi-lingual staff, nearby pay-extra car park, foreign currency exchange.* Accepts all major credit cards.

MODERATE

L150,000–L250,000 DUCA D'ALBA. *Via Leonina 14, 00184. Tel. 6/ 48 44 71, fax 6/ 48 84 840.* This stylish little hotel in a section of Rome is becoming more and more fashionable as time goes by. There are three stories, and each room has been recently refurbished and includes a private bath with tub and shower, direct-dial in-room phone with 24-hour switchboard service, color TV with CNN and the Sky Channel, mini-bar, and air conditioning. The rates include breakfast. *Facilities: 24 rooms, on-site bar, babysitting, fax, laundry, currency exchange, multi-lingual staff.* Accepts all major credit cards.

PANTHEON

EXPENSIVE

L280,000–L500,000 ALBERGO DEL SOLE AL PANTHEON. *Piazza della Rotunda 63, 00186. Tel. 6/ 67 80 441, fax 6/ 68 40 689.* This recently refurbished four-star hotel is one of the oldest in Rome. It has quite a distinguished guest list, from Simone de Beauvoir to Jean-Paul Sartre. Bedrooms are named after famous guests who have slept here. Rooms include a private bath with tub and shower (some with a Jacuzzi), direct-dial private phone with 24-hour switchboard service, color TV with CNN and the Sky Channel, mini-bar, and air conditioning. They are a little on the small side, but very pretty, and some have breathtaking views. *Facilities: 29 rooms, 24-hour room service, on-site bar, wheelchair access, babysitting, fax, laundry, multi-lingual staff, foreign currency exchange, nearby pay-extra car park.* Accepts all major credit cards.

L340,000–L600,000 COLONNA PALACE HOTEL. *Piazza Montecitorio 12, 00186. Tel. 6/ 67 81 341, fax 6/ 67 94 496*. The bedrooms in this centrally located Rome hotel are large and well equipped, each has private bath with tub and shower, direct-dial private phone with 24-hour switchboard service, color TV, and air conditioning. Popular for tourists and politicians, the hotel offers great views from the rooftop garden, and from the Jacuzzi in that rooftop garden. Breakfast is served in a basement that has attractive frescoes. *Facilities: 100 rooms. Breakfast included*. Accepts all major credit cards.

L390,000–L560,000 HOLIDAY INN CROWNE PLAZA MINERVA. *Piazza della Minerva 69, 00186. Tel. 6/ 69 94 1888, fax 6/ 67 94 165*. Not from the same mold as the standard chain hotels, this hotel is known by the locals as simply the Minerva. It's in a good location as it's adjacent to the Pantheon. The rooms have more amenities than a standard room. Each has private bath with tub and shower, direct-dial in-room phone with 24-hour switchboard service, color TV with CNN and the Sky Channel, air conditioning, hair dryer, and mini-bar. The suites have even more to offer. *Facilities: 118 rooms, 16 suites, 24-hour room service, on-site rooftop restaurant and lounge, airport pickup, fitness room, babysitting, fax, laundry, multi-lingual staff, foreign currency exchange*. Accepts all major credit cards.

L250,000–L600,000 HOTEL NAZIONALE A MONTECITORIO. *Piazza Montecitorio 131, 00186. Tel. 6/ 69 50 01, fax 6/ 67 86 677*. This hotel is popular with politicians and tourists alike as its next to the Parliament buildings and close to the Trevi Fountain, the Pantheon, Spanish Steps, and the Vatican. All the rooms include private bath, air conditioning, TV, and mini-bar. Most are spacious and furnished in antiques. The clubby public areas are sure to please, with many cozy nooks that are perfect for conversation and relaxation after a day of sightseeing. *Facilities: 87 rooms, 15 suites, on-site restaurant, on-site bar, laundry, business* *facilities, facilities for the disabled.* Accepts all major credit cards.

MODERATE

L122,000–L163,000 DEL SENATO. *Piazza della Rotonda 73, 00186. Tel. 6/ 67 93 231, fax 6/ 68 40 297.* This hotel is comfortable and is located in the middle of the historical district. There are several rooms with Pantheon views. Rooms have private bath with tub and shower, direct-dial private phone with 24-hour switchboard service, color TV with CNN and the Sky Channel, and air conditioning. Breakfast is included in the price of a room. *Facilities: 53 rooms, breakfast, laundry, no bar.* Accepts all major credit cards.

L170,000–L260,000 HOTEL TRAIANO. *Via 4 Novembre 154, 00187. Tel. 6/ 67 83 862, fax 6/ 67 83 674.* Close to the city center, this hotel is decorated in Roman style. Rooms have private baths with tub and shower, direct-dial private phones with 24-hour switchboard service, and air conditioning. *Facilities: 50 rooms.* Accepts all major credit cards.

L225,000–L290,000 SANTA CHIARA. *Via Santa Chiara 21, 00186. Tel. 6/ 68 72 979, fax 6/ 68 73 144.* This hotel has a great location behind the Pantheon. The guest rooms aren't palatial, but are a good size. Each has a private bath with tub and shower, direct-dial private phone with 24-hour switchboard service, color TV with CNN and the Sky Channel, mini-bar, and air conditioning. *Facilities: 98 rooms, breakfast included, room service.* Accepts all major credit cards.

PIAZZA DI SPAGNA

EXPENSIVE

L318,000–L750,000 GRAND HOTEL PLAZA. *Via del Corso 126. Tel. 6/ 99 21 111, fax 6/ 99 41 575.* This is one of the loveliest old hotels in Rome, with stained-glass skylights, chandeliers, and marble floors. Rooms have private bath with tub and shower, direct-dial private phone with 24-hour switchboard service, color TV with CNN and the Sky Channel, mini-bar, and air conditioning. Some of the rooms are more modern than others, so request desired amenities when you reserve your room. A complimentary breakfast is included with the room. *Facilities: 207 rooms, 5 suites, on-site bar, business services, beauty salon, on-site minister.* Accepts all major credit cards.

L300,000–L450,000 HOTEL DEI BORGOGNONI. *Via del Bufalo 126, 00187. Tel. 6/ 69 94 1505, fax 6/ 69 94 1501.* Each of the rooms in this hotel features private bath with tub and shower, direct-dial private phone with 24-hour switchboard service, color TV with CNN and the Sky Channel, mini-bar, safe, and air conditioning. Some of the rooms overlook the internal garden from their own private terrace. Located just off the Piazza San Silvestro, and close to the Spanish Steps, this hotel is perfect for resting after a hard day of sightseeing. *Facilities: 50 rooms, on-site restaurant, on-site bar, private garage.* Accepts all major credit cards.

✓L400,000–L1,400,000 HOTEL HASSLER. *Piazza Trinità dei Monti 6, 00187. Tel. 6/ 67 82 651 or (800) 223-6800 (U.S.), fax 6/ 67 89 991.* Rated as one of the top foreign hotels in the world, this family-run hotel is done in the traditional grand European style. Each individually decorated room has a private bath with tub and shower, hair dryer, plush robes and toiletries, direct-dial private phone with 24-hour switchboard service, color TV with CNN and the Sky Channel, refrigerator, mini-bar, and air conditioning. There are even extra-large closets and dressing tables. Some of the rooms have private balconies that overlook the city. It is quietly understated, but elegantly decorated with antique furniture, carpets, and paintings. It's location, at the top of the Spanish Steps, makes it a superb choice for shoppers and for those sightseeing. *Facilities: 85 rooms, 15 suites, 24-hour room service,* *two on-site restaurants (Hassler Roof Restaurant and the Hassler Garden), on-site bar, tennis, sun deck, babysitting, laundry, valet, limousine service, in-room messages, multi-lingual staff*. Accepts all major credit cards.

L255,000–L800,000 HOTEL D' INGHILTERRA. *Via Bocca di Leone 14, 00187. Tel. 6/ 69 981, fax 6/ 68 40 828*. Known as the most fashionable of Rome's small hotels, this hotel seems to have an English, clubby atmosphere. It has all of the modern amenities that you need, but still retains a kind of nineteenth-century charm. The rooms are all lovely with high ceilings, but run on the small side. Rooms include private bath with tub and shower, direct-dial private phone with 24-hour switchboard service, color TV with CNN and the Sky Channel, mini-bar, and air conditioning. Some bedrooms have private balconies and are decorated with antiques. It is located right in the middle of the high-fashion district, at the top of the Spanish Steps. *Facilities: 102 rooms, 12 suites, on-site restaurant (the Roman Gardens), on-site bar, babysitting, nearby pay-extra car park, fax, laundry, multi-lingual staff*. AE, CB, DC, MC, V.

L410,000–L450,000 HOTEL DE LA VILLE INTER CONTINENTAL. *Via Sistina 69, 00187. Tel. 6/ 67 331, fax 6/ 67 84 213*. Next to the Hassler, this excellent hotel has deluxe rooms, each with a private bath with tub and shower, direct-dial private phone with 24-hour switchboard service, color TV with CNN and the Sky Channel, mini-bar, and air conditioning. The rooms come in all shapes and sizes, although most are larger than normal, so there's a lot to choose from. Some even have private terraces. It is located very close to all the high-fashion shopping. *Facilities: 195 rooms, on-site restaurant, lounge, on-site bar, room service until 11:00 P.M., garden, laundry, valet service, beauty salon, barber shop*. AE, CB, MC, V.

✓❤L250,000–L550,000 SCALINATA DI SPAGNA. *Piazza Trinità dei Monti 17, 00187. Tel. 6/ 67 93 006, fax 6/*

67 99 582. Cozy and intimate, this hotel has beautiful views of the Spanish Steps. Some of the rooms have private terraces that are wonderful for light meals in warm weather, but these require reservations far in advance. Since it is very romantic, this is a favorite spot for honeymooners. The guest rooms can be a little small, so ask for the larger ones. They all include private bath with tub and shower, direct-dial private phone with 24-hour switchboard service, color TV with CNN and the Sky Channel, and air conditioning. Rates include breakfast. *Facilities: 15 rooms, 1 suite, on-site restaurant, 24-hour room service, babysitting, nearby pay-extra car park, fax, laundry, pets allowed, foreign currency exchange, rooftop garden.* AE, MC, V.

✓❤**L190,000–L410,000 VALADIER HOTEL.** *Via della Fontanella 15, 00187. Tel. 6/ 36 10 559, fax 6/ 67 99 203.* A romantic hotel with all the atmosphere you could need to set the mood and then some, with comfy, inviting couches, art pieces, plush rugs, and carpets. Each room has private bath with tub and shower, direct-dial private phone with 24-hour switchboard service, color TV with CNN and the Sky Channel, mini-bar, and air conditioning. *Facilities: 38 rooms, 24-hour room service, babysitting, on-site restaurant, on-site bar, business facilities.* Accepts all major credit cards.

MODERATE

L185,000–L260,000 CARRIAGE HOTEL. *Via delle Carrozze 36, 00187. Tel. 6/ 69 90 124, fax 6/ 67 88 279.* This charming hotel combines style and value rates with a great location—it's just a few feet from the Piazza di Spagna. Although the rooms can be small, they all have a private bath with tub and shower, private phone, color TV with CNN, and air conditioning. Decorated in antiques, some of the rooms have private terraces, and the public rooms have frescoes and elegant gilded accents. *Facilities: 27 rooms, on-site bar, rooftop garden, fax, babysitting, laundry, multi-lingual staff.* Accepts all major credit cards.

L130,000–L280,000 FIRENZE. *Via due Macelli 106, 00187. Tel. 6/ 67 97 240, fax 6/ 67 85 636.* Close to the Piazza di Spagna, this hotel is elegant, with large bedrooms. Rooms have a private bath with tub and shower, private phone, color TV with CNN and the Sky Channel, and air conditioning. *Facilities: 25 rooms, gardenesque terrace.* AE, MC, V.

L180,000–L280,000 GREGORIANA. *Via Gregoriana 18, 00187. Tel. 6/ 67 94 269, fax 6/ 67 84 258.* It's hard to believe that this art deco hotel in the middle of the high-fashion district used to be a convent. It's located close to the Spanish Steps, and offers a good location for tourists. Since there aren't any public rooms, breakfast and drinks are brought to the guest rooms. The lovely, comfortable rooms each have private bath with tub and shower, direct-dial private phone with 24-hour switchboard service, color TV with CNN and the Sky Channel, mini-bar, and air conditioning. Continental breakfast is included with the room. *Facilities: 19 rooms, babysitting, wheelchair accessible, pets allowed, parking.* No credit cards.

L210,000–L270,000 HOTEL CONDOTTI. *Via Mario de Fiori 37, 00187. Tel. 6/ 67 94 661 or 6/ 67 94 769, fax 6/ 67 90 457.* Dedicated shoppers may want to stay at this hotel. It's in the middle of the designer shopping district, near the Piazza di Spagna. The rooms are a good size and tastefully decorated. They each have a private bathroom, TV, mini-bar, and air conditioning. Some even have their own terrace. Breakfast is included with the room. *Facilities: 17 rooms, babysitting, breakfast room service.* Accepts all major credit cards.

L154,000–L250,000 LOCARNO. *Via della Penna 22, 00186. Tel. 6/ 36 10 841, fax 6/ 32 15 249.* This attractive, cozy, older hotel is located just off the Piazza del Popolo and near great shopping. It often houses the more Bohemian intellectuals and artists. Each simple, comfortable room has a private bath with tub and shower, direct-dial private phone with 24-hour switchboard service, color TV with CNN and the Sky Channel, and air conditioning. There are wrought-iron beds and some antiques, in addition to the overall art nouveau personality of this hotel. *Facilities: 38 rooms, on-site bar, complimentary bicycles, babysitting, business facilities, garden.* Accepts all major credit cards.

L170,000–L300,000 MADRID. *Via Mario de Fiori 93, 00187. Tel. 6/ 69 91 511, fax 6/ 67 91 653.* This charming little hotel has a great location in the heart of the high-fashion boutiques area and close to the Spanish Steps. The rooms can be quite large for doubles, and all rooms have a private bath, TV, radio, and mini-bar. There's also a rooftop terrace where breakfast and drinks are served during warm weather. Rates include breakfast. *Facilities: 26 rooms, 7 suites, air conditioning at extra fee.* Accepts all major credit cards.

L190,000–L250,000 MANFREDI. *Via Margutta 61, 00187. Tel. 6/ 32 07 676, fax 6/ 32 07 736.* This recently refurbished hotel, with marble floors, is a few feet away from the Spanish Steps. The rooms are smallish, but bright and sunny; each with a private bath with shower, direct-dial private phone with 24-hour switchboard service, color TV, and air conditioning. There's also a pretty courtyard for guests to enjoy. *Facilities: 17 rooms, on-site bar, fax, laundry, foreign currency exchange, multi-lingual staff.* AE, MC, V.

L122,000–L170,000 MARGUTTA. *Via Laurina 34, 00187. Tel. 6/ 32 21 046.* This simple hotel offers clean and large rooms. There aren't any frills, but there are pretty wrought-iron beds, and all rooms have a private modern bathroom. *Facilities: 21 rooms, concierge, babysitting, on-site bar, currency exchange, laundry, multi-lingual staff.* Accepts all major credit cards.

L170,000–L220,000 PIAZZA DI SPAGNA. *Via Mario de' Fiori 61, 00187. Tel. 6/ 67 93 061, fax 6/ 67 90 654.* Located just down from the Spanish Steps, in the middle of Rome's designer shopping district, this small hotel has good-sized, unpretentious rooms that all have a private bathroom with tub and shower (some with Jacuzzi), direct-dial private phone with 24-hour switchboard service, color TV, mini-bar, and air conditioning. *Facilities: 16 rooms*. AE, MC, V.

INEXPENSIVE

L80,000–L180,000 PENSIONE SUISSE. *Via Gregoriana 54, 00187. Tel. 6/ 67 83 649, fax 6/ 67 81 258.* This small, clean hotel has several large rooms. Breakfast is served in the rooms, most of which have a private bath with tub and shower, and private phone. A great value, especially for the location. *Facilities: 14 rooms (9 with private bathrooms)*. MC, V.

PIAZZA NAVONA

EXPENSIVE

L330,000–L650,000 RAPHAËL HOTEL. *Largo Febo 2, Piazza Navona, 00186. Tel. 6/ 68 28 31, fax 6/ 68 78 993.* Next to the Piazza Navona, this luxury hotel offers all the comforts of home and then some. It's popular with government officials and tourists alike, as it's near the Senate and Chamber of Deputies, in the center of the historical district. The lobby is full of antiques, and the rooms, although on the small side, do offer modern amenities in a charming atmosphere. The rooms on the top floor offer breathtaking views of Rome, and some even have a private terrace. The individually decorated rooms have parquet floors and marble-sheathed bathrooms with tub and shower, and all rooms have a hair dryer, mini-bar, direct-dial private phone with 24-hour switchboard service, color TV with CNN and the Sky Channel, and air conditioning. Very convenient location and charming atmosphere. *Facilities: 55 rooms, 15 suites, non-smoking rooms, on-site restaurant (Ristorante El Raffaellino—one of the best places to eat in the area), on-site bar, room service, babysitting, laundry, car rentals, foreign currency exchange*. Accepts all major credit cards.

MODERATE

L120,000–L220,000 DUE TORRI. *Vicolo del Leonetto 23-25, 00186. Tel. 6/ 68 76 983, fax 6/ 68 65 442.* This quiet hotel in the artisans' district is near the Piazza Navona. The rooms are larger than normal for this part of Rome, and each has a private bath with tub and shower, direct-dial private phone with 24-hour switchboard service, color TV with CNN, and air conditioning. The public areas are congenial and inviting, but at the same time elegant. Overall, it gives the impression of an Italian house in the country. *Facilities: 26 rooms, on-site bar, babysitting, nearby pay-extra car park, fax, laundry, foreign currency exchange, multi-lingual staff.* AE, DC, MC, V.

L100,000–L220,000 PORTOGHESI. *Via dei Portoghesi 1, 00186. Tel. 6/ 68 64 231, fax 6/ 68 76 976.* This small hotel offers a good value for the money. Each room has a private bath with tub or shower, hair dryer, direct-dial private phone with 24-hour switchboard service, color TV with CNN and the Sky Channel, and air conditioning. There's a pretty terrace where breakfast is served during warm weather. It's just a few minutes' walk from the Piazza Navona, with elegant public rooms. This is a good choice for those interested in convenience more than frills. *Facilities: 27 rooms, fax, laundry, wheelchair accessible, garden terrace, multi-lingual staff.* MC, V.

INEXPENSIVE

L70,000–L113,000 NAVONA. *Via dei Sediari 8, 00186. Tel. 6/ 68 64 203, fax 6/ 68 80 3802.* The Navona is just a few minutes' walk to the Pantheon and across from the Piazza Navona. This hotel gets booked quickly, so reserve in advance. The rooms are basic, but comfortable and pleasant; most have private bathrooms at no extra charge. The owners are friendly, and their Australian son-in-law is extremely helpful. Air conditioning available in the summer months only. *Facilities: 26 rooms (22 with private bathroom), no bar, but alcohol available from the reception desk, multi-lingual staff, babysit-*

ting, wheelchair access (with assistance), fax, foreign currency exchange. AE.

THE QUIRINALE

EXPENSIVE

L250,000–L350,000 QUIRINALE HOTEL. *Via Nazionale 7, 00184. Tel. 6/ 47 07, fax 6/ 48 20 099.* This is a centrally located, deluxe hotel. Rooms have a private bath with tub and shower, direct-dial private phone with 24-hour switchboard service, color TV with CNN and the Sky Channel, and air conditioning. *Facilities: 208 rooms, renovated and fully soundproof banquet and conference facilities, outdoor restaurant and bar in private garden.* AE, DC, V.

MODERATE

L139,000–L190,000 FONTANA. *Piazza di Trevi 96, 00187. Tel. 6/ 67 86 113, fax 6/ 67 90 024.* This converted monastery offers bright and cheery, spacious rooms, some of which have great views of the Trevi Fountain down below. But herein lies a problem—lots of screaming tourists and commotion. If you're looking for a calm retreat, avoid this hotel. Nevertheless, the hotel is nice, and the rooms each have a private bath with tub and shower, direct-dial private phone with 24-hour switchboard service, color TV, and air conditioning. *Facilities: 28 rooms, babysitting, on-site bar, fax, laundry, multi-lingual staff, foreign currency exchange.* Accepts all major credit cards.

L135,000–L187,000 HOTEL BOLIVAR. *Via della Cordonata 6, 00187. Tel. 6/ 67 91 614, fax 6/ 67 91 025.* This three-star hotel is located in the city center. Rooms have a private bath with tub and shower, direct-dial private phone with 24-hour switchboard service, color TV with CNN and the Sky Channel, refrigerator, and air conditioning. *Facilities: 30 rooms.* Accepts all major credit cards.

L150,000–L250,000 HOTEL MIAMI. *Via Nazionale 230, 00185. Tel. 6/ 48 58 27, fax 6/ 48 45 62.* This former duchess's palace is right in the middle of a major district. There are marble floors and inviting public areas. The rooms themselves are bright and cheerful, with private bathroom, mini-bar, TV, and, for an extra charge, you can get air conditioning in your room. *Facilities: 22 rooms, 3 suites.* Accepts all major credit cards.

INEXPENSIVE

L85,000–L140,000 TREVI. *Vicolo del Babuccio 20-21, 00187. Tel. 6/ 67 89 563, fax 6/ 68 41 407.* This centrally located hotel offers neat, clean, if somewhat small, rooms with private bath including tub and shower, direct-dial private phone with 24-hour switchboard service, color TV, mini-bar, and air conditioning. Rates include breakfast, which is served on the rooftop terrace in warm weather. *Facilities: 20 rooms.* Accepts all major credit cards.

STAZIONE TERMINI

EXPENSIVE

✓L340,000–L800,000+ LE GRAND HOTEL. *Via Vittorio Emanuele Orlando 3, 00185. Tel. 6/ 47 09, fax 6/ 47 47 7307.* This, one of the most impressive hotels in Rome, is amazing in the amenities and services that it offers its guests. The guest rooms and public areas are large, all decorated with antiques. The guest rooms are decorated differently, but each has a private marble bath with tub and shower, direct-dial private phone with 24-hour switchboard service, color TV with CNN and the Sky Channel, mini-bar, and air conditioning. Some of the bedrooms are decorated in real, quality antiques, and all are soundproof, with thick carpets and elegant chandeliers. The lobby has cherubs flying around the ceiling, along with baroque touches that emphasize the grandeur of the hotel. *Facilities: 168 rooms, 36 suites, non-smoking rooms, wheelchair access, on-site restaurant (Le*

Restaurant), 2 on-site bars, babysitting service, laundry, massage, sauna, physiotherapy, interpreting service, fax, foreign currency exchange, multi-lingual staff. AE, DC, V.

L295,000–L396,000 HOTEL MASCAGNI. *Via Vittorio Emanuele Orlando 90, 00185. Tel. 6/ 48 90 4040, fax 6/ 48 17 637.* This recently renovated Umbertine palace is located in the most distinguished center of the city. Rooms are decorated with elegant turn-of-the century furniture and each has a private bath with tub and shower, direct-dial private phone with 24-hour switchboard service, color TV with CNN and the Sky Channel, and air conditioning. *Facilities: 40 soundproof rooms, American bar, brunch bar, small conference room.* Accepts all major credit cards.

L295,000–L460,000 HOTEL MEDITERRANEO. *Via Cavour 15, 00184. Tel 6/ 48 84 051, fax 6/ 47 44 105.* Each of the bedrooms in this beautiful hotel is larger than normal, with exposed wood and nice furniture. Rooms have a private bath with tub and shower, direct-dial private phone with 24-hour switchboard service, color TV with CNN and the Sky Channel, mini-bar, and air conditioning. A tribute to art deco in Italy, this ten-story hotel was designed by Mussolini's favorite architect, and includes many Mediterranean-themed statues and other touches. It boasts a rooftop garden. Rates include breakfast. *Facilities: 262 rooms, 10 suites, on-site restaurant, on-site bar, roof garden.* AE, DC, V.

L198,000–L350,000 HOTEL RICHMOND. *Largo Corrado Ricci 36, 00184. Tel. 6/ 99 41 256, fax 6/ 99 41 454.* Located in the center of the historic area near Stazione Termini. Rooms have a private bath with tub and shower, direct-dial phone with 24-hour switchboard service, refrigerator, and air conditioning. *Facilities: 15 rooms.* AE, DC, V.

L230,000–L330,000 HOTEL ROYAL SANTINA. *Via Marsala 22, 00185. Tel. 6/ 44 55 241, fax 6/ 49 41 252.* Located in the center of Rome, this hotel offers hospitality, elegance, and exclusive comforts. Rooms have a private bath with tub and shower, direct-dial private phone with 24-hour switchboard service, color TV with CNN and the Sky Channel, and air conditioning. *Facilities: 118 rooms, including 2 suites, meeting room, bar, restaurant, garage*. Accepts all major credit cards.

L225,000–L405,000 HOTEL SAN GIORGIO. *Via G. Amendola 61, 00185. Tel. 6/ 48 27 341 or (800) 223-9832 in the U.S., fax 6/ 48 83 191*. The very helpful staff in this trend-setting hotel makes it a pleasure to stay in. But it would be a pleasure to stay in anyway, as it was the first Roman hotel to be air-conditioned, and is now soundproof. Great for families, and even connected to a good restaurant. Rooms have a private bath with tub and shower, direct-dial private phone with 24-hour switchboard service, color TV, mini-bar, and air conditioning. Breakfast is included in the rates. *Facilities: 186 rooms, 5 suites, on-site restaurant, on-site bar, garage*. AE, DC, V.

L260,000–L350,000 MASSIMO D'AZEGLIO. *Via Cavour 18, 00184. Tel. 6/ 48 70 270, fax 6/ 48 27 386*. This modern hotel is near the opera, so it's popular with music buffs. Rooms are clean and cozy and have a private bath with tub and shower, direct-dial private phone with 24-hour switchboard service, color TV with CNN and the Sky Channel, mini-bar, and air conditioning. This elegant hotel has a classic facade and is very convenient for public transportation. *Facilities: 210 rooms, on-site restaurant, on-site bar, garage, wine cellar*. AE, DC, V.

L190,000–L390,000 MECENATE PALACE HOTEL. *Via Carlo Alberto 3, 00185. Tel. 6/ 44 70 2024, fax 6/ 44 61 354*. Newly refurbished palace located in the historical center of the city with an impressive view of the Basilica of Santa Maria Maggiore. Rooms have a private bath with shower and tub, direct-dial private phone with 24-hour switchboard service, fax and computer plugs, color TV with CNN and the Sky Channel, and air conditioning. *Facilities: 62 rooms, buffet breakfast, lunch and dinner served, mini-bar, tea and coffee facilities in each room, meeting rooms and panoramic roof garden*. Accepts all major credit cards.

L250,000–L410,000 STARHOTEL METROPOLE. *Via Principe Amedeo 3, 00185. Tel. 06/ 4774, fax 6/ 47 40413.* Each room has a private bath with tub and/or shower, direct-dial private phone with 24-hour switchboard service, color TV with CNN and the Sky Channel, and air conditioning. *Facilities: 269 rooms.* AE, MC. V.

MODERATE

L140,000–L190,000 ABERDEEN HOTEL. *Via Firenze 48, 00184. Tel. 6/ 48 21 092.* Located near the Roma Opera House, it's close to the main tourist attractions and rail connections, plus it's in a safe area because it's in front of the Ministry of Defense. The rooms are tastefully decorated, and have conveniences such as private bath, TV, mini-bar, telephone, and hair dryer. For an extra charge, you can get air conditioning in your room. Rates include a breakfast buffet. *Facilities: 26 rooms.* Accepts all major credit cards.

L225,000–L305,000 ATLANTICO HOTEL. *Via Cavour 23, 00184. Tel. 6/ 47 44 105 or (800) 223-9832 (in the U.S.), fax 6/ 48 24 976.* This hotel is one of the nicest in this area. The rooms are larger than normal, each with air conditioning, TV, telephone, and minibar. The public areas have a pleasantly old-fashioned atmosphere. *Facilities: 74 rooms, on-site restaurant, garage.* Accepts all major credit cards.

L240,000–L275,000 BRITANNIA HOTEL. *Via Napoli 64, 00184. Tel. 6/ 48 83 153 or (800) 448-8355 in the U.S., fax 6/ 48 82 343.* This little hotel offers a great value for its guests, with plenty of amenities for not a lot of money. The rooms have a private bath with tub and shower, direct-dial private phone with 24-hour switchboard service, color TV with CNN and the Sky Channel, safe, scales, sunlamp, and air conditioning. Some rooms also boast private terraces. Because of its location, it's perfect for those who plan to shop till they drop. The decor is better than you would expect, even at higher-priced hotels. Rates include breakfast. *Facilities:*

32 rooms, on-site American bar, babysitting service, private parking. AE, DC, MC.

L120,000–L165,000 FIAMMA HOTEL. *Via Gaeta 61, 00185. Tel. 6/ 48 83 859, fax 6/ 48 18 436.* Great for those on a budget, the rates include breakfast. Located near the Baths of Diocletian, the hotel offers comfortable guest rooms, each with direct-dial in-room phone with 24-hour switchboard service, TV, telephone, private bath/shower room, as well as public rooms accented in marble. Some of the rooms have air conditioning and satellite TV. *Facilities: 79 rooms*. Accepts all major credit cards.

L165,000–L190,000 GLOBUS HOTEL. *Viale Ippocrete 119, 00161. Tel. 6/ 44 57 001, fax 6/ 49 41 062.* Located near the Stazione Termini, this hotel offers exceptional comfort and a roof garden/solarium. Rooms have private bath with tub and shower, direct-dial private phone with 24-hour switchboard service, and color TV with CNN and the Sky Channel. *Facilities: 100 rooms, meeting rooms, garage*. Accepts all major credit cards.

L120,000–L192,000 HOTEL CANADA. *Via Vicenza 58, 00185. Tel. 6/ 44 57 770, fax 6/ 44 50 749.* A member of the Best Western chain, this hotel is pretty standard. It offers comfortable rooms at a mid-range price, each with private bath including tub and/or shower, direct-dial private phone with 24-hour switchboard service, color TV with CNN, and air conditioning. It usually offers good service. *Facilities: 70 rooms, on-site bar, babysitting services, garden area, business facilities, air conditioning*. Accepts all major credit cards.

L140,000–L250,000 HOTEL CENTRO. *Via Firenze 12, 00184. Tel. 6/ 48 28 002, fax 6/ 48 71 902.* This hotel facing the opera house offers comfortable, reasonably-priced rooms each with a private bath with tub and shower, direct-dial private phone with 24-hour switchboard service, color TV with CNN and the Sky Channel, safe, and air conditioning. *Facilities: 38 rooms,*

3 suites, room service, laundry, valet service, nearby parking garage. Accepts all major credit cards.

L120,000–L205,000 HOTEL COROT. *Via Marghera 15-17, 00185. Tel. 6/ 44 70 0900, fax 6/ 44 70 0905.* There's a wide range of accommodations available here, as the hotel occupies a couple of floors of an apartment building. There are also some private rooms available with fewer amenities. The rooms are bright and airy, all in traditional decor, including private bath with shower, direct-dial private phone with 24-hour switchboard service, color TV, and air conditioning. Rates include breakfast. *Facilities: 20 rooms, on-site bar, discounts available*. Accepts all major credit cards.

L110,000–L250,000 HOTEL D'ESTE. *Via Carlo Alberto 4B, 00185. Tel. 6/ 44 65 607, fax 6/ 44 65 601.* This hotel enjoys a good location. It's close to the Termini Station, as well as near the Basilica of Santa Maria Maggiore. Modern in its amenities, the hotel has a decor that gives a turn-of-the-century feeling, with dark wood and brass. Rooms have a private bath with tub and shower, direct-dial private phone with 24-hour switchboard service, color TV with CNN and the Sky Channel, mini-bar, and air conditioning. There are also rooms that can accommodate families. It is quite charming. *Facilities: 40 rooms, rooftop bar/café, on-site restaurant, garden, airport pickup available*. Accepts all major credit cards.

L139,000–L192,000 HOTEL GALILEO. *Via Palestro 33, 00185. Tel. 6/ 44 41 207, fax 6/ 44 41 208.* This hotel specializes in combining good value and comfortable, larger-than-normal accommodations. The rates include breakfast, which is sometimes served on a garden terrace. Rooms have private bath with tub or shower, direct-dial in-room phone with 24-hour switchboard service, color TV with CNN and the Sky Channel, and air conditioning (extra charge). *Facilities: 40 rooms*. Accepts all major credit cards.

✓❤ **L140,000–L300,000 HOTEL GIGLIO DELL' OPERA.** *Via Principe Amedeo 14, 00185. Tel. 6/ 48 44 01 or 6/ 48 80 219, fax 6/ 47 47 023.* This is a three-star, romantic-style hotel located near the Colosseum and Roman Forum. Rooms have a private bath with tub and shower, direct-dial private phone with 24-hour switchboard service, color TV with CNN and the Sky Channel, and air conditioning. *Facilities: 65 rooms, swimming pool, exercise room.* Accepts all major credit cards.

L180,000–L260,000 HOTEL MARCELLA. *Via Flavia 106, 00187. Tel. 6/ 47 46 451 or (800) 223-5608, fax 6/ 48 15 832.* Close to the Piazza della Repubblica, this garden-theme hotel has guest rooms that are plain, but comfortable. Rooms have a private bath with tub and shower, direct-dial private phone with 24-hour switchboard service, color TV with CNN and the Sky Channel, mini-bar, and air conditioning. They also have private sun alcoves. The rates include breakfast. *Facilities: 68 rooms, on-site bar, rooftop sun terrace.* AE, MC, V.

L185,000–L250,000 HOTEL NORD NUOVA ROMA. *Via G. Amendola, 00185. Tel. 6/ 48 85 441 or (800) 223-9832, fax 6/ 48 17 163.* A good value, this family-run chain hotel has comfortable rooms, each with a private bath with tub and shower, direct-dial phone with 24-hour switchboard service, color TV with CNN and the Sky Channel, mini-bar, and air conditioning. It's suitable for families. *Facilities: 159 rooms, air conditioning, parking for 100 cars, on-site bar, nearby restaurant.* Accepts all major credit cards.

L100,000–L180,000 HOTEL PAVIA. *Via Gaeta 83, 00185. Tel. 6/ 48 38 01, fax 6/ 48 19 090.* Once a private villa, this renovated hotel is very charming and popular. To get to the reception area, you pass through a flower-strewn walkway. The rooms are decorated with wood accents in a very tasteful atmosphere. All of the rooms are quiet and have private bath with shower, direct-dial phone with 24-hour switchboard service, color TV, mini-bar, and air conditioning (extra charge). Book early. Rates include breakfast. *Facilities: 50 rooms.* AE, DC, MC, V.

L158,000–L210,000 HOTEL RANIERI. *Via XX Septembre 43, 00187. Tel. 6/ 48 14 467, fax 6/ 48 18 834.* This recently renovated hotel occupies an old building, and has kept its charm. The location here is excellent, as it's within walking distance of the Rome Opera, Vittorio Veneto, and other good tourist attractions. The guest rooms are clean and comfortable, all having a private bath with tub and shower, direct-dial phone with 24-hour switchboard service, color TV, and air conditioning. The public areas are decorated nicely with art pieces. The rates include breakfast, and other meals can be served in the dining room with prior arrangement. *Facilities: 40 rooms.* AE, MC, V.

L90,000–L200,000 HOTEL ROMAE. *Via Palestro 49, 00185. Tel. 6/ 44 63 554, fax 6/ 44 63 914.* This small hotel near Termini Station offers a great value for the amenities that it includes. Each of the comfortable and airy rooms has a private bath with tub and shower, direct-dial private phone with 24-hour switchboard service, color TV, and attractive wood furniture. Breakfast is included in the room rates, and, with its great location, this hotel is hard to beat in the value category. *Facilities: 20 rooms.* Accepts all major credit cards.

L100,000–L180,000 HOTEL SIVIGLIA. *Via Gaeta 12, 00185. Tel. and fax 6/ 44 41 195.* Once a private villa, this lovely neoclassically-designed hotel has simple rooms with high ceilings. Rooms have a private bath with tub and shower, direct-dial private phone with 24-hour switchboard service, color TV, mini-bar, and air conditioning. Some of the rooms have a terrace. Breakfast, which is included in the room rate, is either served in the basement or garden, depending on the weather. *Facilities: 41 rooms.* AE, DC, V.

L100,000–L220,000 HOTEL TIRRENO. *Via S. Martino Al Monti 18, 00184. Tel. 6/ 48 80 778, fax 6/ 48 84 095.* Near the Roman Forum, this hotel was recently renovated. Rooms have a private bath with tub and shower, direct-dial private phone with 24-hour switchboard service, color TV with the Sky Channel and CNN, videotape player, mini-bar, and air conditioning. Transfer to airport on request. *Facilities: 50 rooms, bar.* AE, DC, V.

L198,000–L275,000 HOTEL VALLE. *Via Cavour 134, 00184. Tel. 6/ 48 15 736, fax 6/ 48 85 837.* Relaxing and located right in the historic center. Rooms have a private bath with tub and shower, direct-dial phone with 24-hour switchboard service, color TV with CNN and the Sky Channel, and air conditioning. *Facilities: 35 rooms.* Accepts all major credit cards.

L135,000–L215,000 HOTEL VENEZIA. *Via Varese 18, 00185. Tel. 6/ 44 57 101, fax 6/ 49 57 687.* This excellent little hotel offers rooms that are attractive and bright, some with seventeenth-century reproductions, and all have private bath with tub or shower, direct-dial phone with 24-hour switchboard service, color TV with CNN and the Sky Channel, mini-bar, and air conditioning (off from 11:00 P.M. to 7:00 A.M.). Some even have balconies that overlook the crowded streets below. Recently renovated, the public areas are charming, with brown marble floors. Prices include breakfast. *Facilities: 61 rooms.* Accepts all major credit cards.

L150,000–L180,000 MARGHERA. *Via Marghera 29, 00185. Tel. 6/ 44 54 237, fax 6/ 44 62, 539.* This hotel specializes in providing comfortable rooms at an affordable price. Guest rooms have a private bath with tub and shower, direct-dial private phone with 24-hour switchboard service, color TV, mini-bar, and air conditioning, as well as a trouser press. The guest rooms are immaculate, and the hotel is located across the street from the main Italian tourist office, and very close to the Termini Station. *Facilities: 20 rooms, air conditioning,* *on-site bar, breakfast room service, babysitting, fax, laundry, multi-lingual staff*. Accepts all major credit cards.

L100,000–L220,000 MORGANA HOTEL. *Via Filippo Turati 31-35, 00185. Tel. 6/ 44 67 230, fax 6/ 44 69 142*. Located in the heart of Rome near the Colosseum. Rooms have a private bath with tub or shower, direct-dial private phone with 24-hour switchboard service, color TV with CNN and the Sky Channel, mini-bar, and air conditioning. *Facilities: 70 rooms, shuttle to airport on request*. Accepts all major credit cards.

L130,000–L185,000 VILLA DELLE ROSE. *Via Vicenza 5, 00185. Tel. 6/ 44 51 788, fax 6/ 44 51 639*. Extras such as the beautiful columns in the lobby give away the fact that this was once a private home owned by very wealthy people. The guest rooms are a little on the plain side, but they're a nice size. Each room has a private bath with tub or shower, direct-dial phone with 24-hour switchboard service, and color TV. Air conditioning is available in some rooms. The split-level rooms are good for families, as they allow for extra beds. Great location. Rates include breakfast. *Facilities: 38 rooms, on-site lounge/bar (check out the frescoed ceiling), small pets allowed*. Accepts all major credit cards.

INEXPENSIVE

L40,000–L100,000 CERVIA. *Via Palestro 55, 00185. Tel. 6/ 49 10 57, fax 6/ 49 10 56*. Some of this small hotel's rooms have been refurbished recently and are very nice. The rooms that haven't, however, are simple. With nice public areas, this hotel is pleasant, especially if you have a room with a private bath/shower. *Facilities: 26 rooms, direct-dial private phones with 24-hour switchboard service, on-site bar/breakfast room*. Accepts all major credit cards.

L73,000–L123,000 HOTEL PALLADIUM. *Via Gioberti 36, 00185. Tel. 6/ 44 66 917, fax 6/ 44 66 937*.

Located close to Santa Maria Maggiore Church, these three-star hotel rooms each have private bath with tub and shower, direct-dial phone with 24-hour switchboard service, color TV with CNN and the Sky Channel, refrigerator, and air conditioning. *Facilities: 56 rooms.* Accepts all major credit cards.

TRASTEVERE

EXPENSIVE

L200,000–L450,000 RIPA RESIDENCE. *Via Orti di Trastevere, 00153. Tel. 6/ 58 611, fax 6/ 58 14 550.* Located near some of Rome's oldest homes in the historical area of Trastevere. Rooms have private bath with tub and shower, refrigerator, direct-dial phone with 24-hour switchboard service, color TV with CNN and the Sky Channel, and air conditioning. *Facilities: 180 rooms, bar and restaurant, parking garage.* Accepts all major credit cards.

INEXPENSIVE

L55,000–L58,000 MANARA. *Via Luciano Manara 25, 00152. Tel. 6/ 58 14 713.* This hotel is perfect for budget-bound travelers and those who plan to spend their nights bar-hopping and clubbing in this district. The rooms are simple, bright and clean, and manage to retain a rather old-fashioned ambiance. *Facilities: 7 rooms (only two bathrooms), multi-lingual staff.* No credit cards.

THE VATICAN

EXPENSIVE

L230,000–L370,000 FARNESE. *Via Alessandro Farnese 30. Tel. 6/ 32 12 553, fax 6/ 32 15 129.* This small hotel is a converted mansion within walking distance of St. Peter's Basilica. The rooms are decorated in art deco and have private bath with tub and shower, direct-dial phone with 24-hour switchboard service, color TV with CNN and the Sky Channel, and air conditioning. The rates include breakfast. *Facilities: 24 rooms, on-site bar, garden, parking.* Accepts all major credit cards.

L280,000–L380,000 GIULIO CESARE HOTEL. *Via degli Scipioni 287, 00192. Tel. 6/ 32 10 751, fax 6/ 32 11 736.* This hotel was once the private home of Countess Paterno Solari. The public areas are decorated tastefully with Persian rugs, antiques, chandeliers, and other opulent appointments. The bedrooms are equally lovely, with chandeliers and thick carpets. Rooms have a private bath with tub and shower, direct-dial private phone with 24-hour switchboard service, color TV with CNN and the Sky Channel, mini-bar, and air conditioning. *Facilities: 86 rooms, garden, snack bar, piano bar, terrace.* AE, CB, MC, V.

L260,000–L380,000 HOLIDAY INN ROME-ST. PETER'S. *Via Aurelia Antica 415, 00165. Tel. 6/ 66 42, fax 6/ 66 37 190.* This mini-resort is set in a garden near the center of Rome. The rooms are comfortable, and there are courtesy buses that leave on a schedule for the historical district and airport. Rooms have a private bath with tub and shower, direct-dial private phone with 24-hour switchboard service, color TV with CNN and the Sky Channel, and air conditioning. *Facilities: 321 rooms, 15 suites, Olympic-sized swimming pool, sauna, tennis courts, on-site piano bar.* Accepts all major credit cards.

✓L265,000–L365,000 HOTEL ATLANTE GARDEN. *Via Crescenzio 78, 00193. Tel. 6/ 68 72 361, fax 6/ 68 72 315.* Within walking distance of the Vatican, this hotel is a great value and is highly recommended. Rooms have private bath with tub and shower (some with a Jacuzzi), direct-dial phone with 24-hour switchboard service, color TV, mini-bar, and air conditioning. The rooms are all modern, but still give off a certain nineteenth-century air. Rates include breakfast. *Facilities: 43 rooms, 24-hour room service, free airport transport.* AE, DC, V.

✓L285,000–L580,000 HOTEL ATLANTE STAR. *Via G. Vitelleschi 34, 00193. Tel. 6/ 68 73 233 or (800) 344-1212 (in the U.S.), fax 6/ 68 72 300.* Just across from its sister hotel, the Atlante Garden (above), this hotel offers a great location. Rooms have private bath with tub and shower (some with a Jacuzzi), direct-dial phone with 24-hour switchboard service, color TV with CNN, mini-bar, and air conditioning. Small, deluxe, and posh, it also has the convenience of having one of Rome's best restaurants right on its roof. This restaurant, Les Etoiles Roof Garden Restaurant, has some of Rome's best views, too. *Facilities: 80 rooms, 10 suites, 24-hour room service, on-site restaurant, on-site bar, babysitting, roof garden, beauty salon, secretarial services in English, translation services, guest laundry/valet, foreign currency exchange, pets allowed.* Accepts all major credit cards.

L240,000–L500,000 JOLLY HOTEL LEONARDO DA VINCI. *Via dei Gracchi 324, 00192. Tel. 6/ 32 499 or (800) 221-2626 in the U.S., fax 6/ 36 10 138.* This fabulous hotel offers modern accommodations in a recently refurbished atmosphere. It boasts a wonderful location, across the bridge from the Piazza del Popolo and near St. Peter's. It's popular with business people for its conference facilities. Rooms have a private bath with tub and/or shower, direct-dial private phone with 24-hour switchboard service, color TV with CNN and the Sky Channel, piped-in music, mini-bar, and air conditioning. Rates include buffet breakfast. *Facilities: 245 rooms, 7 suites, room service, two on-site restaurants, on-site bar, snack bar, women's and men's hair salon, guest laundry/valet service, underground parking garage.* AE, MC, V.

L200,000–L340,000 JOLLY HOTEL MIDAS. *Via Aurelia 800, 00165. Tel. 6/ 66 396, fax 6/ 64 18 457.*

Tlx. 6/ 22 821. Situated in green surroundings with pleasant views over the city. Rooms have a private bath with tub and shower, direct-dial private phone with 24-hour switchboard service, refrigerator, mini-bar, room service, color TV with CNN and the Sky Channel, and air conditioning. There's a shuttle service to the airport and city center. *Facilities: 347 rooms (including junior and senior suites), American bar, meeting/conference rooms, three restaurants*. Accepts all major credit cards.

✓L260,000–L360,000 VISCONTI PALACE HOTEL. *Via Federico Cesi 37, 00193. Tel. 6/ 36 84, fax 6/ 32 00 551*. Within walking distance of the Spanish Steps and St. Peter's, this hotel is popular with tourists. Each of the guest rooms in this deluxe facility includes a private bath with tub and shower, direct-dial private phone with 24-hour switchboard service, color TV with CNN and the Sky Channel, mini-bar, and air conditioning. The whole hotel is air-conditioned, and it has conference facilities that attract business people. *Facilities: 250 rooms, parking garage*. AE, DC, V.

MODERATE

L70,000–L272,000 AMALIA. *Via Germanico 66, 00192. Tel. 6/ 39 72 3354 or 6/ 39 72 3356, fax 6/ 39 72 3365*. This hotel offers a very convenient location, close to the Vatican and a major shopping district. The rooms are nice, each with a private bath with tub and shower in marble, hair dryer, direct-dial phone with 24-hour switchboard service, and color TV. Very popular with Italian travelers. *Facilities: 25 rooms, on-site lounge/bar, pets allowed*. AE, MC, V.

L180,000–L250,000 HOTEL CLODIO. *Via Santa Lucia 10, 00195. Tel 6/ 37 21 122, fax 6/ 32 50 7045*. Located near the Olympic Stadium and the Vatican City, and within easy reach of the city center, this hotel has a rooftop garden that provides a panoramic view. Tastefully decorated in the classical style, each of the rooms has a private bath with tub and shower, private phone with 24-hour switchboard service, color TV, and air conditioning. *Facilities: 115 rooms, bar, snack bar, private garage*. AE, DC, MC. V.

✓L150,000–L345,000 HOTEL COLUMBUS. *Via delle Conciliazione 33, 00193. Tel. 6/ 68 65 435, fax 6/ 68 64 874*. This hotel was once the private palace of Pope Julius II, while he was still a cardinal. The lobby and other public areas are very impressive, with walk-in fireplaces, huge, dark furniture, and large, heavy wooden doors. The guest rooms are nice, large, and less imposing. Rooms have private bath with tub or shower, direct-dial phone with 24-hour switchboard service, color TV, mini-bar, and air conditioning. The views from most of the rooms are excellent. Great location and friendly service from a helpful staff. *Facilities: 105 rooms, 4 suites, 24-hour room service, on-site restaurant, babysitting, garden, pets allowed*. AE, DC, MC, V.

L180,000–L280,000 HOTEL PISANA PALACE. *Via della Pisana 374, 00163. Tel. 6/ 66 690, fax 6/ 66 16 1190*. This hotel is located a short distance from the Vatican City. Well-appointed rooms have a private bath with tub and shower, direct-dial private phone with 24-hour switchboard service, TV with CNN and the Sky Channel, and air conditioning. *Facilities: 212 rooms, suites, and junior suites with Jacuzzi, office equipment available, mini-bar, banquet and conference facilities, currency exchange, flower service, restaurant and bar, private parking garage, airport transfer, 24-hour porters*. Accepts all major credit cards.

L195,000–L313,000 HOTEL VILLA PAMPHILI. *Via della Nocetta 105, 00164. Tel. 6/ 5862, fax 6/ 66157747*. Located close to St. Peter's, this hotel overlooks one of Rome's most beautiful parks. Rooms have a private bath with tub and shower, direct-dial private phone with 24-hour switchboard service, color TV with CNN and the Sky Channel, and air conditioning. *Facilities: 248 rooms (including 9 junior suites and one presidential suite), restaurant, pool, laundry*. Accepts all major credit cards.

✓**L180,000–L300,000 SANT' ANNA.** *Via Borgo Pio 134. Tel. 6/ 65 41 602, fax 6/ 65 48 717.* Each room has a private bath with tub and shower, direct-dial private phone with 24-hour switchboard service, refrigerator, color TV with CNN, and air conditioning. *Facilities: 20 rooms.* Accepts all major credit cards.

INEXPENSIVE

L86,000–L120,000 ALIMANDI. *Via Tunisi 8, 00192. Tel. 6/ 39 72 3948, fax 6/ 39 72 3943.* Popular with backpackers because of the budget prices, this small hotel offers clean rooms. Rooms have a private bath with tub and shower, direct-dial phone with 24-hour switchboard service, and color TV with CNN and the Sky Channel. The location, though, is excellent, at the entrance to all the Vatican museums. There's a beautiful roof terrace and garden where you can barbecue. *Facilities: 30 rooms (24 with shower facilities), on-site bar, pets allowed.* Accepts all major credit cards.

L52,000–L80,000 FORTIS GUEST HOUSE. *Via Fornovo 7. Tel. 6/ 32 12 256, fax 6/ 32 12 222.* The rooms at this small hotel are basic, and lack the frills you might be accustomed to. Rooms have a private bath with tub or shower and direct-dial phone. They're clean and comfortable, with a convenient location. Breakfast is included in the rates. *Facilities: 22 rooms (17 with private bathroom).* Accepts all major credit cards.

L45,000–L75,000 LA ROVERE. *Vicolo San Onofrio 5, 00165. Tel. 6/ 65 40 739.* This little hotel is in a very pretty location, although one where there's not a whole lot of action. It is convenient to the Vatican, as well as St. Peter's. There are two terraces, which some of the rooms open onto. For those who plan to party all night, the hotel does close at midnight, but there are front-door keys available. *Facilities: 23 rooms (only 10 showers in the hotel), on-site bar, nearby car park, non-smoking rooms available, safe, foreign currency exchange, multi-lingual staff.* MC, V.

VIA VENETO/PIAZZA BARBERINI

EXPENSIVE

L230,000–L600,000 AMBASCIATORI PALACE. *Via Veneto 62. Tel. 6/ 47 493, fax 6/ 47 43 601.* As the name suggests, this luxury hotel was once a palace. Very popular with business clientele, it has an old-fashioned atmosphere, while still offering modern amenities. Spacious rooms have a private bath with tub and shower, direct-dial private phone with 24-hour switchboard service, color TV with CNN and the Sky Channel, mini-bar, and air conditioning. Many of the rooms even have two bathrooms, as well as a balcony. *Facilities: 145 rooms and suites, non-smoking rooms available, 24-hour room service, on-site restaurant, on-site bar, babysitting, nearby pay-extra car park, guest laundry, wheelchair access, foreign currency exchange, multi-lingual staff.* AE, CB, MC, V.

❤**L280,000–L600,000+ GRAND HOTEL FLORA.** *Via Veneto 191, 00187. Tel. 6/ 48 99 29 or (800) 44-UTELL in the U.S. or (800) 268-7041 in Canada, fax 6/ 48 20 359.* This romantic hotel near the Borghese Gardens is right up there with more expensive hotels in the luxury category. Truly a grand hotel, it seems more like a palazzo, with the public rooms decorated in antiques and Persian carpets. The guest rooms are larger than normal and beautifully furnished. Rooms have a private bath with tub and shower, mini-bar, and air conditioning. Rates include breakfast. *Facilities: 175 rooms, 8 suites, room service, on-site bar, unisex hair salon, guest laundry, valet service.* Accepts all major credit cards.

✓❤**L280,000–L500,000 HOTEL BAROCCO.** *Piazza Barberini 9, 00187. Tel. 6/ 48 72 001, fax 6/ 48 59 94.* This little hotel has wonderful views of the Triton Fountain of Piazza Barberini. Rooms have a private bath with tub and shower, direct-dial private phone with 24-hour switchboard service, color TV, mini-bar, and air conditioning. Some also have work spaces. *Facilities: 28* *rooms, on-site restaurant, on-site bar, business facilities, garden area, pets allowed.* AE, MC, V.

L274,000–L500,000 HOTEL BERNINI BRISTOL. *Piazza Barberini 23, 00187. Tel. 6/ 48 83 051, fax 6/ 48 24 266.* This hotel, although categorized as a luxury hotel, offers nothing really original in that vein. It's more popular with business people than tourists because of the atmosphere. The rooms have modern amenities, such as air conditioning, TV, and mini-bar. It does overlook the Piazza Bernini with the Triton Fountain. Overall, this marble-sheathed hotel is comfortable. *Facilities: 126 rooms, 24-hour room service, on-site restaurant, on-site bar, babysitting, business facilities, garden area.* Accepts all major credit cards.

✓L430,000–L1,100,000 HOTEL EDEN. *Via Ludovisi 49, 00187. Tel. 6/ 47 43 551 or (800) 225-5843 in the U.S. and Canada, fax 6/ 48 21 584.* With a remodeling project completed in 1994, this luxury hotel is one of the most expensive in this category. It's located right in the heart of the city, close to the Spanish Steps and Via Veneto. The rooms are all individually and lavishly decorated with silk-like drapes and beautiful marble bathrooms. All rooms have a direct-dial private phone with 24-hour switchboard service, color TV with CNN and the Sky Channel, mini-bar, safe-deposit box, and air conditioning. There are absolutely stunning views of Rome from some of the rooms, as well as from the rooftop restaurant and bar. *Facilities: 101 rooms, 11 suites, on-site restaurant, on-site bar, fitness center.* AE.

✓L320,000–L5,000,000 HOTEL EXCELSIOR. *Via Veneto 125, 00187. Tel. 6/ 47 08 or (800) 221-2340 in the U.S., fax 6/ 48 26 205.* Arguably one of the most opulent hotels in the world, this place offers all the amenities and luxuries you could possibly desire. Near the U.S. Embassy, this hotel was very popular with 1950s movie stars, and is now "in" with tycoons and rich royalty. All the rooms are large, air-conditioned, and have a marble bathroom (some of these are as big as the huge rooms), direct-dial private phone with 24-hour switchboard service, color TV with CNN and the Sky Channel, and mini-bar. There was a recent refurbishment, so some of the rooms are decorated completely in antiques with gilded touches everywhere, and some are more modern. Either way, you won't be disappointed. *Facilities: 282 rooms, 45 suites, non-smoking rooms available, 24-hour room service, on-site restaurant, on-site bar, babysitting, guest laundry, nearby car park, beauty salon, Turkish bath, sauna, business services, foreign currency exchange, multi-lingual staff, concierge services, pets allowed.* Accepts all major credit cards.

L200,000–L600,000 HOTEL INTERNAZIONALE. *Via Sistina 79, 00187. Tel. 6/ 67 93 047, fax 6/ 67 84 764.* This wonderful little hotel combines all the modern amenities you could need and the charm of a small hotel, all in an excellent location at the top of the Spanish Steps. The guest rooms are all individually decorated with wooden antiques and frescoes, some have balconies, and all have a private bath with tub and shower, direct-dial phone with 24-hour switchboard service, color TV with CNN and the Sky Channel, mini-bar, and air conditioning. The rooms are connected by a series of Gothic hallways. Rates include breakfast. *Facilities: 42 rooms, 2 suites.* AE, CB, MC, V.

L300,000–L400,000 HOTEL SOFITEL. *Via Lombardia 47, 00187. Tel. 6/ 47 80 21, fax 6/ 48 21 019.* Centrally located near Via Veneto and the Villa Borghese gardens. Rooms have a private bath with shower and tub, refrigerator, direct-dial phone with 24-hour switchboard service, color TV with CNN and the Sky Channel, and air conditioning. *Facilities: 124 rooms and suites, restaurant nearby.* Accepts all major credit cards.

✓L280,000–L380,000 IMPERIALE HOTEL. *Via Vittorio Veneto 24, 00187. Tel 6/ 48 26 351, fax 6/ 48 26 352.* Although not as glamorous as the rest of the hotels on this stylish street, it is very charming and the friendly staff makes it seem more so. Relaxed but elegant, this hotel has rooms that are nicely decorated, all with a marble bathroom, as well as TV, mini-bar, and air conditioning. *Facilities: 95 rooms, 24-hour room service, on-site restaurant, on-site bar, babysitting, business facilities, garden area.* AE, DC, V.

L380,000–L1,500,000 MAJESTIC. *Via Veneto 50. Tel. 6/ 48 68 41, fax 6/ 48 80 984.* This older hotel underwent a five-year refurbishment to become one of the top hotels in Rome. It has sheltered many modern stars, from Sylvester Stallone to Luciano Pavarotti. The bedrooms are decorated in a bright, bold style, some even with zigzag carpets. Rooms feature private marble bath with tub and shower (some with a Jacuzzi), direct-dial phone with 24-hour switchboard service, color TV with CNN and the Sky Channel, mini-bar, and air conditioning. Some are also decorated in antiques. *Facilities: 95 rooms and suites, on-site restaurant, on-site bar, garden area, nearby parking garage.* Accepts all major credit cards.

L300,000–L400,000 PULLMAN BOSTON. *Via Lombardia 47. Tel. 6/ 47 8021 or (800) 223-9862 in the U.S., fax 6/ 48 21 019.* Enjoy views of the grounds of the Villa Medici, as well as the Vatican, St. Peter's, and Villa Borghese from the rooftop garden here. This hotel's rooms are pretty large, each with TV, mini-bar, and most with shower facilities. Convenient, with a charming old-fashioned atmosphere. *Facilities: 120 rooms, on-site bar, business facilities, babysitting, garden area.* Accepts all major credit cards.

L290,000–L470,000 REGINA CARLTON. *Via Veneto 72, 00187. Tel. 6/ 47 68 51, fax 6/ 48 54 83.* This hotel manages to keep a wonderfully intimate atmosphere on one of the most stylish streets in Rome. The guest rooms are vibrantly decorated in bright colors. Rooms have a private bath with tub and shower, direct-dial phone with 24-hour switchboard service, color TV, mini-bar, and air conditioning. *Facilities: 130 rooms, on-site restaurant, on-site bar, babysitting, business facilities, concierge.* Accepts all major credit cards.

MODERATE

L120,000–L290,000 DAN VENETO HOTEL. *Via Piemonte 63, 00187. Tel. 6/ 48 24 346, fax 6/ 48 21 534.* Sound-proofed, Venetian-style rooms have a private bath with tub and shower, private phone with 24-hour switchboard service, color TV with CNN and the Sky Channel, and air conditioning. *Facilities: 95 rooms, American bar, breakfast served on terrace/roof garden restaurant, meeting facilities, parking garage.* Accepts all major credit cards.

✓L190,000–L290,000 HOTEL CECIL. *Via Francesco Crispi 55A, 00187. Tel. 6/ 67 97 998, fax 6/ 67 97 996.* This attractive hotel was once the temporary home of Henrik Ibsen. Now the hotel offers clean, comfortable rooms each with a private bath and tub or shower, direct-dial private phone with 24-hour switchboard service, color TV with CNN and the Sky Channel, and air conditioning. *Facilities: 45 rooms, bar, room service, no pool or restaurant.* AE, MC, V.

L120,000–L200,000 HOTEL ELITE. *Via Francisco Crispi 49. Tel. 6/ 67 80 728.* Rooms have a private bath with tub and shower, direct-dial private phone with 24-hour switchboard service, and air conditioning. *Facilities: 25 rooms/suites.* Accepts all major credit cards.

L75,000–L215,000 LYDIA VENIER. *Via Sistina 42, 00187. Tel. 6/ 67 91 744, fax 6/ 67 97 263.* Very popular with students, this little hotel is only a stone's throw away from the Spanish Steps. The rooms are all nicely decorated, if somewhat worn, and some of the rooms have ceiling frescoes. Some rooms have a private bath with tub and shower, and direct-dial phone with 24-hour switchboard service. *Facilities: 17 rooms (six with shower facilities), pets allowed.* Accepts all major credit cards.

L120,000–L265,000 LA RESIDENZA HOTEL. *Via Emilia 22-24, 00187. Tel. 6/ 48 80 789, fax 6/ 48 57 21.* This hotel, converted from a house, offers a very intimate atmosphere, perfect for those who prefer small hotels. The location is wonderful, close to the American Embassy and Villa Borghese. All the rooms are nicely decorated, and have a private bath with tub and shower, direct-dial phone with 24-hour switchboard service, color TV with CNN and the Sky Channel, mini-bar, and air conditioning. Some even have a balcony. The public rooms are elegant and inviting, with Oriental rugs, oil paintings, and rattan furnishings. Rates include continental buffet breakfast. *Facilities: 27 rooms, 6 suites, drinks-only room service, on-site bar, massage, sunbed, Jacuzzi, guest laundry, multi-lingual staff, roof garden.* MC, V.

INEXPENSIVE

✓L97,000–L140,000 HOTEL ALEXANDRA. *Via Vittorio Veneto 18, 00187. Tel 6/ 48 81 943, fax 6/ 48 71 804.* This unique little hotel, once a private home, is one of the least expensive on this fashionable street. All the rooms are individually decorated, some with antiques and others with contemporary wall paintings. Each room has a private bath with tub or shower, color TV with CNN and the Sky Channel, mini-bar, and air conditioning. The rooms on the interior of the hotel have the least traffic noise, but you do sacrifice view. Rates include breakfast. *Facilities: 45 rooms, babysitting service, pets allowed.* Accepts all major credit cards.

L90,000–L130,000 HOTEL GAMBRINUS. *Via Piave 29, 00187. Tel. 6/ 48 71 250, or 6/ 47 42 488, fax 6/ 48 28 800.* Located near Via Veneto. Recently renovated rooms have a private bath with tub and shower, direct-dial private phone with 24-hour switchboard service, refrigerator, color TV with CNN and the Sky Channel, and air conditioning. *Facilities: 38 rooms, mini-bars, hair dryer, safe-deposit box, private fax, buffet breakfast and American bar, transfer from airport to hotel upon request.* AE, DC.

VILLA BORGHESE

EXPENSIVE

✓L300,000–L500,000 ALDROVANDI PALACE HOTEL. *Via Aldrovandi 15, 00197. Tel. 6/ 32 23 993, fax 6/ 32 21 435.* This charming hotel is a must for those who can afford it. It combines all the modern conveniences you could want and an Old World style of service. Rooms have a private bath with tub and shower, direct-dial phone with 24-hour switchboard service, color TV with CNN and the Sky Channel, mini-bar, and air conditioning. The public areas are attractive, with flower-filled vases galore and elegant chandeliers to highlight them. *Facilities: 140 rooms and suites, 1 Royal Suite, non-smoking rooms available, on-site restaurant, on-site piano bar, garden/park area, swimming pool, babysitting, business facilities, parking garage.* AE, MC, V.

L275,000–L396,000 BEVERLY HILLS HOTEL. *Largo Benedetto Marcello 220, 00198. Tel. 6/ 85 42 141, fax 6/ 85 35 0037.* Centrally located near Via Veneto. Newly renovated, comfortable, and fully-equipped rooms include a private bath with tub and shower, refrigerator, direct-dial phone with 24-hour switchboard service, color TV with CNN and the Sky Channel. *Facilities: 180 rooms, conference center.* Accepts all major credit cards.

L180,000–L450,000 DEGLI ARANCI HOTEL. *Via Baraba Oriani 9-11, 00197. Tel. 6/ 80 70 202, fax 6/ 80 70 704.* This smaller hotel, once a private villa, is set on a stylish residential street. Rooms have a private bath with tub and shower, direct-dial phone with 24-hour switchboard service, color TV, mini-bar, and air conditioning. The public areas are fashionable and decorated with touches from ancient Rome, such as classical vases and engravings. Rates include breakfast. *Facilities: 54 rooms, 3 suites, on-site bar.* AE, MC, V.

L210,000–L430,000 HOTEL PARCO DEI PRINCIPI. *Via G. Frescobaldi, 00198. Tel. 6/ 85 4421, fax 6/ 88 45 104.* This hotel is surrounded by a beautiful botanical park. Rooms have a private bath with tub and shower, direct-dial private phone with 24-hour switchboard service, color TV with CNN and the Sky Channel, refrigerator, mini-bar, and air conditioning. *Facilities: 170 rooms and 15 suites (all with balcony and view of pool and private park), three restaurants, 12 meeting rooms, private parking garage.* Accepts all major credit cards.

✓L250,000–L350,000 HOTEL VICTORIA ROMA. *Via Campania 41, 00187. Tel. 6/ 47 39 31, fax 6/ 48 71 890.* This hotel prides itself on its service, and feels that by refusing large groups, it can better serve the individuals who stay here. The guest rooms, although on the small side, are fashionably decorated. Rooms have a private bath with tub and shower, direct-dial phone with 24-hour switchboard service, color TV with CNN and the Sky Channel, mini-bar, and air conditioning. The public areas are bedecked with flowers, Oriental rugs, and paintings. *Facilities: 110 rooms, 4 suites, on-site restaurant, on-site bar, babysitting, business facilities, rooftop garden, pets allowed.* Accepts all major credit cards.

L285,000–L415,000 JOLLY HOTEL VITTORIO VENETO. *Corso d'Italia 1, 00198. Tel. 6/ 84 95 or (800) 221-2626 in the U.S., fax 6/ 88 41 104.* This hotel is a modern statement in steel and concrete. The guest rooms, although compact, are very nicely decorated, perfect for those who prefer more contemporary, as opposed to traditional, decor. Rooms have a private bath with tub and shower, direct-dial phone with 24-hour switchboard service, color TV with CNN, mini-bar, soundproofing, and air conditioning. The location is excellent, with views of the Villa Borghese. *Facilities: 200 rooms, rooms for the disabled, on-site restaurant, sports center, parking garage.* AE, DC, MC. V.

✓L280,000–L540,000 LORD BYRON HOTEL. *Via G. de Notaris 5, 00197. Tel. 6/ 32 20 404, fax 6/ 32 20*

405. This small hotel was once a private villa, and now specializes in discreet, personal service. Elegant, and even sumptuous, in a rather refined sort of way. As it's so close to the Villa Borghese, the location is wonderful. The guest rooms are all individually (and elegantly) decorated, and have a private bath with tub and shower, direct-dial phone with 24-hour switchboard service, color TV with CNN, mini-bar, and air conditioning. Some have balconies. On the coffee table of each bedroom, a complimentary decanter of port greets guests on their arrival. The public areas are beautifully done with vases of flowers everywhere you look, all making it seem more like a private villa than an exclusive hotel. This hotel caters to the very elite of Italy, and shouldn't be passed up. *Facilities: 28 rooms, 9 suites, 24-hour room service, on-site restaurant (Le Jardin—considered one of Rome's best restaurants), on-site piano bar, guest laundry, valet service, concierge desk, car rental desk, parking garage, pets allowed, garden area.* Accepts all major credit cards.

MODERATE

L113,000–L200,000 HOTEL DELLE MUSE. *Via Tommaso Salvini 18, 00197. Tel. 6/ 80 88 333, fax 6/ 80 85 749*. This small hotel is close to Villa Borghese. It's a three-star hotel decorated in a contemporary style with bold and vibrant colors. Rooms include a private bath with tub or shower, direct-dial phone with 24-hour switchboard service, color TV with CNN and the Sky Channel, mini-bar, and air conditioning. The hotel has several different public areas, such as a TV room and a writing room. *Facilities: 61 rooms, on-site garden restaurant, on-site 24-hour bar, car parking garage, garden area.* MC, V.

L170,000–L320,000 HOTEL OXFORD. *Via Boncompagni 89, 00187. Tel. 6/ 48 28 952 or (800) 448-8355 in the U.S., fax 6/ 48 15 349*. This smaller hotel is on the U.S. Embassy's list of preferred hotels in Rome. The guest rooms are slightly old-fashioned, but have brightly colored pieces of furniture. Rooms have a private bath with tub or shower, direct-dial phone with 24-hour switchboard service, color TV with CNN and the Sky Channel, mini-bar, and air conditioning. *Facilities: 57 rooms, 2 suites, on-site restaurant, on-site lounge/bar, babysitting, business facilities, pets allowed.* Accepts all major credit cards.

L180,000–L220,000 VILLA BORGHESE. *Via Pinciana 31, 00198. Tel. 6/ 85 30 0919, fax 6/ 84 42 636.* Not the actual thing, but a villa close to the Villa Borghese, this small hotel is exceedingly charming. The atmosphere is slightly old-fashioned, but so pleasant that even those who prefer more contemporary hotels will be brought into its charm. All the rooms have amenities such as private bathroom, TV, and mini-bar. Many of the upper-floor rooms have beautiful views of Villa Borghese. *Facilities: 31 rooms, 24-hour room service, on-site bar, garden, parking.* Accepts all major credit cards.

OUTER ROME

EXPENSIVE

L230,000–L353,000 ARIS GARDEN HOTEL. *Via Aristofane 101, 00125. Tel. 6/ 52 36 2443, fax 6/ 52 35 2968.* This special hotel is located in a serene, green oasis with a restful and peaceful atmosphere. Rooms have a bath with tub and shower, private phone with 24-hour switchboard service, and air conditioning. There are TVs in the rooms, but the hotel doesn't have a satellite. Enjoy sporting activities in an adjoining area. *Facilities: 72 rooms, 6 meeting rooms, bar and restaurant, sauna, massages, gym, squash, solarium, indoor/outdoor pool, tennis and shooting range.* Accepts all major credit cards.

L370,000–L1,000,000 CAVALIERI HILTON. *Via Cadlolo 101, 00136. Tel. 6/ 35 091 or (800) 445-8667 (in U.S. or Canada), fax 6/ 35 09 2241.* This hotel is a luxury resort fifteen minutes from the center of Rome. It has everything you could possibly require in your accommodations. Each of the rooms has individually controlled heating and air conditioning, an electronic lock, mini-bar, TV with in-house movies, telephone, radio, balcony, and private marble-encased bath, hair dryer, vanity mirror, telephone, and piped-in music. *Facilities: 373 rooms, 17 suites, two on-site restaurants (La Pergola, regarded as one of the best in Rome, and Il Giardino dell Uliveto, a garden restaurant with poolside veranda), room service, 24-hour concierge, outdoor swimming pool, Turkish bath, health club, sauna and massage, tennis courts, jogging paths, indoor arcade of shops, laundry, valet, facilities for the disabled.* Accepts all major credit cards.

L270,000–L900,000 SHERATON GOLF. *22 Viale Parco De' Medici, 00148. Tel. 6/ 52 24 08, fax 6/ 59 40 689.* Located in the parkland area with an 18-hole golf course in the new business area of Rome-EUR, this hotel offers free shuttle service to the airport and city center. Each room has a private bath with tub and shower, direct-dial private phone with 24-hour switchboard service, TV with CNN and the Sky Channel, and air conditioning. *Facilities: 179 rooms, 15 suites, and 56 rooms in a separate chalet. Arcade with boutique, drugstore, souvenirs, restaurant, banquet hall, and club-house restaurant, American bar, and piano bar, fitness center, 18-hole golf course, training course, pro shop, outdoor pool, tennis and squash courts, twelve conference/meeting rooms, car rental service, room service.* Accepts all major credit cards.

L290,000–L450,000 SHERATON ROMA. *Viale del Pattinaggio, 00148. Tel. 6/ 54 53, fax 6/ 59 40 689.* Located in Rome's new business district, this chain hotel offers free shuttle bus service between airport, hotel, and downtown. Rooms have a private bath with tub and shower, direct-dial private phone with 24-hour switchboard service, color TV with CNN and the Sky Channel, and in-house movies. Non-smoking rooms are available. *Facilities: 631 rooms, 24-hour room service, 2 restaurants and pool snack area, piano bar, shopping arcade, conference rooms, sauna, outdoor pool, tennis and squash court, health club.* Accepts all major credit cards.

MODERATE

L150,000–L220,000 HOTEL AMERICAN PALACE EUR. *Via Laurentino 554, 00143. Tel. 6/ 54 19 71, fax 6/ 59 11 740.* Air-conditioned rooms and suites with telephone, and color cable TV. *Facilities: 170 rooms, banquet and conference facilities, buffet breakfast, business center, room service, international currency exchange, fitness center, parking, airport transfer service, restaurant and bar, multilingual staff.* Accepts all major credit cards.

L148,000–L182,000 VILLA DEL PARCO. *Via Nomentana 110, 00161. Tel. 6/ 44 23 7773, fax 6/ 85 40 410.* Although not very close to the center of Rome, it can be easily reached by bus from here. This hotel is located in a nineteenth-century villa and surrounded by a garden. The bedrooms are a nice size and decorated in antiques. Each has air conditioning, mini-bar, TV, radio, and telephone. It offers a pretty good value. *Facilities: 24 rooms, room service, on-site bars, car park.* Accepts all major credit cards.

PART 4

Taste of the Town

DINING OUT

Italian cuisine is nearly the most famous type of cooking, second only to French. Even though you can find Italian restaurants pretty much anywhere in the world because of their popularity, "eating Italian" is a little different in Italy. The Roman locals generally eat light in the morning and have their largest meal in the afternoon. This means that the main meal in restaurants is served from about 1:00 P.M. to 3:00 P.M. Then the evening meal, lighter than lunch, is served in restaurants from about 9:00 P.M. to 11:00 P.M.—pretty late by American standards. This doesn't mean, though, that these are the only times that you can eat. At the more informal restaurants, such as a *trattoria* or a *rosticcerie*, food is served at economical prices. A typical Italian meal is made up of three courses: pasta, then a main course (some type of meat and vegetables), and then dessert. If you're not in the mood to eat a heavy meal, it is socially acceptable to eat just the pasta.

Romans begin the day with a stop for a quick stand-up breakfast that will usually consist of *cappuccino* (espresso topped with steamed milk) or *café latte* (coffee and steamed milk), a croissant, or a flaky pastry *brioche* (a light textured bread) that may be plain or filled. As the day wears on they like to have a mid-morning snack.

Everyone seems to smoke in Europe, and while non-smoking sections are becoming more prevalent, they are often in the least desirable sections of the restaurants.

As the day progresses to lunch time, it seems that everyone eats out. For this meal, cafeterias are popular, but there are hundreds of cafés open. Locals will eat their pasta for lunch (good for digestion), rather than eating it late. During the late afternoon they will have a snack of a fried rice croquette or *supplí*, ice cream, or light sandwiches.

Romans enjoy a relaxing meal and expect waiters to be accommodating without rushing. For a waiter to put a check on the table before you are ready to leave is considered rude. If you haven't been given the check when you are ready to leave, just signal to the waiter. It's not that he's being inattentive, he's just trying to be polite and not rush you.

A traditionally light and inexpensive evening meal will usually consist of pizza (Italian pizza is nothing like the American version) and antipasti (appetizer whose ingredients might include slices of cured meats, seafood, and cooked or seasoned vegetables). The many wine bars serve light meals and are very popular. If you'd like to have a more substantial meal, try a pasta meat selection. Unlike Americans, Romans eat their pastas separately from meat dishes. On Thursdays, a traditional *gnocchi alla Romana* (potato dumplings, tomato sauce, and cheese) is a favorite. On Fridays, fish is very popular and usually very fresh.

Before you order, be sure you calculate the price. The menu pricing is a little different from what most Americans are used to. Usually, restaurants offer a tourist menu or *menu turistico* (be prepared to have to ask for it as they won't voluntarily offer you this cheaper option). This is a large meal at a price that usually includes the pasta starter or soup, then the main meat dish, followed by dessert. Also included in the price is a carafe of wine or mineral water, cover charge, and service, although you should tip in addition to this. This is economical because, although you may not get the best meal in the restaurant, you will get a large portion of food while avoiding additional charges.

Another menu option that's available is the fixed-price meal. This might seem cheaper, but always make sure what that price includes. Often, the price won't include the drink, the bread, or the cover charge, and you'll be billed for this separately, raising the final price.

As Italy is famous for its wines, you will probably want to try several types. Here are a few things you should know. Winemaking wasn't controlled by the government for quality until 1965. Now, wines that are regulated by the government have DOC marked on their label. DOCG is even better and denotes more careful quality control.

You won't have to limit yourself to just wine while in Rome, as Italy has practically any kind of libation that you could want. If you're a liqueur fan, you're in luck because so are the Romans. The most famous of these liqueurs is probably Sambuca (a licorice flavored liqueur), which is made from aniseed and usually served with a coffee bean in it. Italy also makes several different brandies, as well as beer. Another famous drink of the Italians is Campari. It's fruit-punch red and has a kind of bitter herb taste to it. This is usually served with soda over ice.

Most restaurants in Rome close down in August when the locals go on holiday. So if you'll be in Rome that month, be sure to call the restaurant before you make the trip there, only to see a sign that says 'closed' in Italian.

EXPENSE CHART

CATEGORY	COST*
$$$$	L120,000 and over
$$$	L65,000-L120,000
$$	L40,000-L65,000
$	L40,000 and under

*per person for a three-course meal

AVENTINE/PALATINE

$$ ALVARO AL CIRCO MASSIMO

Via dei Cerchi, 53. Tel. 6/ 67 86 112.

Metro/Bus: Bus 53.

Price/Entrée: L50,000.

Open: Tues.–Sun. 1:00–11:00 P.M.

Reservations: Advised.

Atmosphere: Casual.

Credit Cards: Major cards accepted.

Food: Roman/Italian.

Guests may literally "dine out" at outdoor tables here in the summer. Indoors, there's somewhat of a country feeling. It's the perfect setting in which to enjoy the finest fresh fish and game, including *fagiano* (pheasant), *faraona* (guinea hen), or grilled *porcini* (mushrooms).

$ DA BUCATINO

Via Luca della Robbia, 84. Tel. 6/ 57 46 886.

Metro/Bus: Piamide.

Price/Entrée: L35,000.

Open: Daily lunch 12:00 noon–3:00 P.M., dinner 7:00–11:00 P.M.

Reservations: Advised.

Atmosphere: Comfortable.

Credit Cards: No credit cards.

Food: Roman/Italian.

Vegetables and antipasti are very good at this restaurant with an ever-changing menu. Entrées include fish such as *risotto alla pescatore* (rice with an assortment of seafood) or sublime *merluzzo alla diavola* (grilled cod). "*Carretto de la svojature*," as it is called in Rome, means chariot of delight. And it is delightful.

CAMPO DE'FIORI

$$$ CAMPONESCHI

Piazza Farnese, 50. Tel. 6/ 68 74 927.

Metro/Bus: Bus 280.

Price/Entrée: L120,000.
Open: Dinner only Mon.–Sat. 8:00 P.M.–1:00 A.M.
Reservations: Advised.
Atmosphere: Dressy.
Credit Cards: Major cards accepted.
Food: Traditional Italian.

Sophisticated Italian cooking is the specialty here, and the prices reflect the attention to detail. Enjoy a dinner outdoors on the terrace overlooking ancient Roman fountains. Menu selections include corn polenta (a thick porridge made from cornmeal flour) with Alba truffles or *partridge en croûte* (partridge in pastry).

$ LA CARBONARA

Piazza Campo de'Fiori, 23. Tel. 6/ 68 64 783.
Metro/Bus: Bus 64.
Price/Entrée: Appetizers, L8,000–L14,000; main courses, L16,000–L30,000.
Open: Wed.–Mon. lunch 12:00 noon–2:30 P.M., dinner 6:30–10:30 P.M. Closed Tuesdays.
Reservations: Recommended.
Atmosphere: Pleasant.
Credit Cards: Major cards accepted.
Food: Roman/Italian.

Set on the same square as the food market, La Carbonara features a menu that emphasizes fresh, seasonal vegetables. Tasty antipasti, grilled meats, and an excellent rendition of carbonara are best bets. The chef's version of the traditional tomato sauce made with *pancetta* (Italian bacon) is *bucatini all'amatriciana* (hollow coarsely textured spaghetti with a sauce of bacon, tomatoes, and strong pecorino cheese).

$$ IL CARDINALE

Via delle Carceri, 6. Tel. 6/ 68 69 336.
Metro/Bus: Bus 46, 62, or 64.
Price/Entrée: L60,000.
Open: Mon.–Sat. lunch 12:30–2:30 P.M., dinner 8:00–11:30 P.M.
Reservations: Essential.
Atmosphere: Intimate, intriguing.

Credit Cards: AE, DC, EC, MC, V.
Food: Regional dishes.

Set in the former home of a bicycle shop, this restaurant handles regional dishes with flair. The small but well-decorated rooms recall the turn of the century. Served within this elegant setting are dishes including grilled eel, pasta with green tomato and artichoke sauce, a sweetbread casserole with mushrooms, and an anchovy and endive dish, *alicotti con lindivia.*

❤ $$$ IL DRAPPO

Vicolo del Malpasso, 9. Tel. 6/ 68 77 365.
Metro/Bus: Bus 46, 62, or 64.
Price/Entrée: L75,000.
Open: Dinner only, Mon.–Sat. 8:00 P.M.–12:00 midnight. Closed two weeks in August.
Reservations: Required.
Atmosphere: Modern.
Credit Cards: AE.
Food: Sardinian.

The brother and sister who operate this two-room restaurant offer first-rate service in an intimate setting complete with candles and flowers. A typical dinner may be composed of a wafer-thin appetizer called *carte di musica* (sheet music paper), topped with tomatoes, green peppers, parsley, and olive oil; a fresh spring lamb in season; a fish stew made with tuna caviar; or a changing selection of strongly flavored regional specialties.

$ DA GIGGETTO

Via del Portico d'Ottavia, 21-22. Tel. 6/ 68 61 105.
Metro/Bus: Bus 62, 64, 75, or 170.
Price/Entrée: Appetizers, L9,000–L12,000; main courses, L16,000–L21,000.
Open: Tues.–Sun. lunch 12:30–3:30 P.M., dinner 7:30–10:30 P.M.
Reservations: Recommended.
Atmosphere: Pleasant.
Credit Cards: AE, DC, MC, V.
Food: Roman/Italian.

For a traditional meal in an authentic setting, this

restaurant is tops. Dishes such as *carciofi alla giudia* (tender-fried baby artichokes), the cheese concoction, *mozzarella in carrozza* (bread mozzarella), and zucchini flowers stuffed with mozzarella and anchovies are something to remember. Enjoy the codfish, *fettuccini all'amatriciano* (flat noodles with a sauce of bacon, tomatoes, and strong pecorino cheese), shrimps sautéed in garlic and olive oil, tripe, or *saltimbocca* (veal scallop layered with prosciutto and sage).

$ GRAPPOLO D' ORO

Piazza della Cancelleria, 80. Tel. 6/ 68 64 118.
Metro/Bus: Bus to Corso Vittorio Emanuele.
Price/Entrée: L32,000.
Open: Mon.–Sat. lunch 12:00 noon–3:00 P.M., dinner 7:00–11:00 P.M.
Reservations: Recommended.
Atmosphere: Outdoor setting/Casual.
Credit Cards: AE, EC, MC, V.
Food: Roman/Italian.

Resident and foreign artists frequent this restaurant. Tables on the piazza fill quickly, so make a reservation early, and specify your preference for seating. Entrées such as *trippa alla romana* (a tripe dish), *bucatini all'amatriciana* (a spaghetti dish), and *tagliatelle con la trota* (flat egg noodles with trout) are delightful, and the staff is attentive.

$ LA MAJELLA

Piazza del Teatro di Pompeo, 18. Tel. 6/ 68 64 174.
Metro/Bus: Bus 62 or 64.
Price/Entrée: Appetizers, L8,000–L15,000; main courses, L12,000–L20,000.
Open: Mon.–Sat. lunch 12:30–3:00 P.M., dinner 8:00 P.M.–12:00 midnight.
Reservations: Recommended for dinner.
Atmosphere: Pleasant.
Credit Cards: AE, DC, MC, V.
Food: Abruzzi.

Abruzzi mountain food, definitely for a hearty appetite, includes partridge and venison with polenta, suckling pig, and an array of pastas and roasted lamb with herbs. Grilled or fried sea bass, flounder, lobster, and shrimp are among the seafood offered. Famous clientele who have enjoyed the fare served in three old-fashioned dining rooms include the present Pope when he was Polish Cardinal Karol Wojtyla.

$ LE MASCHERE

Via Monte della Farina, 29. Tel. 6/ 68 79 44.
Metro/Bus: Bus 26, 44, 60, 70, or 75.
Price/Entrée: Appetizers, L10,000–L15,000; main courses, L14,000–L25,000.
Open: Dinner only Tues.–Sun. 7:30 P.M.–12:00 midnight.
Reservations: Recommended.
Atmosphere: Casual.
Credit Cards: AE, DC, MC, V.
Food: Calabrian.

Calabrian cuisine is "fiery" cooking, with lots of garlic and red peppers. Offerings include pasta made with broccoli, or flavored with red peppers, garlic, bread crumbs, and more than a touch of anchovy, grilled meats, and swordfish fresh from the sea. Enjoy pizza and a beer if you're not ready for a full meal. For dessert, enjoy sheep cheese or fresh fruit salad.

$$$ PIPERNO

Via Monte de' Cenci, 9. Tel. 6/ 68 86 629.
Metro/Bus: Bus to Via Arenula and to Largo di Torre Argentina.
Price/Entrée: L75,000.
Open: Lunch Tues.–Sun 12:15–2:30 P.M., dinner Tues.–Sat. 8:00–10:30 P.M.
Reservations: Essential.
Atmosphere: Relaxed.
Credit Cards: AE, DC, V.
Food: Roman/Italian.

The atmosphere is casual in this restaurant, where guests may dine in one of three small, wood-paneled rooms or at an outside table. Entrées include *pasta e ceci* (a thick soup of pasta tubes and chick peas), *filetti di baccalà* (cod filet fried in batter), *fiori di zucca* (stuffed zucchini flowers), and artichokes.

$$$ POLESE
Piazza Sforza Cesarini, 40. Tel. 6/ 68 61 709.
Metro/Bus: Bus 42 or 64.
Price/Entrée: L75,000.
Open: Wed.–Mon. 11:30 A.M.–12:00 midnight.
Reservations: Advised on weekends.
Atmosphere: Casual.
Credit Cards: AE, DC, MC, V.
Food: Roman/Italian.

This restaurant is crowded on weekends and summer evenings with guests who know this is a good place to dine under the magnificent trees of Old Rome. Roman specialties include *fettuccine alla Polese* (flat noodles with cream and mushrooms) and *vitello alla fornara* (roast brisket of veal with potatoes).

$ RISTORANTE DEL PALLARO
Largo del Pallaro, 15. Tel. 6/ 88 01 488.
Metro/Bus: Bus 46, 70, or 492.
Price/Entrée: Fixed-price meals, L28,000–L30,000.
Open: Tues.–Sun. lunch 1:00–3:00 P.M., dinner 8:00–11:30 P.M.
Reservations: Recommended for dinner on weekends.
Atmosphere: Pleasant/Casual.
Credit Cards: No credit cards.
Food: Roman/Italian.

This spotless restaurant serves an eight-course meal that's an excellent value. The meal includes bread, a liter of mineral water, and half a liter of the house wine. Antipasti comes first, then a pasta of the day. Meat courses include roast veal, white meatballs, and, on Fridays, dried cod served with potatoes and eggplant. Mozzarella cheese, cake with custard, and fruit in season finish the meal.

$ RISTORANTE DE PANCRAZIO
Piazza del Biscione, 92. Tel. 6/ 68 61 246.
Metro/Bus: Bus 46 or 62.
Price/Entrée: Appetizers, L12,000–L16,000; main courses, L14,000–L35,000; fixed-price menu, L25,000.
Open: Thurs.–Tues. lunch 12:00 noon–3:00 P.M., dinner 7:30–11:15 P.M.

Reservations: Recommended.
Atmosphere: Pleasant.
Credit Cards: AE, DC, MC, V.
Food: Roman/Italian.

This restaurant calls a national monument home. One of its rooms is authentically decorated in the style of an eighteenth-century tavern. Menu items include *risotto alla pescatore*; *saltimbocca*; several versions of scampi; mixed fish fry; and a Roman specialty, *abbacchio al forno* (a dish of roasted baby lamb with potatoes).

$$ TAVERN GIULIA
Vicolo dell'Oro, 23. Tel. 6/ 68 69 786.
Metro/Bus: Corso Vittorio Emanuele.
Price/Entrée: L55,000.
Open: Mon.–Sat. lunch 12:30–3:30 P.M.,
dinner 7:30 P.M.–12:00 midnight. Closed in August.
Reservations: Advised.
Atmosphere: Pleasant.
Credit Cards: AE, DC, EC, MC, V.
Food: Genoese.

A visit to this upscale restaurant is a trip back in time. It's set in a pleasant fifteenth-century house and decorated in the fifteenth-century style. Try the classic Ligurian entrees such as *trenette al pesto* (thin noodles with pesto and potatoes), and *tagliatelle ai funghi*, or the well-known *pasta al pesto* (pasta with a sauce of basil leaves, cheese, garlic, marjoram, and pine nuts). It's also famous for its crème brûlée.

$ VECCHIA ROMA
Via della Tribuna di Campitelli, 18. Tel. 6/ 68 64 604.
Metro/Bus: Bus 64.
Price/Entrée: Appetizers, L15,000–L25,000;
main courses, L20,000–L31,000.
Open: Thurs.–Tues. lunch 12:30–4:00 P.M.,
dinner 8:00 P.M.–12:00 midnight.
Closed Wednesdays and August 7–30.
Reservations: Recommended.
Atmosphere: Charming.

Credit Cards: AE, DC.
Food: Italian.

Rome's beautiful Renaissance buildings are the site of this restaurant, which has a reputation for its fresh seafood. During summer months diners may eat at tables set outside, well-shaded by large umbrellas. Inside, rustic furnishings create a casual, charming ambiance. There are such dishes as a minestrone of the day, antipasti, pastas, and risottos. Fresh cuts of meat including lamb, another specialty, are also offered.

CAPITOL/FORUM/COLOSSEUM

$ ALFREDO ALLA SCROFA

Via della Scrofa, 104A. Tel. 6/ 68 86 163.
Metro/Bus: Piazza di Spagna.
Price/Entrée: Appetizers, L13,000–L20,000; main courses, L18,000–L25,000.
Open: Wed.–Mon. lunch 12:30–3:00 P.M., dinner 7:30–11:30 P.M.
Reservations: Recommended.
Atmosphere: Casual.
Credit Cards: AE, DC, MC, V.
Food: Roman/International.

This restaurant in a sixteenth-century building was established in 1925. Decorated with oak paneling and pictures of famous diners of the past, this restaurant has hosted such notable guests as Tony Curtis, Arthur Miller, Marilyn Monroe, and Mussolini. The uninitiated should order the *maestose fettucine al triplo burro*, which comes with a tableside show in which waiters prepare the dish from their rolling carts with well-choreographed movements.

$ OSTERIA DA NERONE

Via Terme di Tito, 96. Tel. 6/ 47 45 207.
Metro/Bus: Colosseo.
Price/Entrée: L35,000–L40,000.
Open: Mon.–Sat. 7:00–11:00 P.M.

Reservations: Advised.
Atmosphere: Casual.
Credit Cards: No credit cards.
Food: Roman/Italian.

This charming, family-run restaurant offers a delectable fresh antipasto and pasta table. Specialties include *fettuccine al Nerone* (noodles with peas, salami, and mushrooms) and homemade ravioli. Ask for a patio table if the weather is suitable.

$ TRATTORIA L'ALBANESE

Via dei Serpenti, 148. Tel. 6/ 47 40 777.
Metro/Bus: Cavour.
Price/Entrée: Appetizers, L10,000–L15,000; main courses, L15,000–L24,000.
Open: Lunch Wed.–Mon. 12:00 noon–3:00 P.M., dinner Wed.–Sun. 6:30–10:30 P.M.
Reservations: Recommended on weekends.
Atmosphere: Casual.
Credit Cards: DC, MC, V.
Food: Roman/Italian.

Inexpensive and reliable, this restaurant makes great cannelloni and *ravioli di ricotta* (ravioli with ricotta cheese and served with tomato sauce). Enjoy lunch in the garden tucked at the back of the restaurant. This is a good choice if you're exploring central Rome.

PANTHEON

$ ABRUZZI

Via de Vaccaro, 1. Tel. 6/ 67 93 897.
Metro/Bus: Bus 64, 70, or 75.
Price/Entrée: Appetizers, L3,000–L10,000; main courses, L9,000–L18,000.
Open: Sun.–Fri. lunch 12:30–3:00 P.M., dinner 7:30–10:30 P.M.
Reservations: Recommended.
Atmosphere: Casual.
Credit Cards: DC, MC, V.
Food: Abruzzi.

This restaurant has been around for a while, and when you visit you'll see why it's still very popular. Its regional cooking from mountainous Abruzzi is great. Guests are offered a pleasing assortment of cold antipasti, from which you can make your own selections. The garnet red wine is a good start, then try some soup. The main dishes include *saltimbocca.*

$ IL BARROCCIO

Via dei Pastini, 13-14. Tel. 6/ 67 93 797.
Metro/Bus: Bus 119.
Price/Entrée: Appetizers, L11,500–L13,500; main courses, L16,000–L22,000.
Open: Tues.–Sun. lunch 12:30–3:00 P.M., dinner 7:30–11:00 P.M.
Reservations: Recommended.
Atmosphere: Casual.
Credit Cards: AE, DC, MC, V.
Food: Roman/Italian.

Expect to get generous portions of whatever you order here, but service is inconsistent, as is the availability of music from the roving musicians who pass through occasionally. There are two good-size floors ideal for groups. The à la carte items range from bean soup to seafood antipasto. Pizza is a specialty.

$ EAU VIVE

Via Monterone, 85. Tel. 6/ 68 81 095.
Metro/Bus: Bus 64 or 78.
Price/Entrée: Appetizers, L4,000–L12,000; main courses, L18,000–L25,000; fixed-price menus, L15,000, L20,000, and L30,000.
Open: Mon.–Sat. lunch 12:00 noon–2:30 P.M., dinner 8:00–9:30 P.M.
Reservations: Recommended.
Atmosphere: Formal.
Credit Cards: AE, MC, V.
Food: French/International.

This restaurant is devoted to a higher cause. Missionaries, who dress in their native country costumes, operate it. If you're around at 10:00 P.M., you'll hear the wait staff recite a prayer and chant. Tips are used for religious causes. Perhaps that's what led Pope John Paul to dine here when he was still Archbishop of Cracow. An international dish is a daily feature. Frog legs are a specialty, and main dishes range from guinea hen to couscous. The chocolate mousse is a religious experience, too.

$$ FORTUNATO AL PANTHEON

Via del Pantheon, 55. Tel. 6/ 67 92 788.
Metro/Bus: Bus 119.
Price/Entrée: L55,000.
Open: Mon.–Sat. lunch 12:30–3:00 P.M., dinner 7:30–11:30 P.M.
Reservations: Advisable.
Atmosphere: Casual/neat.
Credit Cards: AE, DC.
Food: Roman/Italian.

Locals, politicians, and journalists enjoy this restaurant, which dates back to 1950. Specialties change, but there are several pastas, *penne all'arrabbiata* (short, tubular pasta in a tomato sauce with red pepper flakes) and *risotto alla milanese* (rice with saffron and wine), or risotto with porcini mushrooms. Fish and meat dishes are also served, some with truffles. There are three dining rooms, plus patio seating when weather permits.

$ GIOLITTI

Via Uffici del Vicario, 40. Tel. 6/ 69 91 243.
Metro/Bus: Bus 119 and to Via del Corso and Piazza San Silvestro.
Price/Entrée: Ice cream, L3,000 and up.
Open: Daily 7:00 P.M.–2:00 A.M.
Reservations: Not necessary.
Atmosphere: Casual.
Credit Cards: No cards accepted.
Food: Ice cream.

This ice creamery has a snack counter that's sure to contain something to tame a sweet tooth. It can get crowded at night, when locals and visitors alike turn out for a Giolitti cup of *gelato* topped with whipped cream, ice cream, or sundaes.

$ IL MIRAGGIO

Vicolo Sciarra, 59. Tel. 6/ 67 80 226.
Metro/Bus: Bus 56, 85, 87, or 90B.
Price/Entrée: Appetizers, L9,000–L15,000; main courses, L12,000–L24,000.
Open: Mon.–Sat. lunch 12:30–3:30 P.M., dinner 7:30–10:30 P.M.
Reservations: Recommended.
Atmosphere: Informal neighborhood setting.
Credit Cards: AE, V.
Food: Roman/Sardinian.

Roman cuisine, fresh fish, and tortellini alla papalina are specialties at this restaurant, which is known for its fast service and excellent food. Try the filet of beef with truffles, *rosetta di vitello modo nostro*, or *spiedino all Siciliana* (pieces of meat grilled on a skewer over an open flame, marinated in orange peel and a dry white wine). This is a good place to stop while shopping near the Colonna.

$ QUIRINO

Via delle Muratte, 84. Tel. 6/ 67 94 108.
Metro/Bus: Piazza Barberini.
Price/Entrée: Appetizers, L10,000–L14,000; main courses, L16,000–L24,000.
Open: Mon.–Sat. lunch 12:30–3:30 P.M., dinner 7:30–10:30 P.M.
Reservations: Required.
Atmosphere: Casual.
Credit Cards: AE, V.
Food: Roman/Italian.

Since 1958, this restaurant has been serving strictly "home cooking." Set in an eighteenth-century building that several popes and famous local families have called home, it offers traditional dishes such as brains in butter. Specialties include Sicilian pasta, *pasta alla Norma* (pasta with a sauce of tomatoes, eggplant, and ricotta salinata), and an assortment of dishes that include meat or fish.

PIAZZA DI SPAGNA

✓ $ ANTICO CAFÉ GRECO

Via Condotti, 86. Tel. 6/ 67 91 700.
Metro/Bus: Bus 81, 90, or 90b.
Price/Entrée: Paradiso and light sandwiches, L9,000; cappuccino, L7,500.
Open: Mon.–Sat. 8:00 A.M.–9:00 P.M.
Reservations: Not necessary.
Atmosphere: Nineteenth century.
Credit Cards: No credit cards.
Food: Café style.

With its carved wood bar and silk-covered walls, this café has a nineteenth-century atmosphere, but it actually has been serving drinks since 1760. This is a wonderful place to relax and enjoy a cup of cappuccino at a marble table. Waiters wear black tailcoats.

$ DAL BOLOGNESE

Piazza del Popolo, 1-2. Tel. 6/ 36 11 426.
Metro/Bus: Flaminio.
Price/Entrée: Appetizers, L13,000–L24,000; main courses, L18,000–L28,000.
Open: Tues.–Sun. lunch 12:45–3:00 P.M., dinner 8:15–11:00 P.M. Closed Sunday for dinner; closed Mondays; closed most of August.
Reservations: Required.
Atmosphere: Casual.
Credit Cards: AE, DC.
Food: Bolognese.

This is a popular spot with actors, models, and artists. I suggest you try the savory Parma ham or the melon and prosciutto to begin the meal. Main course specialties include *tagliatelle alla bolognese* (flat egg noodles in meat sauce), lasagna verde, and the *costoletta alla bolognese* (veal cutlet fried with a slice of ham or bacon).

$ CAFÉ ALEMAGNA

Via del Corso, 181. Tel. 6/ 67 89 135.
Metro/Bus: Bus to Corso Vittorio Emanuele.
Price/Entrée: Pastries start at L1,500; coffee at L1,000.

Open: Daily 7:00 A.M.–10:00 P.M.
Reservations: Not necessary.
Atmosphere: Casual.
Credit Cards: No cards accepted.
Food: Café style.

This monumental café with black stone floors and crystal chandeliers is a popular place for busy shoppers and locals in a hurry. Stop by for a quick bite, or sit and enjoy a pastry and cup of coffee. There is a sandwich bar, a caféteria, and a dining room with waiter service.

$$ LA CAMPANA

Vicolo della Campana, 18. Tel. 6/ 68 67 820.
Metro/Bus: Bus to Piazza Augusto Imperatore and Lungotevere Marzio.
Price/Entrée: L50,000.
Open: Tues.–Sun. lunch 12:30–2:45 P.M., dinner 7:30–10:45 P.M. Closed Mondays and August.
Reservations: Dinner reservations advised.
Atmosphere: Relaxing.
Credit Cards: AE, DC, V.
Food: Roman/Italian.

Rome's oldest restaurant dates back to 1518. Stables once stood where the two dining rooms are today. Known for reasonable prices, the restaurant offers a menu that includes specialties like *vignarola* (sautéed fava beans, peas, and artichokes), rigatoni with prosciutto and tomato sauce, and *olivette di vitello con purée.*

$ CANOVA CAFÉ

Piazza del Popolo. Tel. 6/ 63 61 2231.
Metro/Bus: Flaminio.
Price/Entrée: Coffee, L1,100; meal, L38,000.
Open: Food served 12:00 noon–3:30 P.M., bar 7:00 A.M.–1:00 AM. Closed Mondays.
Reservations: Not necessary.
Atmosphere: Casual.
Credit Cards: No cards accepted.
Food: Café style.

This bustling café has a sidewalk terrace for people-watching, and a snack bar, restaurant, and a wine shop inside. Tour the courtyard in the summer. The ivy-covered walls and flowering plants create a fresh, verdant atmosphere. Walls inside are covered with expensive accessories for sale.

$$$ FRATELLI MENGHI

Via Flaminia, 57. Tel. 6/ 32 00 803.
Metro/Bus: Bus 90, 90b, 95, or 119.
Price/Entrée: L65,000.
Open: Mon.–Sat. 11:30 A.M.–8:00 P.M.
Reservations: Advised.
Atmosphere: Casual.
Credit Cards: No cards accepted.
Food: Roman/Italian.

Trust the neighborhood locals. They are the main clientele for this longtime family-owned restaurant that specializes in Roman fare. Try the minestrone, "the thick soup," *pasta e ceci*, and *involtini* (meat roulades), and you'll see why they keep coming back.

$ DA MARIO

Via della Vite, 55-56. Tel. 6/ 67 83 818.
Metro/Bus: Piazza di Spagna.
Price/Entrée: Appetizers, L10,000–L14,000; main courses, L14,000–L20,000.
Open: Mon.–Sat. lunch 12:30–3:00 P.M., dinner 7:30–11:00 P.M. Closed in August.
Reservations: Recommended.
Atmosphere: Casual.
Credit Cards: AE, DC, MC, V.
Food: Roman/Florentine.

Guests enjoy fast service in this air-conditioned restaurant with dark, rustic decor. Central to the Piazza di Spagna, it's a good place for serious shoppers to refuel. Popular for its prices on game specialties, it also offers *pappardelle* (a wide noodle dish), beefsteak, and roasted quail with polenta.

$$ NINO

11 Via Borgognona. Tel. 6/ 67 95 676.
Metro/Bus: Piazza di Spagna.

Price/Entrée: Average, L55,000.
Open: Mon.–Sat. lunch 12:30–3:00 P.M., dinner 7:30–11:00 P.M. Closed August.
Reservations: Advised.
Atmosphere: Busy.
Credit Cards: Major cards accepted.
Food: Tuscan.

Local artsy types favor this restaurant for its extensive wine list and hearty food. This charming Tuscan restaurant offers specialties such as grilled veal liver, quail, *fagioli cotti al fiasco*, *codfish alla livornese* (codfish cooked in wine, tomatoes, and spices), zampone, and *zuppa di fagioli alla Francovich* (thick Tuscan white bean soup with garlic). Popular with the bus crowd, Nino welcomes large groups.

$ OSTERIA MARGUTTA

Via Margutta, 82. Tel. 6/ 32 31 025.
Metro/Bus: Piazza di Spagna.
Price/Entrée: Appetizers, L12,000–L16,000; main courses, L18,000–L23,000.
Open: Mon.–Sat. lunch 12:30–3:00 P.M., dinner 7:30–10:30 P.M.
Reservations: Recommended.
Atmosphere: Casual.
Credit Cards: AE, DC, MC, V.
Food: Roman/Italian.

An old-fashioned tavern, this is a great place to drop by for a plate of antipasti. If you're hungry, stay and order dishes such as roast beef, lamb with green peppercorns, or a juicy steak. Sundays are a good time to visit; you'll catch a weekly art show on the street outside.

$ OTELLO ALLA CONCORDIA

Via della Croce, 81. Tel. 6/ 67 91 178.
Metro/Bus: Piazza di Spagna.
Price/Entrée: Appetizers, L8,000–L14,000; main courses, L16,000–L25,000.
Open: Sat.–Thurs. lunch 12:30–2:45 P.M., dinner 7:30–10:45 P.M. Closed August.

Reservations: Required.
Atmosphere: Rustic.
Credit Cards: No credit cards accepted.
Food: Roman/Italian.

This restaurant has a beautiful courtyard, which is a wonderful place to dine in good weather. Whether enjoyed inside or out, there are plenty of choices for guests here, and each menu item is delicious. *Spaghetti alle vongole veraci* (spaghetti with a mussel, tomato, and garlic sauce), breast of turkey with mushrooms, roasted baby lamb, eggplant parmigiana, and a selection of grilled or sautéed fish dishes are among the tempting dishes offered.

$$$ RANIERI

Via Mario de' Fiori, 26. Tel. 6/ 67 91 592.
Metro/Bus: Bus 52, 53, 56, 81, or 90.
Price/Entrée: Average, L73,000.
Open: Mon.–Sat. lunch 12:30–3:00 P.M., dinner 7:30–11:00 P.M.
Reservations: Advised.
Atmosphere: Traditional.
Credit Cards: AE, DC, EC, MC, V.
Food: Italian/French.

The veal cutlet entrée served with asparagus and mushrooms has been pleasing guests at this restaurant since the nineteenth century. The queen's former cook opened Ranieri in 1843, and the well-received dishes haven't changed much. Another specialty is *gnocchetti alla parigina, mignonettes alla Regina Vittoria.*

$ IL RISTORANTE 34

Via Mario de Fiori, 34. Tel. 6/ 67 95 091.
Metro/Bus: Piazza di Spagna.
Price/Entrée: Appetizers, L10,000–L20,000; main courses, L15,000–L21,000.
Open: Lunch Tues.–Sun. 12:30–3:00 P.M., dinner Tues.–Sat. 7:30–10:30 P.M. Closed August 6–26.
Reservations: Required.
Atmosphere: Elegant.
Credit Cards: AE, DC, MC, V.
Food: Roman/Italian.

The menu here is as elegant as the decor. Nestled in the heart of Rome's famous shopping district, this restaurant offers dishes designed to tempt the taste buds. Noodles with caviar and salmon, pasta and lentil soup, risotto with chunks of lobster, two kinds of *entrecôte* (a cut of steak taken from between the ribs), meatballs in a sauce with fat mushrooms, or pasta in pumpkin-flavored cream sauce are among flavorful dishes served here. Deep red wallpaper and a high ceiling make for a dramatic, elegant setting.

$–$$ EL TOULÀ

Via della Lupa, 29B. Tel. 6/ 68 73 498.
Metro/Bus: Bus 26, 90, or 913.
Price/Entrée: Appetizers, L16,000–L22,000; main courses, L33,000–L52,000; fixed-price menu, L90,000.
Open: Lunch Mon.–Fri. 1:00–3:00 P.M., dinner Mon.–Sat. 8:00–11:00 P.M. Closed August.
Reservations: Required for dinner.
Atmosphere: Elegant, jacket and tie required.
Credit Cards: AE, DC, MC, V.
Food: Roman/Venetian.

Archways with ornate moldings and high, elaborately decorated ceilings set the tone for a very sophisticated evening at this restaurant. The menu changes monthly to take advantage of seasonal items. Dishes may include *fegato* (liver) *alla Veneziana* (thinly sliced calves' liver fried with salt, pepper, and onions), calamari stuffed with vegetables, bigoli pasta in squid ink, *bacalari* (codfish mousse served with polenta), and fish soup made with monkfish and clams. If you would like to try a variety of entrées, you may request a mixed plate.

PIAZZA NAVONA

$ DA BAFFETTO

Via del Governo Vecchio, 114. Tel. 6/ 68 61 617.
Metro/Bus: Corso Vittorio Emanuele.
Price/Entrée: Average, L15,000.

Open: Mon.–Sat. 6:30 P.M.–12:45 A.M.
Closed Sundays and August.
Reservations: No reservations.
Atmosphere: Casual.
Credit Cards: No credit cards accepted.
Food: Roman/Italian.

Look for the line outside to find this restaurant on one of Rome's most popular shopping streets. The pizza here is the most popular in the city. A simple interior and slow service are evidence that the pizza is the main attraction.

$$$ IL CONVIVIO

Via dell' Orso, 44. Tel. 6/ 68 69 432.
Metro/Bus: Corso del Rinascimento.
Price/Entrée: Average, L80,000.
Open: Mon.–Sat. lunch 1:00–2:30 P.M.,
dinner 8:00–10:30 P.M.
Reservations: Necessary.
Atmosphere: Casual.
Credit Cards: AE, DC, EC, MC, V.
Food: Italian.

Reputed to be one of Rome's finest, this restaurant pleases its guests time after time in a tranquil, sophisticated setting. Modern, creative treatment of classic Italian and Roman dishes is its specialty. The menu changes with the seasons, but offers such dishes as shellfish with tarragon and lamb with thyme. An extensive wine list is available.

HOSTARIA DELL'ORSO

Via dei Soldati, 25. Tel. 6/ 68 30 7074.
Price/Entrée: Appetizers, L25,000–L35,000;
main course, L45,000–L65,000.
Open: Dinner only Mon.–Sat.
7:30 P.M.–12:00 midnight.

Set in one of the prettiest centuries-old buildings in Rome, this formal restaurant is the third member of a trio that, in combination, offers something for everyone. Hostaria dell'Orso serves international cuisine, and it's on the street level. The dimly lit, comfortable Blu Bar and La Cabala, a disco for titled young Romans, are upstairs. It's near the Piazza Navona (closed Sundays). Reservations are recommended.

$ MONTEVECCHIO

Piazza di Montevecchio, 22. Tel. 6/ 68 61 319.
Metro/Bus: Bus 70 or 492.
Price/Entrée: Appetizers, L12,000–L15,000; main courses, L20,000–L30,000.
Open: Tues.–Sun. lunch 1:00–3:00 P.M., dinner 8:00–11:30 P.M. Closed August 10–25.
Reservations: Required.
Atmosphere: Casual.
Credit Cards: AE, MC, V.
Food: Roman/Italian.

This restaurant is somewhat hidden, but worth the extra time it may take you to hunt for it. High ceilings and walls lined with bottles of wine are part of the casual decor. Menu offerings include such items as roebuck with polenta, roast Sardinian goat, and several veal dishes.

$$ ORSO 80

Via dell'Orso, 33. Tel. 6/ 68 64 904.
Metro/Bus: Bus 70, 87, or 64.
Price/Entrée: L50,000.
Open: Tues.–Sun. 7:30–10:00 P.M. Closed August 10–20.
Reservations: Advised.
Atmosphere: Casual.
Credit Cards: AE, DC, MC, V.
Food: Roman/Italian.

Antipasti lovers know about this place, which offers a homemade egg pasta with your entrée. Set in old Rome on a street famous for the workshops of artisans, it is also well-known for its seafood dishes. A Roman specialty dessert makes the perfect ending.

$$$ PAPA GIOVANNI

Via dei Sediari, 4. Tel. 6/ 68 65 308.
Metro/Bus: Corso de Rinascimento.
Price/Entrée: L100,000 and up.

Open: Mon.–Sat. 1:00–2:30 P.M., 8:00–11:00 P.M. Closed August and December.
Reservations: Required.
Atmosphere: Casual.
Credit Cards: MC, V.
Food: Roman/Italian.

This restaurant offers some of the best lighter Roman cuisine in the city. Set in a country-style atmosphere, it offers such dishes as exotic salads, *cacio e pepe*, salt cod and tripe, and concoctions with truffles. After the light fare, try a dessert like ricotta soufflé with strawberry sauce, hot chocolate, and sorbets.

$–$$ PASSETTO

Via Giuseppe Zanardelli, 14. Tel. 6/ 68 80 6569.
Metro/Bus: Bus 70, 87, or 492.
Price/Entrée: Appetizers, L10,000–L18,000; main courses, L16,000–L50,000.
Open: Tues.–Sat. lunch 12:30–3:30 P.M., dinner 7:30–11:30 P.M.
Reservations: Recommended.
Atmosphere: Romantic.
Credit Cards: AE, DC, MC, V.
Food: Roman/International.

Excellent, highly professional service and romantic decor complete with crystal chandeliers create an experience that won't soon be forgotten. The food is just as memorable. You'll like such entrées as sea bass, or *rombo passetto* (a similar fish to sole) cooked in a cognac and pine nut sauce. Seasonal fruit served with thick cream is a favorite. In the summer, enjoy dining on the terrace.

$ TRE MAGHI

Piazza Pasquino, 77-78. Tel. 6/ 68 30 7704.
Metro/Bus: Corso Vittorio Emanuele.
Price/Entrée: Average, L40,000.
Open: Mon.–Sat. lunch 12:30–3:00 P.M., dinner 7:30–11:00 P.M.
Reservations: Not necessary.
Atmosphere: Casual.

Credit Cards: No credit cards.
Food: Vegetarian.

The heavens, or rather the alignment of the stars in them, dictate the offerings on this restaurant's macrobiotic menu. Consequently, dishes change monthly according to the stars. The food is great, regardless of the astrological sign at the time, but skeptics may be happier elsewhere.

$ TRE SCALINI

Piazza Navona, 30. Tel. 6/ 68 79 148.
Metro/Bus: Bus 64.
Price/Entrée: Appetizers, L16,000–L20,000; main courses, L22,000–L35,000.
Open: Thurs.–Tues. lunch 12:15–3:30 P.M., dinner 7:15–11:15 P.M. Closed December and February.
Reservations: Recommended.
Atmosphere: Pleasant.
Credit Cards: AE, DC, MC, V.
Food: Roman/Italian.

Ask to be seated on the ground floor by the bar, or on the upper floor of this very well-known restaurant. Established in 1882, it has house specialties that include *canfallo in passitte* (butterfly-shaped pasta in an herb and cheese sauce), *saltimbocca*, risotto with porcini, risotto with pesto, roast duck with proscutti, spaghetti with clams, many choices of fish, including a carpaccio of sea bass, and roast lamb.

THE QUIRINALE

$$ BIRRERIA TEMPERA

Via San Marcello, 19. Tel. 6/ 67 86 203.
Metro/Bus: Bus 56, 60, 62, 85, 90, 90b, 95, or 492.
Price/Entrée: L50,000.
Open: Mon.–Sat. 6:00 P.M.–2:00 A.M.
Reservations: No reservations.
Atmosphere: Casual.
Credit Cards: No credit cards.
Food: Roman/Italian.

This bustling, old-fashioned beer hall is a favorite with local business people and students. It's a good place to relax, enjoy a beer, and have a light bite to eat. The menu includes salads, sandwiches, pastas, and daily specials.

$ COLLINE EMILIANE

Via Avignonesi, 22. Tel. 6/ 48 17 538.
Metro/Bus: Piazza Barberini.
Price/Entrée: Appetizers, L8,000–L14,000; main courses, L16,000–L25,000.
Open: Sat.–Thurs. lunch 12:30–2:45 P.M., dinner 7:30–10:45 P.M. Closed August.
Reservations: Required.
Atmosphere: Casual.
Credit Cards: No credit cards.
Food: Emilian.

This family-run restaurant right off the piazza offers some of the best pasta in Rome. Not a restaurant that takes the distinction lightly, it has a house specialty that includes an inspired *tortellini alla panna* with truffles (round pockets of dough filled with minced meats, cheeses, and spices served with a cream and cheese sauce). Main courses include *braciola di maiale* (boneless rolled pork cutlets that have been stuffed with ham and cheese, breaded, and sautéed); *maccheroncini al funghetto*; and *tagliatelle alla bolognese*.

STAZIONE TERMINI

$ CANTINA CANTARINI

Piazza Sallustio, 12. Tel. 6/ 48 55 28.
Metro/Bus: Via XX Settembre.
Price/Entrée: Average, L30,000.
Open: Mon.–Sat. lunch 12:30–3:00 P.M., dinner 8:00–10:30 P.M. Closed August.
Reservations: Recommended.
Atmosphere: Upscale.
Credit Cards: AE, DC, V.
Food: Roman/Italian.

This restaurant has an upscale atmosphere, but its prices are definitely more mainstream. Meat entrées are offered Monday through Thursday, and fish is the fare on Friday and Saturday. Seating is hard to come by, but you'll know why once you get a chance to try the food.

❤ $$$ CORIOLANO

Via Ancona, 14. Tel. 6/ 44 24 98 63.
Metro/Bus: Bus 36 or 36b.
Price/Entrée: L65,000 and up.
Open: Mon.–Sat. 7:00 P.M.–2:00 or 3:00 A.M. Closed August 1–25.
Reservations: Advised.
Atmosphere: Jacket and tie.
Credit Cards: AE, DC, MC, V.
Food: Italian.

Antiques and tables covered in fine linen create an elegant atmosphere that makes dining here truly an event. Light homemade pastas, choice olive oil, and market-fresh ingredients combine to make flavorful dishes such as *tagliolini all'arogosta* (thin noodles topped with lobster sauce), one of the specialties.

$ COTTINI

Via Merulana, 287. Tel. 6/ 47 40 768.
Metro/Bus: Bus 93 from Stazione Termini.
Price/Entrée: L30,000.
Open: Tues.–Sat. 7:00 A.M.–9:00 P.M.
Reservations: No reservations.
Atmosphere: Casual.
Credit Cards: No credit cards.
Food: Cafeteria style.

This corner café has salads, hot pastas, and main courses that are freshly made from fine ingredients, plus a large coffee bar and an in-house bakery, which sells its wares at a pastry counter.

$ SCOGLIO DI FRISIO

Via Merulana, 256. Tel. 6/ 48 72 765.
Metro/Bus: Bus 93 from Stazione Termini.

Price/Entrée: Appetizers, L11,000–L18,000; main courses, L18,000–L22,000; fixed-price menus, L60,000–L100,000.
Open: Dinner only, daily 7:30–11:00 P.M.
Reservations: Recommended.
Atmosphere: Nautical.
Credit Cards: AE, DC, MC, V.
Food: Neapolitan.

Decor is nautical but nice at this Neapolitan restaurant, which is a great place to see what genuine pizza is all about. A guitar player and a strolling tenor add to the friendly atmosphere, but food is the main attraction to be sure. Try a pizza with clams and mussels, the chicken cacciatore, or veal scallopine.

$$$ TAVERNA FLAVIA

Via Flavia, 9. Tel. 6/ 47 45 214.
Metro/Bus: Castro Pretorio, bus to Via XX Settembre.
Price/Entrée: Average L65,000.
Open: Mon.–Sat. lunch 12:30–3:00 P.M., dinner 7:30–11:30 P.M. Closed August 13–18.
Reservations: Required.
Atmosphere: Ritzy.
Credit Cards: AE, DC, EC, V.
Food: Roman/Italian.

Locals and film stars mix easily in this festive restaurant. Walls are covered with pictures of famous people who have dined here in past years, and it's still a very popular place for all types. Specialties such as *insalata Veruschka* are wonderful, and the wine list is generous.

$ TAVERNA FLAVIA DI MIMMO

Via Flavia, 9. Tel. 6/ 47 45 214.
Metro/Bus: Piazza della Republica.
Price/Entrée: Appetizers, L10,500–L16,000; main courses, L18,000–L40,000.
Open: Mon.–Sat. lunch 1:00–3:00 P.M., dinner 7:30 P.M.–1:30 A.M.
Reservations: Recommended.
Atmosphere: Roman-style.

Credit Cards: AE, DC, MC, V.
Food: Roman/International.

Frank Sinatra ate here years ago, and you can choose from among the very same selections he was offered. Very Roman and traditional, this restaurant hasn't changed much since it opened, and it doesn't need to. It features a different regional dish each night, and specialties include a risotto with scampi and spaghetti al whiskey.

$ TRATTORIA ELETTRA

Via Principe Amedeo, 72-74. Tel. 6/ 47 45 397.
Metro/Bus: Stazione Termini.
Price/Entrée: Appetizers, L8,000–L10,000; main courses, L10,500–L18,000.
Open: Sun.–Fri. lunch 12:00 noon–3:30 P.M., dinner 7:00–11:30 P.M. Closed August 5–28.
Reservations: Not required.
Atmosphere: Casual.
Credit Cards: AE, DC, MC, V.
Food: Roman/Italian.

Cheerful and well-run, this family-owned establishment offers good prices and delicious, uncomplicated food. Enjoy the risotto with asparagus in a cream sauce, followed by a main meat dish of beef or poultry.

$ TRIMANI WINE BAR

Via Cernaia, 37b. Tel. 6/ 44 69 630.
Metro/Bus: Piazza della Repubblica or Castro Pretorio.
Price/Entrée: Salads and platters of light food, L12,000–L19,000; glasses of wine, L5,000–L15,000.
Open: Mon.–Sat. lunch 11:30 A.M.–3:00 P.M., dinner 5:30 P.M.–12:00 midnight. Closed three weeks in August and December 25–January 1.
Reservations: Not required.
Atmosphere: Elegant.
Credit Cards: AE, DC, MC, V.
Food: Continental.

Set on the outskirts of Rome's historic district, this wine bar has elaborate decor that takes its inspiration from classical Rome. Live music adds to the refined setting, whose ambiance tends to make guests want to linger. Selections from the diverse menu may include vegetarian pastas, salad niçoise, herb-laden bean soups, slices of quiche, Hungarian goulash, and gazpacho.

TRASTEVERE

✓ $–$$ ALBERTO CIARLÀ
Piazza San Cosimato, 40. Tel. 6/ 58 18 668.
Metro/Bus: Bus 44, 75, or 170.
Price/Entrée: Appetizers, L18,000–L30,000; main courses, L30,000–L60,000.
Open: Mon.–Sat. lunch 12:45–2:30 P.M., dinner 8:30 P.M.–12:30 A.M.
Reservations: Required, especially on weekends.
Atmosphere: Elegant/pricey.
Credit Cards: AE, DC, MC, V.
Food: Seafood.

This restaurant, one of Rome's finest, is located at the edge of a very large square, where tables are set for dining al fresco in warm weather. A display of seafood on ice near the entryway gives guests an idea of what's to come. The filet of sea bass is without peer, and specialties include well-flavored sushi, salmon Marcel Trompier with lobster sauce, spaghetti with clams, *ravioli di pesce* (ravioli with fish), and an array of shellfish. The wine list is excellent and extensive.

$$ DA CHECCO ER CARRETTIERE
Via Benedetta, 10. Tel. 6/ 58 17 018.
Price/Entrée: L60,000.
Open: Tues.–Sat. 9:30 A.M.–2:20 P.M. and 6:30 P.M.–12:00 midnight. Closed Sundays and dinner Mondays.
Reservations: Advised.
Atmosphere: Casual.
Credit Cards: AE, DC, MC, V.
Food: Roman/Italian.

The staff makes guests feel right at home in this restaurant with the country-cozy ambiance. Seafood is the main feature on the menu, but there are traditional meat dishes, too. Specialties include a well-seasoned mashed potato and tomato mixture; pastas such as *spaghetti allo carrettiera*, with black pepper, sharp cheese, and olive oil; and linguine with scampi.

✓ $$ DA CICERUACCHIO

Via del Porto, 1. Tel. 6/ 58 06 046.
Metro/Bus: Bus 23 or 145.
Price/Entrée: L40,000–L65,000.
Open: Tues.–Sun. 8:00 P.M.–12:00 midnight.
Reservations: Advised.
Atmosphere: Relaxed.
Credit Cards: AE, DC, MC, V.
Food: Grilled, charbroiled.

Guitarists and singers are featured in the evenings at this touristy but fun restaurant. Set in a former jail with stone walls, it is heavy on atmosphere, and the food's not bad either. Charbroiled steaks and chops are the specialty, and menu selections include bean soup, scampi with curry, and other charbroiled meats.

$ LA CISTERNA

Via della Cisterna, 13. Tel. 6/ 58 12 543.
Metro/Bus: Bus 44, 75, or 170.
Price/Entrée: Appetizers, L14,000–L22,000; main courses, L20,000–L40,000.
Open: Dinner only, Mon.–Sat. 7:00 P.M.–12:00 midnight.
Reservations: Recommended.
Atmosphere: Indoor/outdoor dining.
Credit Cards: AE, DC, MC, V.
Food: Roman/Italian.

This restaurant has been a favorite with the locals since the 1930s. There are sidewalk tables for outside dining, and a series of rooms inside. Specialties include antipasti, roast meat dishes, and fresh fish. Take time to view the murals.

$$ DA MEO PATACCA

Piazza dei Mercanti, 30. Tel. 6/ 58 33 1086.
Metro/Bus: Bus 170.
Price/Entrée: L60,000.
Open: Daily 8:00–11:30 P.M.
Reservations: Accepted.
Atmosphere: Colorful/carnival-like.
Credit Cards: AE, DC, MC, V.
Food: Roman/Italian.

The emphasis here is on fun and family. Extremely colorful and casual, the tavern is decorated with wagon wheels, peppers, and garlic. Specialties include wild boar, wild hare, quail, corn on the cob, pork and beans, thick-cut sirloins, and chicken on a spit. Frivolity is encouraged.

$$ PARIS

Piazza San Calisto, 7/a, Trastevere. Tel. 6/ 58 15 378.
Metro/Bus: Viale Trastevere.
Price/Entrée: Average, L60,000.
Open: Tues.–Sat. lunch 12:00 noon–3:00 P.M.,
dinner 8:00–11:30 P.M. Closed three weeks in August.
Reservations: Advised.
Atmosphere: Casual.
Credit Cards: AE, DC, EC, MC.
Food: Roman/Jewish.

Ask for a table on the piazza if the weather's right when you visit this restaurant. It offers simple, classic dishes such as homemade *pasta e ceci* and *minestra di arzilla* (sting ray soup), homemade fettuccine, fried artichokes, and fried cod. Its most remarkable offerings, however, are the homemade desserts, which are hard to find in most Rome restaurants today.

✓ $ ROMOLO NELLA GIARDINA DELLA FORNARINA

Via Porta Settimiana, 8. Tel. 6/ 58 18 284.
Metro/Bus: Bus 23 or 280.
Price/Entrée: Appetizers, L10,000–L13,000;
main courses, L19,000–L25,000.
Open: Tues.–Sun. lunch 12:00 noon–3:00 P.M.,
dinner 7:30 P.M.–12:00 midnight. Closed August 5–25.

Reservations: Recommended for dinner.
Atmosphere: Casual.
Credit Cards: AE, DC, MC, V.
Food: Roman/Italian.

Once popular with the celebrity crowd, this restaurant has been a gem since 1848. The decor is cozy, with lots of wood and polished brass. Begin your meal with fettuccine with meat sauce, followed by *scalloppine al marsala* (thin slices of veal coated with flour and sauteéd in butter) or deviled chicken, and the dessert of your choice. Ask for a dining spot in the garden if it is open during your stay.

✓ $ SABATINI I

Piazza Santa Maria in Trastevere, 10. Tel. 6/ 58 12 026.
Metro/Bus: Bus 44, 75, or 170.
Price/Entrée: Appetizers, L14,000–L22,000; main courses, L20,000–L40,000.
Open: Lunch served daily 12:00 noon–3:00 P.M., dinner served daily 8:00 P.M.–12:00 midnight.
Reservations: Recommended.
Atmosphere: Casual.
Credit Cards: AE, DC, MC, V.
Food: Roman/seafood.

Make your reservations in advance for this popular, very busy place located on a charming square where you can dine during summer months. Stenciled walls and beamed ceilings inside take their inspiration from classical Rome. Choose from a large table of antipasti, then enjoy an entrée from the selection of dishes such as fresh fish, shellfish, grilled scampi, spaghetti with seafood, and *pollo con pepperoni* (chicken cooked with green and red peppers). Have a glass of wine over dinner.

$ TRATTORIA VINCENZO

Via della Lungaretta, 173. Tel. 6/ 58 82 876.
Metro/Bus: Bus 23.
Price/Entrée: Appetizers, L3,000–L12,000; main courses, L12,000–L25,000.
Open: Lunch Tues.–Sun. 12:00 noon–2:45 P.M., dinner Tues.–Sat. 7:30–10:45 P.M.

Reservations: Not required.
Atmosphere: Casual.
Credit Cards: AE, DC, MC, V.
Food: Seafood.

Seafood dishes are the best here; the food is inexpensive, and everyone knows it. The restaurant is especially crowded on Sunday afternoons, when flea market mavens are here. Enjoy the stew, *ravioli di ricotta e spinaci* (ravioli stuffed with spinach and ricotta cheese), *spaghetti alla carbonara*, or *saltimbocca alla romana.*

THE VATICAN

$ ARMANDO

Via delgi Ombrellari, 41. Tel. 6/ 68 61 602.
Metro/Bus: Bus 64.
Price/Entrée: L40,000.
Open: Tues.–Thurs.
Reservations: Advised for dinner.
Atmosphere: Casual.
Credit Cards: AE, DC, MC, V.
Food: Roman/Italian.

Tourists know this family-run restaurant well. Set in the heart of the working-class area of the Vatican, Armando is a great place for a casual meal. Such Roman dishes as *pasta e ceci* and *petto alla fornara* (roast veal breast) served with potatoes are on the menu.

$ BIBO ASTORIA 73

Piazza Cola di Rienzo, 60. Tel. 6/ 36 10 007.
Metro/Bus: Bus 70, 81, 492, or 910.
Price/Entrée: Appetizers, L6,500–L13,000; main courses, L8,000–L16,000; sandwiches, L5,000–L8,500.
Open: Breakfast is served starting at 7:00 A.M.
Reservations: Required.
Atmosphere: Casual.
Credit Cards: AE, MC, V.
Food: International/Italian.

Informality is the order of the day at this restaurant. It isn't a fancy place, but it has a good reputation nevertheless. Guests may eat here morning, noon, and night. There are oversize omelets for breakfast, and pizzas, spaghetti, or hamburgers for lunch and dinner. The covered winter garden is something to see.

✓ $$$ LES ETOILES

Located in the Hotel Atlante Star, via die Bastion 1. Tel. 6/ 68 93 434.

Metro/Bus: Owtoviano.
Price/Entrée: L100,000.
Open: Daily 7:00–10:30 P.M.
Reservations: Advised.
Atmosphere: Jacket and tie.
Credit Cards: AE, DC, MC, V.
Food: Roman/Italian.

You'll find some surprises awaiting you at this restaurant. Perched atop the Hotel Atlante Star, it serves great Italian cuisine, and offers one of the best views in the city. Whether you dine on the garden patio or inside the restaurant, the scenery is magnificent, with St. Peter's Dome as a highlight. The chef changes the menu, based on what's available at the market. Enjoy fresh seafood, pasta dishes with porcini mushrooms or seasonal vegetables, or a choice of grilled meats.

$ MATRICIANO

Via dei Gracchi, 55. Tel. 6/ 32 12 327.

Metro/Bus: Lepanto.
Price/Entrée: Appetizers, L8,000–L12,000; main courses, L16,000–L22,000.
Open: Daily lunch 12:30–3:00 P.M., dinner 8:00–11:30 P.M. Closed August 2–29 and Wednesdays (Nov.–Apr.) and Saturdays (May–Oct.).
Reservations: Required, especially for dinner.
Atmosphere: Casual.
Credit Cards: AE, DC, MC, V.
Food: Roman/Italian.

This family-run restaurant is a great place in which

to unwind after a long day of sightseeing or shopping. Near St. Peter's, it has a casual, comfortable atmosphere that makes it easy to relax. The specialty of the house is named after the restaurant, or is the restaurant named after the specialty? Regardless, try the *matriciana* dish, which is bucatini pasta served with bacon, tomatoes, and basil. Other excellent dishes offered are *scallopa alla valdostana*, baby lamb, and *tripa* (tripe) *alla romana*.

$ RISTORANTE GIARDINACCIO

Via Aurelia, 53. Tel. 6/ 63 13 67.
Metro/Bus: Bus 46, 62, or 98.
Price/Entrée: Appetizers, L7,000–L14,000; main courses, L20,000–L31,000.
Open: Wed.–Mon. lunch 12:15–3:30 P.M., dinner 7:15–11:00 P.M.
Reservations: Recommended, especially on weekends.
Atmosphere: Casual.
Credit Cards: AE, DC, MC, V.

Next to St. Peter's, this popular country tavern draws much of its appeal from its flaming grills and wood-accented decor. Quail, goat, and mutton goulash, as well as pasta and many vegetarian dishes are among the specialties here.

$ RISTORANTE PIERDONATI

Via della Conciliazione, 39. Tel. 6/ 68 80 3557.
Metro/Bus: Bus 64 from Stazione Termini.
Price/Entrée: Appetizers, L10,000–L19,000; main courses, L16,000–L30,000; set menu, L25,000.
Open: Fri.–Wed. lunch 12:00 noon–3:30 P.M., dinner 7:00–10:30 P.M. Closed August.
Reservations: Not required.
Atmosphere: Casual.
Credit Cards: AE, MC, V.
Food: Roman/Italian.

The former home of Cardinal della Rovere, and now the headquarters of the Knights of the Holy Sepulchre, this restaurant is more than a century old. Guests dine in a room with an arcade ceiling. Specialties include calf liver, stewed veal, and *ravioli bolognese* (ravioli with meat sauce), but for a true Roman dining experience, order the tripe. You won't regret it.

VIA VENETO/PIAZZA BARBERINI

$$ ANDREA

Via Sardengna, 26. Tel. 6/ 48 21 891.
Metro/Bus: Bus 58.
Price/Entrée: L58,000.
Open: Mon.–Sat. Closed Sun., Mon. for lunch, and three weeks in August.
Reservations: Advised.
Atmosphere: Casual.
Credit Cards: AE, DC, MC, V.
Food: Italian.

Ernest Hemingway and King Farouk dined here, and now it's a favorite among Italian powerbrokers. The literary and the mighty couldn't be wrong. The service is friendly; the house wine is excellent; and the setting is intimate. The menu features such dishes as spaghetti with seafood and truffles, homemade *tagliolini* (thin noodles) with shrimp and spinach sauce, and *carciofi all'Andrea* (artichokes simmered in olive oil). Save room for the delectable desserts.

$ AURORA 10 DA PINO IL SOMMELIER

Via Aurora, 10. Tel. 6/ 47 42 779.
Metro/Bus: Piazza Barberini.
Price/Entrée: Appetizers, L15,000–L19,000; main courses, L18,000–L29,000.
Open: Tues.–Sun. lunch 12:00 noon–3:00 P.M., dinner 7:00–11:00 P.M.
Reservations: Recommended.
Atmosphere: Nice.
Credit Cards: AE, DC, MC, V.
Food: Roman/Sicilian.

Originally a Maronite convent, this restaurant counts powerful diplomats and film stars among its converts. It offers more than 250 types of wine from Italy. The menu has a variety of pasta or risotto, salad "Aurora," fish fry, and swordfish in herb sauce, among other offerings.

$ CÉSARINA

Via Piemonte, 109. Tel. 6/ 48 80 828.
Metro/Bus: Bus 56.
Price/Entrée: Appetizers, L9,000–L15,000; main courses, L18,000–L29,000.
Open: Mon.–Sat. lunch 12:30–3:00 P.M., dinner 7:30–11:00 P.M.
Reservations: Recommended.
Atmosphere: Nice.
Credit Cards: AE, DC, MC, V.
Food: Emilian/Roman.

Since it was established, this restaurant has expanded into three dining rooms, with seating for more than two hundred. Specialties include veal cutlet with ham and cheese, *saltimbocca*, and *costoletta alla bolognese*. Or choose from among a trio of handmade pastas served with a medley of sauces. The well-mannered, attentive staff offers excellent service.

$$ GEORGE'S

Via Marche, 7. Tel. 6/ 48 45 75.
Metro/Bus: Piazza Barberini.
Price/Entrée: Appetizers, L13,000–L18,000; main courses, L42,000–L48,000.
Open: Mon.–Sat. 7:30 P.M.–12:00 midnight.
Reservations: Required.
Atmosphere: Relaxed.
Credit Cards: AE, DC, MC, V.
Food: International.

Directly off the Via Veneto, this restaurant boasts an English-speaking staff and a relaxing atmosphere. Casual is key. When weather permits, everything is moved outside to the garden. This is a good place to stop for a drink and enjoy the piano music at the bar. Marinated mussels, veal, smoked Scottish salmon, and steak dishes are among flavorful offerings here.

$ GIARROSTO TOSCAN

Via Campania, 29. Tel. 6/ 58 21 899.
Metro/Bus: Bus 90B, 95, 490, or 495.
Price/Entrée: Appetizers, L12,000–L18,000; main courses, L18,000–L21,000.
Open: Thurs.–Tues. lunch 12:30–3:00 P.M., dinner 7:30–11:30 P.M.
Reservations: Required.
Atmosphere: Nice/polite.
Credit Cards: AE, DC, MC, V.
Food: Tuscan.

Guests from Via Veneto find this restaurant very attractive, so expect to wait awhile to be seated. A great antipasti is brought to the table for you to choose from: little meat balls, melon with prosciutto, an omelet, mozzarella, and Tuscan salami. Main course specialties include oysters, grilled steak seasoned with oil, and fresh fish (seafood varies in price according to weight). Save room for dessert.

$ PICCOLO ABRUZZO

Via Sicilia, 237. Tel. 6/ 48 20 176.
Metro/Bus: Bus 490 or 495.
Price/Entrée: Appetizers, L8,000–L14,000; main courses, L13,000–L22,000.
Open: Lunch Mon.–Fri. 12:30–3:00 P.M., dinner Mon.–Sat. 7:00 P.M.–12:00 midnight.
Reservations: Highly recommended.
Atmosphere: Casual.
Credit Cards: AE, MC, V.
Food: Abruzzi.

Regulars know to plan to eat here before or after the rush if they want a relaxing dinner. This place is small and very popular, so it's usually crowded. The dining room is warm, with rustic brick and stucco and the scent of garlic, salt-cured hams, and Mediterranean herbs in the air. Begin with a pasta, then a meat course, then cheese, and dessert.

$$ SANS SOUCI

Via Sicilia, 20. Tel. 6/ 48 21 814.
Metro/Bus: Piazza Barberini.

Price/Entrée: Appetizers, L25,000–L30,000; main courses, L48,000–L56,000.
Open: Dinner only, Tues.–Sun. 8:00 P.M.–1:00 A.M.
Reservations: Required.
Atmosphere: Elegant/sophisticated.
Credit Cards: AE, DC, MC, V.
Food: French.

This is a good choice if you're after a really special evening. It is one of Rome's most elegant and sophisticated places to dine. The ever-changing menu offers the latest creations from the kitchen. Fine foods here emphasize seasonal delicacies such as porcini mushrooms, fresh spring asparagus blended with ricotta and served with white truffle sauce, fresh goose, grilled sea bass, or lamb. Remember to save room for the remarkable desserts.

$$ TULLIO

Via San Nicola da Tolentino, 26. Tel. 6/ 48 18 564.
Metro/Bus: Piazza Barberini or Via XX Settembre.
Price/Entrée: L50,000.
Open: Lunch 12:30–3:00 P.M., dinner 7:30–11:00 P.M. Closed Sundays and August.
Reservations: Advised.
Atmosphere: Relaxed.
Credit Cards: AE, DC, MC, V.
Food: Tuscan.

"Simple" correctly describes both the decor and the menu at this pleasant, air-conditioned restaurant, and both are well-done. Prices are very reasonable for Tuscan dishes such as *pasta e fagioli* (pasta and white beans), grilled steaks and chops, and *fagioli alluccelletto* (beans with tomato sage).

VILLA BORGHESE/VILLA GIULIA

$–$$ AL CEPPO

Via Panama, 2-4. Tel. 6/ 84 19 696.
Metro/Bus: Bus 4, 52, or 53.
Price/Entrée: Appetizers, L12,000–L18,000; main courses, L18,000–L45,000.

Open: Tues.–Sun. lunch 1:00–3:00 P.M.,
dinner 8:00–11:00 P.M.
Reservations: Highly recommended.
Atmosphere: Pleasant.
Credit Cards: AE, DC, MC, V.
Food: Roman/Italian.

Romans, rather than foreigners, are most of the clientele at this restaurant near Piazza Ungheria. Just two blocks from Villa Borghese, the Al Ceppo, or "The Log," restaurant is a favorite. Enjoy the scene as the chef cooks lamb chops, liver, and bacon in an open fireplace. Dishes include the very special *rabbit à la Marchiginana* stuffed with veal, pine nuts, and pistachio nuts, handmade pasta, *taglioline monteconero*, monkfish with rosemary, or *fish cartaccio* (fish baked in parchment envelope with onions, parsley, and herbs). Desserts are delectable.

✓ $$ RELAIS LE JARDIN

Located in the Le Byron Hotel, Via G. de Notaris, 5. Tel. 6/ 36 13 041.
Metro/Bus: Bus 52.
Price/Entrée: Appetizers, L28,000–L46,000;
main courses, L42,000–L56,000.
Open: Mon.–Sat. lunch 1:00–3:00 P.M.,
dinner 8:00–10:30 P.M. Closed Sundays and August.
Reservations: Required.
Atmosphere: Jacket and tie preferred.
Credit Cards: AE, DC, MC, V.
Food: Roman/Italian.

The decor is lighthearted, but extremely classy, a fitting backdrop for this restaurant, which is renowned for its traditional yet imaginative menu and excellent service. Seafood is always in evidence, but its treatment changes based on availability of ingredients. Specialties include risotto with a seafood/vegetable sauce, noodle pie with salmon and asparagus, seafood crêpes, and fresh salmon with asparagus. Don't miss the desserts.

OUTER ROME

$$ AMBASCIATA D' ABRUZZO

Via Pietro Tacchini, 26. Tel. 6/ 80 78 256.
Metro/Bus: Bus 26, 52, 53, or 168.
Price/Entrée: All you can eat, L50,000.
Open: Mon.–Sat. lunch 1:00–3:30 P.M., dinner 7:00–11:30 P.M.
Reservations: Recommended.
Atmosphere: Pleasant.
Credit Cards: AE, DC, MC, V.
Food: Abruzzi.

This is an all-you-can-eat restaurant, difficult to come by in Rome, but a great value and lots of fun. Make reservations or you may have to wait in line. Dishes include grilled fish, antipasti, spaghetti, salads, and baked ham, served in a very informal setting. Guests also have their choice of desserts.

$ CHECCHINO DAL 1887

Via di Monte Testaccio, 30. Tel. 6/ 57 46 318.
Metro/Bus: Bus 27.
Price/Entrée: Appetizers, L10,000–L14,000; main courses, L12,000–L25,000.
Open: Lunch Tues.–Sun. 12:30–3:00 P.M., dinner Tues.–Sat. 8:00–11:00 P.M. Closed Sundays for dinner, Mondays, August, and a week at Christmas.
Reservations: Recommended.
Atmosphere: Outdoor style.
Credit Cards: AE, DC, MC, V.
Food: Roman/Italian.

The English-speaking staff is friendly and ready to help you choose a traditional Roman specialty and sample some of the city's best wines. Popular for dishes such as grilled baby lamb chops, Roman-style tripe, pasta and bean soup, it also offers specialties such as *rigatoni con pajata, coda alla vaccinara* (pieces of ox-tail stewed in a tomato sauce seasoned with celery), *fagioli con cotiche* (Haricot beans cooked in tomato sauce with slices of pork crackling), and *la cocina povera.* Salads, soups, steaks, grills, and ice cream are also served here.

✓ $ HOSTARIA L' ARCHEOLOGIA

Via Appia Antica, 139. Tel. 6/ 78 80 494.
Metro/Bus: Bus 118.
Price/Entrée: Appetizers, L10,000–L16,000; main courses, L12,000–L22,000.
Open: Fri.–Wed. lunch 12:30–3:30 P.M., dinner 8:00–10:30 P.M.
Reservations: Recommended.
Atmosphere: Eighteenth century.
Credit Cards: AE, DC.
Food: Roman/Italian.

Groups are welcome to tour this restaurant's interesting wine cellar and stay to enjoy Roman cuisine. This family-run restaurant offers cozy seating warmed by the fireplace in cold weather, and wonderful outdoor dining in the summer. Decorated with strings of garlic, corn, and copper pots hung beneath the beamed ceiling, it's a comfortable, casual place.

Notes

ENTERTAINMENT AFTER DARK

If you're expecting Rome evenings to be wild and scandalous, you'll be surprised to find that this is *far* from the truth. You will generally find more tourists than locals at the livelier nightclubs. Most Romans are happier just "hanging out" with friends, chatting and drinking a little wine, instead of partying at a nightclub.

Nightclubs in Rome change with the trends and whims of the party culture. Clubs may change ownership, music, prices, themes, or even close down all together. Fortunately, the local paper, called *La Repubblica,* gives an update on club news in the Thursday edition called "Trovaroma." Ask at your hotel's front desk or the concierge for the paper.

Many clubs will charge a cover charge or have a minimum drink order. Sometimes the cover charge includes the first drink, so ask before you pay. The cover charges are expensive, because unlike many Americans, most Romans don't drink in large quantities when they go out. Generally, drinks are expensive, with the first usually being the highest. Subsequent drinks may go down in price, but not by much. Anyone sixteen years or older can be served alcoholic drinks in Rome.

Clubs in the area of Via Veneto and Piazza di Spagna are generally more expensive and cater to better clientele. For the younger crowd, the places to visit are in the Trastevere and Testaccio areas.

> **SMOKING**
> **It seems *everyone* smokes in Rome, especially the nighttime crowd. You'll really notice it in the clubs where the ventilation isn't very good. Be warned: the more popular the club, the bigger the crowd, and the smokier the room.**

Rome is beautiful at night. You'll notice the fountains lit up and the water seems to sparkle. It's also much quieter in the evening and there seems to be a special mystic quality about the ancient city. This quality may just be the reason for the calming effect Romans seem to be under when the sun goes down.

AVENTINE/PALATINE

BULLI E PUPI

On Aventine Hill at 11/A Via San Saba. Tel. 6/ 57 82 022.
Admission/Cost: L20,000 cover charge.
Open: Tues.–Sun. 11:00 P.M.–4:00 A.M.

Not a place for the executive types, but their children or the young at heart might like it. Dress is casual and the music spans a wide range, with an emphasis on disco and dance tunes.

✓ TERME DI CARACALLA

Via delle Terme di Caracalla. Tel. 6/ 48 11 601.
Admission/Cost: Opera, L30,000–L65,000; ballet, L25,000–L50,000.
Open: Call for opening times.

Attend summer performances of grand opera, usually from the first of July to the middle of August, at the Baths (Terme) of Caracalla. Sponsored by the Roman Opera House, the season is likely to include Verdi's *Aïda*, which is appropriate in this grand setting. *Aïda's* grand finale is the glorious "double scene" in which the floodlit upper part represents the Temple of Vulcan, and the part underneath, the tomb.

Tickets are sold at the Teatro dell'Opera. You can

purchase unreserved seats, but you'll need to take along a pair of binoculars.

CAMPO DE'FIORI

MUSIC INN
Largo dei Fiorentini, 3. Tel. 6/ 65 44 934.
Admission/Cost: L35,000 (including one drink).
Open: Thurs.–Sun. 8:30 P.M.–1:00 A.M.
Closed in August.

Some of the biggest names in jazz, both European and American, have performed here. The Music Inn is considered among the leading jazz clubs of Rome.

CAPITOL/FORUM/COLOSSEUM

ST. LOUIS MUSIC CITY
Via del Cardello, 13/A. Tel. 6/ 47 45 076.
Admission/Cost: L10,000 (including club membership). Drinks, L6,000–L10,000.
Open: Tues.–Thurs. 9:00 P.M.–2:00 A.M.

Live performances, especially good jazz, and occasionally some soul and funk, can be heard here. The large complex, complete with a bar and fast food restaurant, is decorated in U.S. and U.K. kitsch. Despite the noise from the restaurant, it's a place where many young and talented musicians get their start.

PANTHEON

HEMINGWAY
Piazza delle Coppelle, 10. Tel. 6/ 68 80 4135.
Admission/Cost: Drinks, L18,000.
Open: Mon.–Sat. 9:00 A.M.–3:00 A.M.
Closed Aug. 9–19.

Sophistication is all at Hemingway. First, you have to know how to find it. It's tucked behind a door off one of the most obscure piazzas in Rome. Inside, the emerald entryway sets the stage for more nineteenth-century decor. Soaring vaulted ceilings shimmer from the reflection of various glass chandeliers. The club imitates a Liberty-style salon, complete with murals and portraits of voluptuous, reclining odalisques. The arts crowd, painters, writers, and creative dilettantes sprawl in overstuffed armchairs and listen to classical music.

ZELIG

Via Monterone, 74. Tel. 6/ 68 79 209.
Admission/Cost: L35,000.
Open: Nightly until 2:00 A.M.

Personalities here are as ever-changing as the main figure in the movie by the same name. The younger crowd frequents this disco.

PIAZZA DI SPAGNA

ENOTECA FRATELLI ROFFI ISABELLI

Via della Croce, 76. Tel. 6/ 67 90 896.
Admission/Cost: Glass of wine, L3,000–L10,000; Grappa, L5,500.
Open: Mon.–Sat. 11:00 A.M.–12:30 A.M.

Come taste the wine in a bar that seems like it was made for just that. Set behind an unimposing facade, this place in the chic shopping district offers a wealth of Italian wines, brandies, and grappa. Perfect for experiencing the spirits of Italy, this place has postage-stamp tables in back, and an impressive display of wines, which are stacked on shelves in every available corner. Darkly antique in personality, it's a great spot to head after visiting the nearby Spanish Steps.

GILDA

Via Mario dei Fiori, 97, near Piazza di Spagna. Tel. 6/ 67 84 838.
Admission/Cost: (including one drink): Sun.–Thurs. L35,000, Fri.–Sat. L40,000. Meals, L85,000.

Open: Restaurant, Tues.–Sat. 9:30 P.M.–3:30 A.M.; nightclub, Tues.–Sat. 10:30 P.M.–3:30 A.M.

This nightspot is hot. Famous clientele and performers alike are the norm for this combination nightclub, disco, and restaurant. A great place for people-watching, Gilda counts famous Italian actors and politicians, and celebrities from Sylvester Stallone to Prince Albert of Monaco among its patrons. There's a new piano bar, dance floors, and a restaurant that offers Italian and international cooking.

PIAZZA NAVONA

❤ ARCILIUTO

Piazza Monte Vecchio, 5. Tel. 6/ 68 79 419.
Admission/Cost: (including one drink), L35,000; subsequent drinks, L15,000.
Open: Mon.–Sat. 10:00 P.M.–1:00 A.M.
Closed July 20–Sept. 5.

For a really special, intimate evening, this place is hard to beat. Thought to be the former studio of Raphael, it is one of the most romantic spots in Rome. Guests enjoy drinks by candlelight as a guitarist and lutist perform. Neapolitan love songs, old Italian madrigals, and current hits from New York's Broadway or London's West End are presented in an elegant atmosphere. Only drinks are served.

BAR DELLA PACE

Via della Pace, 3-5. Tel. 6/ 68 61 216.
Admission/Cost: Whiskey, L11,000.
Open: Tues.–Sun. 3:00 P.M.–2:30 A.M.

Bar della Pace, located near Piazza Navona, dates to the beginning of the twentieth century. Outside, the ivy-screened facade disguises tables on the terrace. Inside, wood, marble, and mirrors make for an elegant ambiance. Definitely in an impressive neighborhood, it shares this area of Rome with Santa Maria della Pace, a church with sybils by Raphael, and a cloister designed by Bramante. Staff here tends to be elitist, so expect somewhat frosty service if you're not famous or decked out in a designer wardrobe.

BLU BAR

Via dei Soldati, 25. Tel. 6/ 68 64 250.

Admission/Cost: First drink, L35,000; subsequent drink, L20,000.

Open: Mon.–Sat. 10:30 P.M.–3:00 or 4:00 A.M. (depending on business).

Located in the same establishment as the Hostaria dell'Orso, the Blu Bar lives up to its name. Moody but mellow, this hideaway features the inspired music of two pianists and a guitarist. Cocktails are the main focus, and jacket and tie are required.

LA CABALA

Via dei Soldati, 25. Tel. 6/ 68 64 221.

Admission/Cost: First drink, L30,000; subsequent drinks, L20,000.

Open: Mon.–Sat. 10:30 P.M.–3:00 or 4:00 A.M. (depending on business).

Just one floor above the Hostaria dell'Orso, La Cabala is brimming with a well-dressed, over-twenty-five crowd. Disco, and all that goes along with it, is the emphasis here.

TARTARUGHINO

Near Piazza Navona at 1 Via della Scrofa. Tel. 6/ 68 64 131.

Admission/Cost: From L8,000 on up.

Open: Nightly 9:00 P.M.–3:00 A.M.

The political set favors this small, stylish, expensive restaurant and piano bar. Many power brokers and other cutting edge types frequent this place, but there's no dancing.

LA VETRINA

Via della Vetrina, 20. No phone.

Admission/Cost: L35,000.

Open: Thurs.–Tues. 10:00 P.M.–2:00 A.M.

Popular with the nightclub crowd, this bar revamps

itself several times a year. It tends to be somewhat bohemian, complete with art exhibits, live music, and the occasional poetry reading.

STAZIONE TERMINI

DRUID'S DEN

Via San Martino Monto, 28. Tel. 6/ 48 80 258.
Admission/Cost: Pint of beer, L7,000.
Open: Daily 6:00 P.M.–12:30 A.M.

This den near Piazza Santa Maria Maggiore and the train station is popular for its casual, Irish atmosphere reminiscent of a student union bar. Occasionally rowdy, it's Rome's answer to an Irish pub, with music and brew to match. A group of young Irishmen one night did the Irish jig to the delight of other patrons.

FIDDLER'S ELBOW

Via dell Olmata, 43. Tel. 6/ 48 72 110.
Admission/Cost: Pint of Guinness, L7,000.
Open: Tues.–Sun. 4:30 P.M.–12:15 A.M.

Reputedly the oldest pub in the capital, the Fiddler's Elbow has a young, lively crowd that's not quite as rowdy as the Druid's Den. It's near Piazza Santa Maria Maggiore and the railway station.

TEATRO DELL'OPERA

Piazza Beniamino Gigli, 2. Tel. 6/ 48 1601.
Admission/Cost: Opera, L26,000–L160,000; ballet, L15,000–L18,000; symphonic concerts, L20,000–L50,000.
Open: Usually November–May.

If you are in Rome during opera season, attend a performance at the historic Rome Opera House, located off Via Nazionale. Performances of the Rome Opera Ballet can be seen at the Teatro dell'Opera. Tickets go on sale two days before a performance is scheduled.

TRIMANI WINE BAR

Via Cernaia, 37/b. Tel. 6/ 44 69 630.
Admission/Cost: Wine, L25,000–L50,000.

Open: 11:30 A.M.–3:00 P.M. and
5:30 P.M.–12:00 midnight.

One of Rome's most esteemed wine shops offers this annex. Family-operated, it offers great wines for sampling at the counter, and light, fixed-price meals of meat, cheeses, pasta, or cakes in the upstairs dining area. Dress is casual.

TRASTEVERE

BIG MAMA

Vicolo San Francesco a Ripa, 18. Tel. 6/ 57 44 020.
Admission/Cost: One time membership card, L20,000; plus cover, L10,000–L30,000, depending on the act. Drinks, L5,000–L21,000.
Open: Nightly 9:00 P.M.–1:30 A.M.
Closed July–September.

Big-name musicians and tomorrow's jazz and blues greats like to hang out at this hot spot. Hot and crowded, it has some of the best live music in Rome, including jazz, blues, African, and rock. There is also a bar and snack food.

CAFÉ-BAR DI MARZIO

Piazza di Santa Maria in Trastevere, 158.
Tel. 6/ 58 16 095.
Admission/Cost: Whiskey begins at L11,000; coffee, L3,000.
Open: Tues.–Sat. 7:00 A.M.–2:30 A.M.

Indoor and outdoor tables at this café at the edge of the square offer great views of the famous fountain. Warm and hospitable, it is strictly a café (not a restaurant). The dress code is casual.

FANTASIE DI TRASTEVERE

Via di Santa Dorotea, 6. Tel. 6/ 58 81 671.
Admission/Cost: Full meal, L75,000; first drink, L30,000.
Open: Mon.–Sat. 8:00–11:00 P.M.

In this unusual place, the setting is the "people's theater," where the famous actor, Petrolini, made his debut. Folk singers and musicians perform in provincial attire, while guests dine on hearty regional cuisine. Some songs are old Roman and Neapolitan favorites; others are esoteric. It's a great place to enjoy an authentic taste of uninhibited Roman nightlife.

PASQUINO

Viclo del Piede, 19, Piazza Santa Maria in Trastevere. Tel. 6/ 58 03 622.

Admission/Cost: Tickets, L7,000.

Open: Four screenings daily between 4:00 and 11:00 P.M.

Get in touch with home at this small theater. It shows relatively new English-language films. Just a block from Piazza Santa Maria in Trastevere, it's a great place to catch a show. Then, visit one of the cafés on the square, where you can admire the charm of the village, the architecture, and the scene around the fountain. Phone the theater if you want to know what's playing.

SCARABOCCHIO

Piazza Ponziani, 8. Tel. 6/ 58 00 495.

Admission/Cost: (including one drink), L25,000.

Open: Tues.–Sun. 10:00 P.M.–3:00 A.M.

This club offers a sensory sensation with its funky music and huge video screens. Scarabocchio is a popular spot for the eighteen and older set, but don't plan on going if you're interested in conversation. Music is the main attraction.

THE VATICAN

ACADEMY OF ST. CECILIA

Via della Conciliazione, 4. Tel. 6/ 67 80 742.

Admission/Cost: Symphonic music, L20000–L45,000; chamber music, L20,000–L35,000.

Open: Call for opening times.

Take Bus #30 to the concerts given by the orchestra of the Academy of St. Cecilia at Piazza di Villa Giulia.

The site of the Etruscan Museum, it holds concerts from the end of June to the end of July; in the winter they are held in the concert hall on Via della Conciliazione.

ALEXANDERPLATZ

Via Ostia, 9. Tel. 6/ 37 29 398
Admission/Cost: No cover charge. Whiskey, L10,000; a full meal, L38,000.
Open: Mon.–Sat. 9:00 P.M.–2:00 A.M.

There's no entry fee to this restaurant, bar, and jazz club. One of the most well-established jazz and blues clubs in Rome, it features Italian and foreign musicians nightly.

FOLLIA

Via Ovidio, 17. Tel. 6/ 68 30 8435.
Admission/Cost: L20,000–L30,000.
Open: Tues.–Sun. 11:30 A.M.–3:00 A.M.

Romans in the know regard this club as a fairly essential place to go in the hopes of happening upon Italian TV celebrities, who have been known to wind up here for one reason or another. The decor is a pseudo-country-house concept, which somehow seems an appropriate backdrop for the sophisticated young crowd. Disco music and a piano bar are the entertainment.

FONCLEA

Via Crescenzio, 82/a. Tel. 6/ 68 96 302.
Admission/Cost: Meals, L35,000; drinks, L7,000–L10,000.
Open: Nightly 8:00 P.M.–2:30 A.M. Music 10:30 P.M.–12:30 A.M.

This diverse spot near Castel Sant'Angelo has a pub atmosphere. It serves Mexican and Italian food, and is a venue for live music ranging from jazz to Latin American, depending on who's on the schedule.

VIA VENETO/PIAZZA BARBERINI

✓ HARRY'S BAR

Via Veneto, 148. Tel. 6/ 48 46 43.
Admission/Cost: Meals, L60,000–L80,000; whiskey, L10,000–L12,000.
Open: Mon.–Sat. 11:30 A.M.–1:30 A.M.
Closed August 1–10.

No relation to the world-famous Harry's Bars in Florence, Venice, Paris, and other cities, Harry's Bar is the chicest watering hole along this popular street. The Rome Harry's is elegant, with tapestry walls, elaborate wood paneling, curvy plastering, and sconces. The food here is superb, with an exorbitant price tag to match. Enjoy a summer meal at one of the sidewalk tables.

JACKIE O'

Via Boncompagni, 11. Tel. 6/ 48 85 457.
Admission/Cost: Cover charge, L30,000; average drink, L20,000.
Open: Mon.–Sat. restaurant, 9:00 P.M.; disco, 11:00 P.M.–3:30 A.M.

This Via Veneto classic named for the late great Jackie Onassis was recently renovated and refurbished. It's the primary choice for dinner and/or disco dancing by the rich and famous. The restaurant is expensive.

NOTORIOUS

Via San Nicolà da Tolentino, 22. Tel. 6/ 47 46 888.
Admission/Cost: (including one drink), L35,000.
Open: Tues.–Sun. 11:00 P.M.–4:00 A.M.

It's fashionable to show up late to this, one of the most popular discos in Rome. Some of the most beautiful locals frequent this spot, dressed in their best disco attire, to dance to the never-live music. It's usually crowded, but the experience is worth it, if dancing's your thing.

OPEN GATE

Via San Nicola da Tolentino, 4. Tel. 6/ 47 46 301.
Admission/Cost: L30,000–L35,000.
Open: Tues.–Sun. 10:30 P.M.–4:00 A.M.

Dancing starts at midnight at this disco, piano bar, and restaurant that attracts the over-twenty-five set. Glitter and glitz are the main attraction. This place became a legend during the 1950s, and now it's a popular spot for upscale debutante parties.

VELENO

Via Sardegna, 27, off Via Veneto. Tel. 6/ 49 35 83.
Admission/Cost: (including one drink): Men, L22,000 Tues.–Sat., 32,000 Fri.–Sat.; women, free.
Open: Tues.–Sun. 10:00 P.M.–4:00 A.M.

Rap, soul, and funk music make this a hot dance spot. It's mostly popular with the local motor scooter crowd. Veleno, or Poison, is a favorite on the celebrity circuit. Theme evenings keep things interesting here.

OUTER ROME

CAFFÈ LATINO

Via di Monte Testaccio, 96. Tel. 6/ 57 44 020.
Admission/Cost: L35,000.
Open: Tues.–Sun. 10:00 P.M.–3:30 A.M.

Located in the trendy Testaccio neighborhood, this club offers jazz, soul, and spicy salsa music in a small space that tends to get overheated. The sophisticated thirty-something crowd comes here for the concerts (mainly jazz) and separate video room and bar for socializing.

DIVINA

Via Romagnosi, 11A. Tel. 6/ 36 11 348.
Admission/Cost: (including one drink), Tues.–Thurs. L35,000, Fri.–Sat. L40,000.
Open: Tues.–Sat. 11:00 P.M. to either 4:00 or 5:00 A.M.

Many people come here looking for Gil's, a famous club that once stood on this spot and is now part of Roman nightlife history. Many stay at Divina, where you're sure to have a romantic evening. It's a relaxing piano bar, with several small rooms lined with mirrors. Don't just show up here. Some nights are by invitation only, and you're not allowed in unless you're a friend of the club (frequent patron). Be sure to make a reservation.

FRANKIE-GO
Via Schiaparelli, 29-30. Tel. 6/ 32 21 251.
Admission/Cost: L30,000.
Open: Wed.–Thurs. 11:00 P.M.–4:00 A.M.,
Fri.–Sat. 11:00 P.M.–5:00 A.M.

A template of House of Parioli's rich young narcissists best describes this club. The under-thirty crowd sometimes includes young actors. Beauty pageants, theme parties, and other special events are common, and there is a restaurant. The entrance is on Via Luciani 52.

THE PIPER 90
Via Tagliamento, 9. Tel. 6/ 84 14 459.
Admission/Cost: L20,000–L30,000.
Open: Wed.–Sat. 10:00 P.M.–5:00 A.M.,
Sun. 3:30–7:30 P.M. and 10:00 P.M.–5:00 A.M.

One of Rome's first discos, this place is a "must" for anyone interested in disco history. The drinking age in Rome is sixteen, but fourteen-year-olds are admitted to this club, where dress is casual. Teenagers like the disco, music, live groups, and pop videos. Occasionally, there's ballroom dancing for the older crowd.

SPAGO
Via di Monte Testaccio. Tel. 6/ 57 44 999.
Admission/Cost: L35,000.
Open: Thurs.–Sat. 10:30 P.M.–3:30 A.M.

It's best to take a taxi to this hard-to-find spot. The crowd here is trendy and sophisticated, with Roman yuppies blended in for good measure. Saturday night disco dancing is the main attraction.

Notes

PART 5

Around Town

SIGHTS TO SEE

AVENTINE/PALATINE

BATHS OF CARACALLA

Via delle Terme di Caracalla, 52. Tel. 6/ 57 58 302.
Admission: L6,000.
Open: Apr.–Sept., Tues.–Sat. 9:00 A.M.–6:00 P.M., Sun. and Mon. 9:00 A.M.–1:00 P.M.; Oct.–Mar., Tues.–Sat. 9:00 A.M.–3:00 P.M., Sun. and Mon. 9:00 A.M.–1:00 P.M.
Metro/Bus: Bus 90 or 118 from the Stazione Termini.

The baths that once covered this twenty-seven-acre site would rival many spas or health clubs of today. Built in the third century, its facilities included a changing room, gymnasium, steam rooms, and a library next to the pool rooms. Pools were individually heated by an underground heating system. Only brick ruins remain today. View the baths during the day, and enjoy the opera in the evening.

PROTESTANT CEMETERY

Via Caio Cestio, 6. Tel. 6/ 57 41 900.
Admission: No admission charge, but a L1,000 offering is customary.
Open: Mar.–Sept., Thurs.–Tues. 8:00–11:30 A.M. and 3:30–5:30 P.M.; Oct.–Feb., Thurs.–Tues. 8:00–11:30 A.M. and 2:30–4:30 P.M.
Metro/Bus: St. Paul's. Bus 13, 27, or 30.

Non-Catholics, famous and otherwise, who lived and/or died in Rome are buried in this cemetery. You may recognize the names of such notables as John Keats and the Italian Communist leader, Antonio Gramsci, as you wander among the monuments, but don't let the history here distract you: pickpockets prey on the engrossed, so guard your belongings as you look around.

PYRAMID OF CAIUS CESTIUS

Piazzale Ostiense.
Admission: No admission charge.
Open: Open for outside viewing only. No set hours.
Metro/Bus: Piramide. Bus No. 30.

One of Rome's most curious sights is the tomb of a wealthy Roman who died in 12 B.C. It is built of brick and faced with marble. You can wander around and take pictures outside.

CAMPO DE'FIORI

GHETTO E SINAGOGA (JEWISH GHETTO AND SYNAGOGUE)

Lungotevere dei Cenci. Tel. 6/ 68 75 051.
Admission: No admission charge.
Open: 9:30 A.M.–2:00 P.M., 3:00–5:00 P.M.
Closed Saturdays and Jewish holidays.
Metro/Bus: Bus 23, 97, 774, or 780.

In 1556, Jews were brought into this high-walled enclosure as slaves, and forced to live here. Today it is a shopping area that specializes in Roman-Jewish offerings, and there are several restaurants. The synagogue was built in 1874.

ISOLA TIBERINA (TIBER ISLAND)

Admission: No admission charge.
Open: Daily.
Metro/Bus: Bus 23, 97, 774, or 780.

The hospital is still standing on this 900-foot island that was once thought to be the home of the Greek god of healing. Sick people would travel here seeking relief. Located in the oldest part of the city, the island still is accessible from the ghetto by a footbridge that dates to 62 B.C. It is the oldest bridge still in use on the Tiber River. A small park on the down-river point of the island is an excellent place to enjoy a picnic, or just to relax.

PIAZZA CAMPO DE'FIORI

Near Piazza Farnese.
Admission: No admission charge.
Open: Mon.–Fri. 7:00 A.M.–1:30 P.M.
Metro/Bus: Bus 46, 62, 70, 81, 87, 90, 90b, 186, 492, or 926.

You'll enjoy seeing how the locals shop at this colorful market. While you're taking in a slice of authentic life here, select from cheeses, salamis, ripe fruit and vegetables, and fresh flowers.

CAPITOL/FORUM/COLOSSEUM

ARCH OF CONSTANTINE

Next to the Colosseum, Piazzale del Colosseo.
Admission: No admission charge.
Open: Open to public for outside viewing.
Metro/Bus: Colosseo.

Who would've thought that this arch, dedicated in 315 A.D. to celebrate Constantine's victory three years earlier over Maxentius, his co-emperor, would someday sit amidst swirling, bothersome traffic? Despite the twentieth-century's contribution to the area, the arch is beautiful, meticulously carved, and well-preserved.

BASILICA DI SAN CLEMENTE

Piazza di San Clemente, via Labicana, 95. Tel. 6/ 73 16 723.
Admission: Church, free; grottoes, L2,000.
Open: Mon.–Sat. 9:00 A.M.–12:00 noon and 3:30–6:00 P.M., Sun. 10:00 A.M.–12:30 P.M. and 3:30–6:30 P.M.
Metro/Bus: Colosseo.

This twelfth-century church is the third on this site. It holds centuries of fascinating history. A church dating back to the fourth century sits beneath the "newer" one. An even older shrine, the Temple of Mithras, which housed an all-male fertility cult in the first century, sits at the very bottom.

CARCERE MAMERTINO (MAMERTINE PRISON)

Via San Pietro in Carcere.
Admission: No admission charge.
Open: Daily 9:00 A.M.–12:30 P.M. and 4:00–7:00 P.M.
Metro/Bus: Colosseo.

Legend has it that St. Peter was imprisoned here and used the miraculous spring to baptize the other inmates. Indeed, this is among the oldest sites in Rome. Some of the oldest structures in Rome are at the site of the dungeons. Years ago this was a state prison. It later became a chapel named San Pietro in Carcere.

CHIESA DI SAN PIETRO IN VINCOLI (ST. PETER IN CHAINS)

Piazza di San Pietro in Vincoli, 4A. Tel. 6/ 48 82 865.
Admission: No admission charge.
Open: Mon.–Sat. 7:00 A.M.–12:30 P.M. and 3:30–6:00 P.M., Sun. 7:00–11:45 A.M. and 3:00–7:00 P.M.
Metro/Bus: Via Cavour. Bus 11, 27, or 81.

The chains that restrained St. Peter in Palestine are exhibited at this church, which was founded for that purpose. Michelangelo's statue of Moses and some of his other famous pieces, as well as the tomb of Julius II, are also here.

COLOSSEUM

Piazzale del Colosseo. Tel 6/ 68 75 036.
Admission: Street level, free; upper levels, L6,000.
Open: Hours vary monthly. Call for specific hours.
Metro/Bus: Colosseo.

This, Rome's grandest and most celebrated monument, dates to between 72 and 81 A.D. The 137-foot-tall colosseum has centuries of history. Gladiators did battle here. Criminals received their punishments at the jaws of lions. Battle scenes were staged here. Renaissance construction workers helped themselves to marble from the structure when they needed it for St. Peter's, setting in motion the eventual destruction of a large portion of the outer wall. The colosseum was remodeled in the nineteenth century, so visitors will see this "newer" version when they visit.

FORI IMPERIALI (IMPERIAL FORUMS)

Via XXIV Maggio.
Admission: No admission charge.
Open: By applying to Sorprintendenza Archeologica di Roma.
Metro/Bus: Colosseo.

Caesar began the Fori Imperiali as a civic center when the city outgrew the Foro Romano. The forum and market are major attractions in this area. The Trajans' forum is not open to visitors. The Trajans' column is 138 feet high, composed of nineteen marble blocks. The three-story market built by Trajans served as a sort of ancient shopping mall and business center, with 150 shops and commercial exchanges. Most of its rooms are empty now, but it is still interesting to visit.

FORO ROMANO (ROMAN FORUM)

Via dei Fori Imperiali. Tel. 6/ 67 80 782.
Admission: Adults, L10,000; children under 12, free.
Open: Hours vary monthly. Call to verify times. Closed Tuesdays and Sunday afternoons and January 16–February 15.
Metro/Bus: Colosseo. Bus 27, 30, 85, 87, or 88.

This area was the flourishing center of Roman life in ancient times until the Imperial Forum took away its prestige. Rich in history, its highlights include the Victorious Arch of Septimius Severus, the Arch of Titus, and the Temple of Antoninus and Faustina. Since this place was used as a quarry for many years, there are only fragments of monuments, crumbling temples, and stones on the site where Caesar was glorified. Visitors may purchase detailed plans of the original forum.

LARGO ARGENTINA

Via del Portico d'Ottavia, 29. Tel. 6/ 67 10 2070.
Admission: No admission charge.

Open: Visits must be arranged in advance.
Call for appointment.
Metro/Bus: Corso Vittorio Emanuele II.

If you'd like to visit the remains of four ancient temples of the Area Sacra di Largo Argentina, you must make arrangements ahead of time. Uncovered during the early 1920s, this area needs major restoration.

MONUMENTO A VITTORIO EMANUELE II (MONUMENT TO VICTOR EMMANUEL II)

Piazza Venezia.
Admission: No admission charge because it is not open to the public.
Open: The inside is not open to the public.
Metro/Bus: From Termini Station, Bus 64, 65, 70, 75, or 170. From Piazza Barberini, Bus 56, 60, or 492.

Pope Paul II and Benito Mussolini once lived here. The monument was built in 1911 to celebrate the unification of Italy. It holds the Tomba del Milite Ignoto (Tomb of the Unknown Soldier from World War I).

PIAZZA DEL CAMPIDOGLIO

Via del Teatro di Marcello.
Admission: No admission charge.
Open: Closed Sundays and Mondays.
Metro/Bus: Colosseo.

Michelangelo designed this magnificent square at the smallest of the seven hills for Pope Paul III, but at one time it was the site of an asylum for fugitive slaves. The collection of sculptures here must be seen.

SANTA MARIA D'ARACOELI

Capitoline Hill. Tourist office 6/ 49 711.
Admission: No admission charge.
Open: Daily 7:00 A.M.–12:00 noon and 4:00–7:00 P.M.
Metro/Bus: Bus 46, 89, or 92.

Enter through the Piazza del Campidoglio to avoid climbing over one hundred steep, marble steps that lead to this historical building. Built during the thirteenth century for the Franciscans, it has a nave and two aisles, a Renaissance ceiling, and eleven pillars in each of the two rows inside. Romans have believed this site to be sacred ever since the Gauls were executing a sneak attack and would have succeeded but a flock of noisy geese warned the villagers, who then successfully defended themselves. Located in the church is a Bufalini Chapel, a masterpiece of Pinturicchio in frescoes, and a famous wood carving of the Santo Bambino which is believed to be the source of many miracles.

SANTA MARIA IN COSMEDIN

Piazza della Verità, 18. Tel. 6/ 67 81 419.
Admission: No admission charge.
Open: Daily 9:00 A.M.–12:00 noon and 3:00–5:00 P.M.
Metro/Bus: Bus 57, 95, or 716.

Tourists visit this church mainly to see the "Mouth of Truth," or "Bocca della Verità," which was originally a drainage-hole cover. It is, however, a beautiful sixth-century medieval church in its own right, with an impressive bell tower and painstakingly crafted mosaics.

PANTHEON

CHIESA DI SANT'IVO ALLA SAPIENZA

Corso, 40 Rinascimento. Tel. 6/ 68 64 987.
Admission: No admission charge.
Open: 10 A.M.–12:00 noon Sunday mornings only.
Metro/Bus: Corso de Rinascimento.

Borromini's masterpiece was completed in 1650 A.D. after eight years of work. Sunlight illuminates the dome, which has six windows.

PALAZZO DORIA PAMPHILI

Piazza Grazioli, 5. Tel. 6/ 67 97 323.
Admission: Gallery, L10,000; apartments, L5,000.
Open: Tues. and Fri.–Sun. 10:00 A.M.–1:00 P.M.
Metro/Bus: Flaminio.

The facade dates from the seventeenth century, and gilded furniture, crystal chandeliers, and Renaissance tapestries are everywhere. Some of the majestic apartments surrounding the gallery of the palace and the central court are leased to tenants. The Galleria Doria Pamphili contains a beautiful patrician art collection, in which Velázquez's *Portrait of Innocent X* is a highlight. There are shops at street level.

THE PANTHEON

Piazza della Rotonda. Tel. 6/ 36 98 31.
Admission: No admission charge.
Open: July–Sept., daily 9:00 A.M.–6:00 P.M.; Oct.–June, Mon.–Sat. 9:00 A.M.–4:00 P.M., Sun. 9:00 A.M.–1:00 P.M.
Metro/Bus: Bus 64, 170, or 175 to largodi Torre Argentina.

Over 2,000 years old, this building was founded by Agrippa in 27 B.C., and is the only one of Rome's ancient buildings that is fully intact today. The walls of this ancient Roman building are twenty-five feet thick. They once were "guarded" by white marble statues of pagan gods around the perimeter. While still relatively new, it became a Christian church in 606 A.D., and housed the tombs of Raphael and the two Kings of Italy.

PIAZZA DI SPAGNA

KEATS-SHELLEY MEMORIAL

Piazza di Spagna, 26. Tel. 6/ 67 84 235.
Admission: Children and adults. L5,000.
Open: June–Sept., Mon.–Fri. 9:00 A.M.–1:00 P.M. and 3:00–6:00 P.M.; Oct.–May, Mon.–Fri. 9:00 A.M.–1:00 P.M. and 2:30–5:30 P.M.
Metro/Bus: Piazza di Spagna.

Keats spent the last few months of his life in this eighteenth-century house at the foot of the Spanish Steps. His close friend, the painter Joseph Severn, tended to him until death. The Keats apartment houses a museum, which displays a death mask of Keats and a carnival mask worn by Byron, along with relics from Byron, Keats, and Shelley.

MURA DI ROMA ANTICA (ANCIENT ROMAN WALLS)

Porta San Sebastiano, 18. Tel. 6/ 70 47 5284.

Though they no longer serve their intended function, the Aurelian Walls wind around the city for twelve miles, an ever-present reminder of the conditions of ancient Rome. The magnificent gates at the Porta San Sebastiano mark the beginning of Via Appia Antica. They were repaired during the fifth century and restored in the sixth century. Archaeological finds are on display in the Museo delle Muro, which is set within two medieval tower gates.

PIAZZA DI SPAGNA

Piazza di Spagna, 26. Tel. 6/ 67 84 235.
Admission: Public square, no charge.
Open: Open weekdays 12:30–2:30 P.M.
Metro/Bus: Piazza di Spagna.

Foreigners really like this area, which, with its French church, Roman sites, and American McDonald's, truly is international in flavor. One of the most enjoyable picture settings of eighteenth-century Rome was named after a palace that housed the Holy See to the Spanish Embassy. It was actually built by the French to connect their quarters above with the Spanish area below. In its center is a fountain shaped as a leaking boat, designed by Pietro Bernini, father of Giovanni Lorenzo Bernini. The Spanish Steps are a meeting place for young people, musicians, artists, and crafts people. One of the city's most noticeable landmarks, the Church of the Trinità dei Monti, is at the top of the steps.

PIAZZA NAVONA

PIAZZA NAVONA

Piazza Navona.
Admission: Public square, no charge.
Open: You can visit anytime.
Metro/Bus: Bus 62, 64, 46, 70, 81, 87, 90, 90b, 186, or 492.

Bernini's *Fontana dei Fiumi* (Fountain of the River) is a fitting centerpiece for one of Rome's premier public squares since the first century A.D. An excellent representation of Roman baroque, it remains untouched by the progress of new buildings or traffic. Plan to end up here around lunch time, and dine at one of the many restaurants and cafés that surround the square. The Chiesa di Sant' Agnese in Agone is on the west side.

THE QUIRINALE

The Quirinale became a popular location for the homes of ancient Romans and popes. The Quirinale is the highest of Rome's seven hills. During historic times plagues were prevalent in the low city areas and those who could afford it located high above the city.

CHIESA DI SAN CARLO ALLE QUATTRO FONTANE (CHURCH OF ST. CHARLES AT THE FOUR FOUNTAINS)

Corner of Via del Quirinale and Via della Quattro Fontane.
Admission: No admission charge.
Open: Mon.–Sat. 9:00 A.M.–1:00 P.M.,
Mon.–Fri. 4:00–6:00 P.M.
Metro/Bus: Bus 52, 53, 56, 60, 61, 62, 95, or 492.

Borromini had his first important commission at this small church, which, along with the adjacent convent, was started in 1634. Oddly-shaped strongboxes make the dome of the church. They are lit by concealed windows, and appear to float above the arched walls.

FONTANA DI TREVI (TREVI FOUNTAIN)

Piazza di Trevi.
Admission: Public fountain, no charge.
Open: Open to public for viewing any time.
Metro/Bus: Bus 52, 53, 58, 60, 61, 62, 71, 95, or 492.

The Hollywood movie, *Three Coins in a Fountain*, popularized this fountain in a tiny square, but its history goes back much farther than that. Designed by Nicola Salvi, it was the last important monumental baroque work in Rome. It took thirty years to build and was finished in 1762. Legend has it that if a coin is tossed in the fountain, the person will return to Rome some day.

PALAZZO DEL QUIRINALE

Palazzo del Quirinale.
Admission: This square is open to the public. The Palazzo del Quirinale offers only outside viewing.
Open: The inside is not open to the public.
Metro/Bus: Bus 52, 53, 56, 60, 61, 62, 71, 81, 95, or 119.

The Palazzo del Quirinale, begun in 1574 and completed in 1740, is the official residence of the Italian president. Each day at 4:00 P.M. you can view a changing of the guard with a military band and a small parade. The Quirinale is the highest of the seven ancient hills of Rome. The Palazzo del Quirinale tops the summit and is Rome's largest and most spectacular square. Steep marble steps lead to Santa Maria d'Aracoeli, where the famous Pinturicchio fresco depicting the life of St. Bernard of Siena, and the wood carving of Santo Bambino are kept.

STAZIONE TERMINI

BASILICA DI SANTA MARIA MAGGIORE

Piazza di Santa Maria Maggiore. Tel. 6/ 48 31 95.
Admission: No admission charge.
Open: Apr.–Sept., daily 7:00 A.M.–8:00 P.M.; Oct.–Mar., daily 7:00 A.M.–7:00 P.M.
Metro/Bus: Stazione Termini.

The elegant eighteenth-century facade of this church can be misleading. One of the four patriarchal basilicas of Rome, it was founded by Pope Liberius in 358 A.D., then repaired by Pope Sixtus III from 432-440 A.D. The church is a treasure trove of art, but it's greatest asset is the mosaics.

SANTA MARIA DEGLI ANGELI

Piazza della Repubblica, 12. Tel. 6/ 48 80 812.
Admission: No admission charge.

Open: Daily 7:30 A.M.–12:00 noon and 4:00–6:30 P.M.
Metro/Bus: Piazza della Repubblica.

Michelangelo was commissioned to transform the great central hall of the decaying third-century Baths of Diocletian into the Church of Santa Maria degli Angeli. It is next to the Museo Nazionale Romano.

TRASTEVERE

BASILICA DI SAN CLEMENTE

Corner of Via San Giovanni Laterano and Piazza San Clemente. Tel. 6/ 70 45 1018.
Admission: There is a charge to see the excavations.
Open: Daily 9:00 A.M.–12:30 P.M. and 3:30–6:30 P.M.
Metro/Bus: Colosseo. Bus 81, 85, 93, or 186.

This, one of Rome's most intricate buildings, is a church built on top of another church. Below the twelfth-century structure is a frescoed church from the fourth century and ruins of several other buildings. The frescoes in the Chapel of St. Catherine are among the church's greatest art treasures. The lower church is badly decayed, but visitors may still see frescoes dating back to the ninth century.

BASILICA OF SAN GIOVANNI IN LATERANO

Piazza di San Giovanni, 4. Tel. 6/ 69 86 433.
Admission: No admission charge.
Open: Daily 7:00 A.M.–6:00 P.M.
Metro/Bus: Bus 91.

This church, not St. Peter's, is the cathedral of Rome. Earthquakes, fire, and war are all part of the history of this church, which Catholics the world over refer to as the "mother church." Constantine founded it in the fourth century.

OPEN AIR FLEA MARKET

Trastevere Rail Station to Porta Portese.
Admission: No admission charge.
Open: Sunday 6:30 A.M.–2:00 P.M.
Metro/Bus: Bus 170, 280, 718, or 719.

Sundays from dawn to about 1:00 or 2:00 P.M. is the time for Rome's flea market. On the outskirts of Trastevere, it's a loud, crowded, and disorderly place. Come early for the best finds, and feel free to haggle.

THE VATICAN

BASILICA DI SAN PIETRO (ST. PETER'S)

Piazza San Pietro.
Admission: No admission charge.
Open: Daily 7:00 A.M.–7:00 P.M.;
Oct.–Mar. 7:00 A.M.–6:00 P.M.
Metro/Bus: Bus 23, 30, 32, 49, 51, or 64.

Allow extra time to see everything here. Remember to dress appropriately. Shorts or very short shirts that don't cover the shoulders, back, or stomach are not allowed. Constantine built the first church here, on the site where it was thought that St. Peter was killed and buried. During the second century, Emperor Constantine ordered a shrine to be erected on St. Peter's tomb. Michelangelo's beautiful 435-feet-high dome is here, although he died before its completion. Giacomo della Porta finished the project. Carlo Maderno modified it in the early part of the seventeenth century. Facing the altar, look to the right of the portico and you'll see the Holy Door that only the Pope can open and close every twenty-five years at the start and end of each Jubilee Year. You can also view the famous *Pietá* by Michelangelo. Views of the Pope's back yard can be seen from the dome. Take the elevator, then the steps to reach the top.

CASTEL SANT'ANGELO

On the Tiber at largo Castello. Tel. 6/ 68 75 036.
Admission: All ages, L8,000.
Open: Tues.–Sun. 9:00 A.M.–1:00 P.M.
Closed Mondays.
Metro/Bus: Ottaviano. Bus 23, 46, 62, 64, 87, 98, 280, or 910.

Built during the second century as a tomb for the Emperor Hadrian, it was used as an imperial tomb until the time of Caracalla, and later converted into a prison. There is a secret passage that leads to the Vatican, and popes throughout the years have taken refuge here. Set in a landmark area on the Tiber, it faces the St. Angelo Bridge, which is accented with statues of angels, including two reproductions of originals by Bernini. Today, the building is a museum with art works and various relics on display.

JANICULUM HILL

Via della Lungara.
Admission: No admission charge.
Open: Open to public daily. No set hours.
Metro/Bus: Bus 41 from Ponte Sant' Angelo.

The site of the battle that took place between Pope Pius IX and Guiseppe Garibaldi in 1870, this hill offers one of the best views in the area. Plan to arrive just before sundown for a spectacular vista.

PIAZZA SAN PIETRO (ST. PETER'S SQUARE)

Piazza San Pietro. Tel. 6/ 69 84 466.
Admission: Guided tour of the tombs, L10,000.
Open: Apr.–Sept., daily 7:00 A.M.–7:00 P.M.;
Oct.–Mar., daily 7:00 A.M.–6:00 P.M.
Metro/Bus: Bus 23, 30, 32, 49, 51, or 64.

Giovanni Lorenzo Bernini, famous for his use of the baroque style in Rome, created this square, which is an excellent example of seventeenth-century architecture. Fountains at both ends of the square have waters that flow from the four-hundred-year-old aqueduct, Acqua Paola. You may see the Pope on Wednesday mornings between 10:00–11:00 A.M. during warm months. During winter months, he addresses the public in the Paul IV Hall near the south side of St. Peter's. Ask for a free ticket at the Prefecture of the Pontifical Household at the extreme northern colonnade of St. Peter's Square.

THE SISTINE CHAPEL

Viale Vaticano. Tel. 6/ 69 88 3333.
Admission: Adults, L13,000; children, L8,000.

Open: Oct.–June, Mon.–Sat. 8:45 A.M.–1:45 P.M., July–Sept. and Easter week, Mon.–Sat. 8:45 A.M.–4:45 P.M.
Metro/Bus: Ottaviano.

Michelangelo's frescoes here are famous worldwide. The artist had been working on a tomb for the Pope when Julius II commanded that he switch his attentions to creating the fresco murals on the ceiling and walls of the chapel. The tedious, physically strenuous work exacted a toll on the artist, permanently damaging his eyesight. Best known here are the nine panels he painted based on his interpretation of the Book of Genesis. Of these, the most famous scene depicts the expulsion of Adam and Eve from the Garden of Eden. Monsignor Biagio was offended by the nudes painted by Michelangelo, and took his objections to the Pope. The artist, Daniele de Volterra, was instructed to paint a draped cloth on each to cover the nudity.

The chapel was on the brink of collapse, from both the weather and its age, before restoration began in the 1990s. The work touched off a controversy in the art world, but, through painstaking efforts, the fresco has been reattached and the ceilings repaired.

THE VATICAN GARDENS

Admission: L16,000 per person.
Open: Mar.–Oct. 10:00 A.M.;
Nov.–Feb., Tues., Thurs., and Sat., 10:00 A.M.
Metro/Bus: Ottaviano.

Book a tour of these magnificent gardens in person. No reservations are taken by phone. Spread over fifty-eight acres, the gardens separate the Vatican from the outside world. The lush, carefully tended gardens are filled with brilliantly colored flowers, woodlands of massive oaks, and aged fountains and pools, all accessed by winding paths. The Casino of Pius IV originally was the summer home of Pope Pius IV. It was built in 1560.

VATICAN LIBRARY

Admission: Special permit required. Admission fee charged, except last Sunday of the month.

Open: Mon.–Sat., and last Sun. of the month 8:45 A.M.–1:00 P.M.; July–Sept. and Easter, Mon.–Fri.: 8:45 A.M.–4:00 P.M., Sat. 8:45 A.M.–1:00 P.M. Closed public and religious holidays.
Metro/Bus: Ottaviano.

Another treasure among the Vatican complex, this library has beautiful frescoes. Historic artifacts and manuscripts are displayed here under glass. Visit the Sistine Salon to see sketches by Michelangelo and Botticelli.

VATICAN TOURIST OFFICE

On the left side of Piazza San Pietro, near the Arco delle Campane. Tel. 6/ 69 88 4466.
Admission: Adults, L13,000; children, L8,000. No admission charge first Sun. of each month.
Open: Museums, Oct.–June, Mon.–Sat. 8:45 A.M.–1:45 P.M.; July–Sept. and Easter week, Mon.–Sat. 8:45 A.M.–4:45 P.M. Ticket sales stop one hour before closing time.
Metro/Bus: Ottaviano. Bus 23, 30, 32, 49, 51, 64, 70, 81, 490, 492, 495, 907, 990, 991, or 994.

Your key to the Vatican sights is this office. Maps are for sale, and staff is on hand to answer any of your questions concerning St. Peter's or the Vatican museums.

VILLA DORIA PAMPHILI

Admission: No admission charge.
Open: Daily from dawn to dusk.
Metro/Bus: Bus 23, 30, 32, 49, 51, or 64.

About the size of Central Park in New York City, this Roman park offers a rare patch of green in the capital city. Once the property of Princess Orietta Pamphili, the park opened to the public in 1971.

VIA VENETO

CIMITERO MONUMENTALE DEI PADRI CAPPUCCINI

In the church of the Immaculate Conception, Via Veneto, 27.

Admission: L1,000.
Open: Apr.–Sept. 9:00 A.M.–12:00 noon and 3:00–6:30 P.M.; Oct.–Mar., daily 9:30 A.M.–12:00 noon and 3:00–6:00 P.M.
Metro/Bus: Piazza Barberini.

Skulls and crossbones are just the beginning at this cemetery. Bones are the art medium here. The many artworks crafted from skeletal remains are interesting, but may not be attractive to the squeamish.

VIA VITTORIO VENETO

Via Veneto.
Admission: This is a street open to the public.
Metro/Bus: Bus 52, 53, 56, 58, or 60 along Via del Tritone.

Stop for lunch, shop to your heart's content, or glance at the flowers and trees along the famed Via Veneto. Though it still has elegant hotels and fashionable bars, the street has lost some of the glitter and glamour from the *La Dolce Vita* days of the '60s. The street ascends from Piazza Barberini to the Villa Borghese.

VILLA BORGHESE

VILLA BORGHESE

Top of Via Veneto.
Admission: There is a charge to get in the museums.
Open: Closed Mondays and for a long afternoon break, 1:00–4:00 P.M.
Metro/Bus: Bus 3, 4, 52, 53, 57, 95, 490, 495, or 910.

Rome's finest public park has two museums, hills, lakes, and vistas. Created during the seventeenth century, it's a beautiful place to enjoy a breezy walk, go to the petting zoo, or attend a Sunday morning concert. The Galleria Nazionale d'Arte, with its important collection of Italian and foreign art from the nineteenth and twentieth centuries, is here. A splendid late-Renaissance palace built for Julius III as a summer villa is the home of Rome's museum of Etruscan art, the Museo Nazionale Etrusco di Villa Giulia.

OUTER ROME

SAN PAOLO FUORI LE MURA

Via Ostiense. Tel. 6/ 54 10 341.
Admission: No admission charge.
Open: Cloisters, Mon.–Sat. 9:00–11:45 P.M.; Basilica, Mon.–Sat. 9:00 A.M.–1:00 P.M. and 3:00–6:00 P.M.
Metro/Bus: San Paolo Basilica. Bus 23, 170, 318, or 673.

St. Paul is thought to be buried at this beautiful church. Constantine erected a small basilica over the saint's tomb. Visitors pass through a massive atrium to reach the church, whose interior is cold and imposing, not at all like the character of the old basilica. A great fire gutted the church in 1823, but there are still many art treasures here. The Triumphal Arch has mosaics dating from the fifth century, and an elaborate Gothic tabernacle sits over the traditional tomb of St. Paul. Monks sell souvenirs from a treasure shop in the church.

TOMB OF ST. SEBASTIAN

Via Appia Antica, 136. Tel. 6/ 78 87 035.
Admission: L8,000; children under 10, free.
Open: Wed.–Mon. 9:00 A.M.–12:00 noon and 2:30–5:30 P.M.
Metro/Bus: Bus 118 or 218.

Built near the site of a quarry, the catacombs extend for miles underground. The church was built here during the fourth century, and this is the only catacomb in Rome that's open regularly. St. Peter's and St. Paul's bodies were hidden in these catacombs.

GALLERIES

ACCADEMIA DI SAN LUCA

Piazza dell' Accademia di San Luca, 77. Tel. 6/ 67 89 243.
Admission: No admission charge.
Open: Mon., Wed., Fri., and the last Sun. of the month 10:00 A.M.–1:00 P.M.
Metro/Bus: Bus 52, 53, 56, 58, 60, 61, 62, 71, 81, 95, 118, or 492.

There are more than 1,000 pieces of art at this academy, which the painter Girolamo Muziano founded in 1577. Paintings and sculptures by artists including Guercino, Rubens, and Raphael are here.

BORGHESE GALLERY

Villa Borghese. Tel. 6/ 85 48 577.
Admission: L4,000.
Open: Winter 9:00 A.M.–2:00 P.M.; summer 9:00 A.M.–7:00 P.M.
Metro/Bus: Bus 910 from Stazione Termini or 56 from Piazza Barberini.

Set on the grounds of the beautiful park, the gallery is housed in the Casino Borghese and contains paintings, sculptures, and a statue. The ground floor is the only one open, because the gallery is undergoing restoration, but you'll be able to see sculptures by Bernini here.

CASINO DELL'AURORA PALLAVICINI

Via XXIV Maggio, 43. Tel. 6/ 48 27 224.
Admission: No admission charge.
Open: The first of every month 10:00 A.M.–12:00 noon and 3:00–5:00 P.M.
Metro/Bus: Colosseo. Bus 44, 46, 56, 60, 62, 64, 65, 70, 75, 81, 90, 90b, 170, 186, or 492.

You can visit the private collections in the Galleria Pallavicini with its baroque ceiling fresco of Aurora by Guido Reni. Open the first of every month, the Galleria doesn't charge admission, but you must obtain special permission to enter.

GALLERIA COLONNA

Via della Pilotta, 17. Tel. 6/ 67 94 362.
Admission: L5,000; groups over 10, L4,000.
Open: Sat. only 9:00 A.M.–1:00 P.M.
Metro/Bus: Colosseo. Bus 44, 46, 56, 60, 62, 64, 65, 70, 75, 81, 90, 90b, 170, 186, or 492.

This excellent collection of important patrician art includes works by such greats as Tintoretto, Veronese, and Van Dyck. The stately baroque galleries are works of art themselves. Four arches connect the gallery to the gardens of Villa Colonna.

GALLERIA DORIA PAMPHILI

Piazza del Collegio Romano. Tel. 6/ 67 94 365.
Admission: Gallery, L6,000; apartments, L4,000.
Open: Tues., Fri., Sat., Sun. 10:00 A.M.–1:00 P.M.
Metro/Bus: Flaminio.

Pamphili Pope Innocent X's sister-in-law, Donna Olimpia Maidalchini, started this patrician art collection, which includes three paintings by Caravaggio, Bernini's portrait bust of the Pope, and works by Titian.

GALLERIA NAZIONALE D'ARTE ANTICA

Via delle Quattro Fontane, 13. Tel. 6/ 48 14 591.
Admission: Adults, L6,000; children under 18, free.
Open: Tues.–Sun. 9:00 A.M.–7:00 P.M.
Metro/Bus: Piazza Barberini.

The National Gallery has locations at the Palazzo Barberini and the Palazzo Corsini. Each features a different collection of nineteenth- and twentieth-century Italian art by the same famous artists.

GALLERIA SPADA

Via Capodiferro, 3. Tel. 6/ 68 61 1558
Admission: L4,000; EC citizens under 18 or over 60, and art historians and architecture students, free.
Open: 9:00 A.M.–2:00 P.M.; Tues. and Sat. 9:00 A.M.–7:00 P.M.; Sun. 9:00 A.M.–1:00 P.M.
Metro/Bus: Bus 44, 46, 62, 64, 65, 70, 87, 90, 186, 492, or 926.

Cardinal Bernardino Spada began the fine patrician

art collection on display here. There are many fine paintings from the seventeenth and eighteenth century, and works from Guercino, Rubens, and many other excellent artists.

MUSEUMS

ANTIQUARIUM FORENZE

Piazza Santa Maria Nova, 53. Tel. 6/ 67 90 333.
Admission: Adults, L10,000; children under 12, free (if accompanied by an adult).
Open: Often closed in the winter; summer 9:00 A.M.–6:00 P.M.
Metro/Bus: Colosseo. Bus 11, 27, 81, 85, 87, or 186.

Your ticket to the Roman Forum also grants entrance to this museum, which occupies two floors of the Church of Santa Francesca Romana. Excavations from the forum are on display.

CAPITOLINE MUSEUMS

Piazza del Campidoglio. Tel. 6/ 67 10 3069.
Admission: L10,000.
Open: 9:00 A.M.–1:30 P.M., Sun. 9:00 A.M.–1:00 P.M. winter Tues. and Sat. 5:00–8:00 P.M., Sat. 8:00–11:00 P.M. Closed Mondays.
Metro/Bus: Bus 46, 89, or 92.

Two palaces house a collection of classical sculptures and works by Caravaggio, Titian, and others. Founded during the fifteenth century, it is the world's first public museum.

MUSEO DELLA CIVILTÀ ROMANA

Piazza G. Agnelli. Tel. 6/ 59 26 135.
Admission: L5,000.
Open: Tues.–Thurs. 9:00 A.M.–1:30 P.M. and 3:00–6:00 P.M., Sun. 9:00 A.M.–1:00 P.M.
Metro/Bus: Linea B to EUR Fermi.

This museum devoted to Roman civilization over the years includes monuments, photographs, and drawings.

An impressive scale model shows the city as it appeared in the time of Constantine.

MUSEO NAZIONALE ETRUSCO DI VILLA GIULIA

Piazzale di Villa Guilia. Tel. 6/ 32 01 951.
Admission: L8,000.
Open: 9:00 A.M.–2:00 P.M., Wed.
9:00 A.M.–7:30 P.M., Sun. 9:00 A.M.–1:00 P.M.
Metro/Bus: Bus 19 or 30.

Mostly devoted to Etruscan art, this museum in a palace is a treasure trove of jewelry, bronzes, vases, and household objects from that period. Leave identification at the ticket counter if you would like a private viewing of the Castellani Collection.

MUSEO DEL PALAZZO VENEZIA

Via del Plebescito, 118. Tel. 6/ 67 98 865.
Admission: L8,000.
Open: 9:00 A.M.–2:00 P.M., Sun. 9:00 A.M.–1:00 P.M. Closed Mondays.
Metro/Bus: Bus 64, 65, 70, 75, or 170 from Termini Station. From Piazza Barberini, 56, 60, or 492.

Mussolini called this complex headquarters during a crucial time in recent history, but now it is a museum. See collections of medieval art, ceramics, weapons, jewelry, Neapolitan crib figures, tapestries, bronze, and many other beautiful items.

MUSEUM OF FOLKLORE

Piazza S. Egidio, 1b. Tel. 6/ 58 16 563.
Admission: L3,750; students, L2,500.
Open: Tues.–Thurs. 9:00 A.M.–1:00 P.M. and 5:00–7:30 P.M., Sun. 9:00 A.M.–12:30 P.M.
Closed Mondays.
Metro/Bus: Bus 23, 56, 65, or 280.

Once a convent, this museum displays ancient sculpture, pictures of Roman scenes, and other art. Upstairs, there's a display that shows Rome as it was two hundred years ago.

WALKS AND TOURS

When you're not familiar with a city, it's always a good idea to take a tour. If you schedule the tour close to your arrival, you'll get an overview of the city. Then you can decide where you'd like to spend more of your vacation time. Most hotels in Rome can arrange for multilingual guides or interpreters for tours of many famous sites. Taped tour commentaries can be rented at some of the museums or sites.

BUS TOURS

Bus tours offer a good, comprehensive overview of major sites in Rome and the surrounding areas. The **Italian Tourist Agency, CIT,** *Piazza della Republica 68, tel. 6/ 47 941*, and many private firms offer tours of all the major sites and trips to other points of interest. Guests may arrange to be picked up and dropped off at their hotels.

Tours typically are offered in three-hour segments. Buses are air-conditioned, sixty-passenger coaches with English-speaking tour guides. Various operators give tours focusing on, among other things, ancient Rome, Christian Rome, Classical Rome, or the Vatican. Some also offer excursions outside the city; however, these require a lot of stamina, because the tours generally leave your hotel at 7:00 A.M. and return at 11:00 P.M.

ATAC 110 TOURIST BUS

Piazza dei Cinquecento. Tel. 6/ 46 951.
Cost: L6000.
Hours of Operation: Leaves at 3:30 P.M. daily from April through October. 2:30 P.M. Sat. and Sun. only during November through March.

Rome's municipal bus company, ATAC, which is operated by the city transport authority, provides a three-hour sightseeing tour, the least expensive, organized tour of Rome. Beginning at Termini, the ATAC tour takes in forty-five major sites and important monuments. There is a multilingual brochure that gives highlights. Tours on ATAC bus 110 depart from Piazza dei Cinquecento. There are five stops in route. Tickets are available from the ATAC information booth in the square.

AMERICAN EXPRESS

Piazza di Spagna, 38. Tel. 6/ 67 641.
Cost: City, L40,000–L56,000; Tivoli, L52,000; Pompey, Naples and Capri, L160,000.
Credit Cards: AE.
Hours of Operation: Mon.–Fri. 9:00 A.M.–5:30 P.M., Sat. 9:00 A.M.–12:30 P.M.

You may take a coach tour of the main Roman sites and also excursions to the popular and beautiful Tivoli, Pompey, Naples, and Capri.

APPIAN LINE

Piazza Esquilino 6. Tel. 6/ 48 84 151.
Cost: City, L30,000–L58,000; Naples and Pompey, L135,000.
Credit Cards: AE, MC, V.
Hours of Operation: Buses leave Mon.–Fri. 9:00 A.M. and 4:00 P.M.

This company organizes bus tours of Rome and excursions outside the city daily. Book in advance and arrive fifteen minutes before your scheduled departure for Rome trips. The half-day tours to Tivoli include a visit to the impressive Hadrian's Villa.

ENJOY ROME

Via Varese 39. Tel. 6/ 44 51 843.
Cost: L40,000 on up.
Credit Cards: AE, MC, V.
Hours of Operation: Mon.–Fri. 8:30 A.M.–6:00 P.M., Sat. 8:30 A.M.–1:00 P.M.

This friendly English-speaking company is a useful resource for information and advice about the many aspects of traveling in Rome. It has a phone line open until 10:00 P.M. each weekday evening, and can arrange bus tours. It is located near the main railway station.

GREEN LINE TOURS
Via Farini 5a. Tel. 6/ 48 27 480.
Cost: Three-hour tours, L40,000; day trips, L180,000.
Credit Cards: AE, DC, V.
Hours of Operation: Daily 6:30 A.M.–9:00 P.M.

This is where you can sign up for a coach tour of Rome or any of a number of day trips outside town.

HELICOPTER TOURS

CENTRO SPERIMENTALE DAVIAZIONE
Via Salaria 825, Aeroporto dell'Uribe.
Tel. 6/ 88 64 0035, fax 6/ 88 32 84 27.
Cost: Call or fax for information concerning the cost of a helicopter tour.
Credit Cards: None accepted. Cash only.
Hours of Operation: Mon.–Fri. 9:00 A.M.–6:00 P.M.

Reserve this helicopter tour a week in advance, and plan to take the tour with a minimum of five passengers. This twenty-minute helicopter flight offers a bird's-eye view of Rome.

HORSE-DRAWN CARRIAGES

Cost: Around L80,000 per hour.
Credit Cards: Not accepted. Cash only.
Hours of Operation: Daily during daylight hours only.

For a relaxing tour of the town, hire a carriage in the Piazza di Spagna, Piazza Navona, St. Peter's Square, Via Veneto, or Villa Borghese. Carriages accommodate up to five passengers and can be rented by the hour, half-day or full-day, for about L80,000 per hour. Check that the cost is an hourly, rather than per person, rate.

PRIVATE TOURS

RUBEN POPPER

Via dei Levii. Tel. 6/ 76 10 901.

Follow in the footsteps of this English-speaking German who has lived in Rome over thirty years, as he leads walking tours of the city.

PETER ZALEWSKI

Via Cristoforo Colombo, Marcellina di Roma.
Tel. 6/ 774 425 451.

History and archaeology buffs may enjoy a tour conducted by this group. A team of professionals in both fields will lead private English-speaking tours or excursions of Rome and outlying areas.

WALKING TOURS

Rome's cultural associations of the museums and monuments offer free Sunday morning walking tours with guides. This is a charming way to learn about the city if you have a working knowledge of the Italian language. Check daily newspapers for announcements.

AMERICAN EXPRESS

Piazza di Spagna, 38. Tel. 6/ 67 641.
Cost: L40,000–L56,000
Credit Cards: AE.
Hours of Operation: Mon.–Fri. 9:00 A.M.–5:30 P.M., Sat. 9:00 A.M.–12:30 P.M.

This group organizes city tours with English-speaking guides. The walking tours last three to four hours.

ENJOY ROME

Via Varese, 39. Tel. 6/ 44 51 843.
Cost: L23,000.
Credit Cards: Not accepted.
Hours of Operation: Mon.–Fri. 8:30 A.M.–6:00 P.M., Sat. 8:30 A.M.–1:00 P.M.

This friendly English-speaking company is a useful

resource for information and advice about the many aspects of traveling in Rome. It has a phone line open until 10:00 P.M. each weekday evening, and can arrange walking tours. It is located near the main railway station.

ROMAN CATHOLIC FATHERS OF ATONEMENT

Via Santa Maria dell'Anima. Tel. 6/ 68 79 552.
Cost: No charge.
Credit Cards: Not applicable.
Hours of Operation: Friday morning tours.

Enjoy a free, English-speaking lecture on Thursday mornings or a walking tour of the city and the Vatican on Friday mornings with these ecumenical Fathers of Atonement. There is no charge for the lectures and tours, but donations are appropriate and appreciated.

SECRET WALKS IN ROME

Via dei Quattro Cantoni, 6. Tel. 6/ 39 72 8728.
Cost: Membership fee, L3,000, plus L12,000 each walking tour; 20% discount for students; children under 15 are free when accompanied by an adult.
Credit Cards: None accepted.

The less well-known sights of Rome come alive on these tours conducted by English-speaking actors and residents. This company also arranges bicycle tours.

Notes

SHOPPING

Rome has many interesting shops, but rarely will you find great bargains. A good rule of thumb for Rome bargain shopping is to buy Italian made items. Some of the better buys are on leather goods, including shoes; plus silk neck ties and custom made clothing. Some great shopping areas are just beyond the Spanish Steps.

You'll find that the shopping hours are very different from those in the States. Shops will usually open between 9:00 and 9:30 A.M., then close for lunch at about 1:00 P.M. During the summer months, they will re-open at 4:00 P.M. and stay open until 8:00 P.M. During the winter months, they will re-open at 3:30 P.M. The higher-priced stores and those on Villa Borgognona generally stay open through lunch. It's not unusual to find smaller stores closed on Monday mornings during the summer months or Saturday afternoons in the winter. Shops rarely are open on Sundays.

The best time to find a sale in Rome is in January. Since there aren't as many tourists here at that time, it means less competition and more to choose from, as well as lower prices.

CLOTHING SIZES

CHILDREN'S CLOTHING SIZES

American	2-3	4-5	6-6x	7-8	10	12	14	16
British	2-3	4-5	6-7	8-9	10-11	12	14	14+
Italian	2-3	4-5	6-7	8-9	10-11	12	14	14+

CHILDREN'S SHOE SIZES

American	7 1/2	8 1/2	9 1/2	10 1/2	11 1/2	12 1/2	13 1/2	1 1/2	2 1/2
British	7	8	9	10	11	12	13	1	2
Italian	24	25 1/2	27	28	29	30	32	33	34

HAT SIZES

American	6 3/4	6 7/8	7	7 1/8	7 1/4	7 3/8	7 1/2
British	6 5/8	6 3/4	6 7/8	7	7 1/8	7 1/4	7 3/4
Italian	54	55	56	57	58	59	60

SHIRT SIZES FOR MEN (COLLAR SIZES)

American	14 1/2	15	15 1/2	16	16 1/2	17	17 1/2	18
British	14 1/2	15	15 1/2	16	16 1/2	17	17 1/2	18
Italian	36	38	39	41	42	43	44	45

SHOE SIZES FOR MEN

American	7	7 1/2	8	8 1/2	9	10 1/2	11	11 1/2
British	6	7	7 1/2	8	9	10	11	12
Italian	39	40	41	42	43	44	45	46

SUIT SIZES FOR MEN

American	34	36	38	40	42	44	46	48
British	34	36	38	40	42	44	46	48
Italian	44	46	48	50	52	54	56	58

SOCKS

American	9 1/2	10	10 1/2	11	11 1/2
British	9 1/2	10	10 1/2	11	11 1/2
Italian	38-39	39-40	40-41	41-42	42-43

BLOUSE & SWEATER SIZES FOR LADIES

American	6	8	10	12	14	16	18
British	31	32	34	36	38	40	42
Italian	81	84	87	90	93	96	99

DRESS, COAT & SKIRT SIZES FOR LADIES

American	6	8	10	12	14	16	18
British	8	10	12	14	16	18	20
Italian	38	40	42	44	46	48	50

SHOE SIZES FOR LADIES

American	5	6	7	8	9	10
British	3	4	5	6	7	8
Italian	36	37	38	39	40	41

SHOPPING DISTRICTS

You'll find the more elegant stores on Rome's famous shopping street, Via Condotti. It's located just below the Spanish Steps and runs to the intersection of Via del Corso.

PANTHEON

Most of the stores that you will find in this area sell religious articles and paraphenalia.

PIAZZA DI SPAGNA

This is the main shopping area in Rome, complete with just about everything you could want. This is where the Spanish Steps are located, and it is under these steps that the most exclusive shopping can be found.

PIAZZA NAVONA

Here you can find all sorts of oddities, along with furniture and even a great toy store. This is also a good area if you'd like to invest in antiques.

THE QUIRINALE

The only interesting shop in this area is a terrific hat maker, Borsalino.

STAZIONE TERMINI

This is a good last-minute place to go shopping. It has all the odds and ends that you may have forgotten while shopping elsewhere.

TRASTEVERE

The main draw here for shoppers is an open-air flea market.

THE VATICAN

Here you'll find a fabulous kids' clothing store, as well as a food shop, and some wonderful mosaics. There are also numerous sidewalk stands and little stores that sell all types of papal items. Most stores will even send your purchase to be blessed by the Pope (this usually takes twenty-four hours).

VIA VENETO

This is the center for leather goods, great shoes, and a good variety of fashion stores.

OUTER ROME

You'll find a good wine store (Enoteca Rocchi), as well as an Italian department store (Standa).

> **Shopping Caution. Don't let your shopping expedition end up a disaster. Pickpockets and Gypsy kids will be persistent in trying to steal your wallet, purse, or purchases. Don't leave purses on the back of restaurant chairs. Secure most of your cash, credit cards, jewelry, and passport in the hotel safe deposit box.**

PANTHEON

ANNA MARIA GUADENZI

Piazza della Minerva, 69A. Tel. 6/ 67 90 431.

Rome's oldest religious shop has a warm, welcoming feeling. Historic art and artifacts as well as religious items are sold here. Look for works depicting Mary, the Mother of Jesus, rosaries, chalices, and paintings of saints. Open: Monday 3:30–7:30 P.M., Tues.–Sat. 9:00 A.M.–1:00 P.M. and 3:30–7:30 P.M.

PIAZZA DI SPAGNA

ALDO DI CASTRO

Via del Babuino, 71. Tel. 6/ 67 94 900.

Aldo di Castro is the largest dealer of antique prints and engravings in Rome, so this is a good place to find something really special. Depending on the age and rarity, items can range from $25 to $1,000. Open: Mon. 3:30–7:30 P.M., Tues.–Sat. 10:00 A.M.–1:00 P.M. and 3:30–7:30 P.M.

ANATRIELLO DEL REGALO

Via Frattina, 123. Tel. 6/ 67 89 601.

Handcrafted silver objects are the specialty here. This store has one of the most impressive collections of unusual new and antique silver in Italy. It features antique silver from Switzerland, Germany, and England, and the new handiwork of Italian silversmiths. Open: Mon. 3:30–7:30 P.M., Tues.–Sat. 9:00 A.M.–1:00 P.M. and 3:30–7:30 P.M.

BENETTON

Via Condotti, 19. Tel. 6/ 67 97 982.

Known worldwide for its colorful sweaters, this store at the Spanish Steps features children's clothing. It offers rugby shirts, jeans, and accessories in a variety of styles and colors for the kids. Open: Mon. 3:30–7:30 P.M., Tues.–Sat. 10:00 A.M.–7:30 P.M.

BUCCONE

Via Ripetta, 19. Tel. 6/ 36 12 154.

This historic wine shop is thought to have one of the best selections of fine wines in Rome. Open: Mon.–Sat. 8:30 A.M.–1:30 P.M. and 3:30–8:00 P.M.

BULGARI

Via Condotti, 10. Tel. 6/ 67 93 876.

One visit to this store is all you need to see why Bulgari has been the most respected and distinguished jeweler in Rome since 1890. For more than one hundred years, its jewelers have been making carefully crafted, original designs. Open: Mon. 3:00–7:00 P.M., Tues.–Sat. 10:00 A.M.–7:00 P.M.

CARLO PALAZZI

Via Borgognona, 7E. Tel. 6/ 67 89 143.

This custom tailor makes suits and shirts for men. With fine fabrics and expert tailoring, this company provides clothing that any man would be proud to wear. Open: Mon. 3:30–7:30 P.M., Tues.–Sat. 9:30 A.M.–1:00 P.M. and 3:30–7:30 P.M. In July and August, closed Saturday afternoons instead of Monday mornings.

CESARI

Via del Babuino, 195. Tel. 6/ 36 13 451.

Fine lingerie, linens, towels, and handkerchiefs are Cesari's specialty. Ask to have an item embroidered or monogrammed. Open: Mon. 3:30–7:30 P.M., Tues.–Sat. 9:00 A.M.–1:00 P.M. and 3:30–7:30 P.M.

LA CICOGNA

Via Frattina, 138. Tel. 6/ 67 91 912.

Fabulous children's fashions, clothing for expectant mothers, and baby accessories are the specialties here. It carries just about anything that you could imagine a child would need. Open: Mon.–Sat. 9:30 A.M.–7:30 P.M.

THE COLLEGE

Via Vittoria, 52. Tel. 6/ 67 84 073.

Children's fashions are the primary subject at The

College. There is, however, apparel for men and women in limited quantity. Open: Mon. 3:30–7:30 P.M., Tues.–Sat. 9:30 A.M.–1:00 P.M. and 3:30–7:30 P.M.

DOMINICI

Via del Corso, 14. Tel. 6/ 36 10 591.

The entire family is sure to leave this store well-shod. It offers a variety of colors and styles of men's, women's, and children's shoes. Open: Mon. 3:30–8:00 P.M., Tues. –Sat. 9:30 A.M.–1:00 P.M. and 3:30–8:00 P.M.

FEDERICO BUCCELLATI

Via Condotti, 31. Tel. 6/ 67 90 329.

World-renowned for its gold and silverware, Buccellati also offers fine handmade jewelry. It is one of Italy's finest gold- and silversmiths. Open: Tues.–Sat. 10:00 A.M.–1:30 P.M. and 3:00–7:00 P.M.

FENDI

Via Borgognona, 36A-39. Tel. 6/ 67 97 641.

The central store of this well-known leather goods specialist covers a block. This family-owned business, operated by the five Fendi sisters, has burgeoned into a quarter of a billion dollar business annually. If you're visiting anytime during January and July, don't miss the great sale. Known primarily for fine, expensive leather goods, Fendi also sells clothing, furs, gift items, and home furnishings. Open: Mon. 3:30–7:30 P.M., Tues.–Sat. 9:30 A.M.–7:30 P.M.

GIANFRANCO FERRÉ

Via Borgognona, 6. Tel. 6/ 67 97 445.

Some of the world's most fashion-conscious men wear the Ferré label. Everything is expensive in this famous line of clothing for men, even the T-shirts. Open: Mon.–Thurs. 9:30 A.M.–1:00 P.M. and 3:30–7:30 P.M., Fri. and Sat. 9:30 A.M.–7:30 P.M.

GIANNI VERSACE UOMO

Via Borgognona, 36. Tel. 6/ 67 95 292.

You'll find a deluxe assortment of fashion-forward

men's wear and well-designed household items such as pillows and dishes at this store. Open: Mon. 3:30–7:30 P.M., Tues.–Sat. 9:00 A.M.–1:30 P.M. and 3:30–7:30 P.M.

GUCCI

Via Condotti, 8. Tel. 6/ 67 90 405.

One of the best-known names in high-class leather goods. Gucci sells such items as handbags, suitcases, shoes, and desk accessories. Moderately expensive. The gift wrap is beautiful. Open: Mon. 3:00–7:00 P.M., Tues.–Sat. 10:00 A.M.–7:00 P.M.

THE LION BOOKSHOP

Via del Babuino, 181. Tel. 6/ 32 25 837.

Rome's oldest book shop selling English-language and children's books, the Lion specializes in the literature of England and America. It's a good place for browsers and serious buyers. Open: Mon.–Sat. 9:30 A.M.–1:30 P.M. and 3:30–7:30 P.M.

MAX MARA

Via Condotti, 46. Tel. 6/ 67 93 638.

There's at least one of these chain stores in just about every city that you visit in Italy. It offers a great selection of Italian casual wear. Though it's not inexpensive, Italian clothing costs about 30% less in Italy than in the United States. Open: Mon. 3:00–9:00 P.M., Tues.–Sat. 10:00 A.M.–7:00 P.M.

OLIVER

Via del Babuino, 61. Tel. 6/ 67 98 314.

Stylish men and women will be pleased with this store. It has a tempting selection of easy-going sportswear. Open: Mon. 3:00–7:00 P.M., Tues.–Sat. 10:00 A.M.–7:00 P.M.

LA RINASCENTE

Via del Corso, 189. Tel. 6/ 67 97 691.

This, Italy's answer to the department store, advertises on billboards and in the newspaper. Shop here for clothing, hosiery, cosmetics, perfume, and many other goods, or simply stroll through and compare it with your favorite store back home. Open: Mon. 2:00–7:30 P.M., Tues.–Sat. 9:30 A.M.–7:30 P.M.

RIZZOLI

Largo Chigi, 15. Tel. 6/ 67 96 641.

Rizzoli is just the store for multilingual bibliophiles. It has one of the largest collections of Italian language books, and plenty of titles in German, Spanish, French, and English. Open: Mon. 2:30–7:30 P.M., Tues.–Sat. 9:00 A.M.–2:00 P.M. and 2:30–7:30 P.M.

SALVATORE FERRAGAMO

Via Condotti, 73-74 & Via Condotti, 66. Tel. 6/ 67 81 130.

Salvatore Ferragamo is one of the world's top shoe stores. These stores stock classic yet fashion-conscious shoes, as well as women's clothing and leather goods. Their silk signature scarves are quite a feature. Open: Mon. 3:00–7:00 P.M., Tues.–Sat. 10:00 A.M.–7:00 P.M.

SERGIO VALENTE BEAUTY CENTER

Via Condotti, 11. Tel. 6/ 67 94 515.

The English-speaking staff at this beauty center can take care of your pampering while you're in Rome. Hair coloring, styling, facials, manicures, and massages are offered. Open: Tues.–Sat. 9:30 A.M.–6:00 P.M.

VALENTINO

Via Mario de Fiori, 22. Tel. 6/ 67 83 656.

Shopping at Valentino is an event. Everyone who shops here leaves feeling very special indeed. But, like many great experiences, this one comes with a pretty hefty price tag. Open: Mon. 3:00–7:00 P.M., Tues.–Sat. 10:00 A.M.–7:00 P.M.

VANILLA

Via Frattina, 37. Tel. 6/ 67 90 638.

Those who like a little adventure in their wardrobe will like this boutique especially for women. It specializes in handmade, elaborate designs and avant-garde, imaginative creations. Open: Mon. 3:30–7:30 P.M., Tues.–Sat. 9:30 A.M.–7:30 P.M.

PIAZZA NAVONA

LA CITTÀ DEL SOLE

Via della Scrofa, 65. Tel. 6/ 68 75 404.

This toy store can overload the senses. The selection ranges from simple to extravagant, and prices run from cheap to exorbitant. Children and adults alike are sure to find many, many things to interest them. Open: Mon. 3:00–8:00 P.M., Tues.–Sat. 10:00 A.M.–7:30 P.M.

GALLERIA CORONARI

Via dei Coronari, 59. Tel. 6/ 68 69 917.

This is a great place to find a one-of-a-kind something for your home. The collection of treasures here includes jewelry, paintings, dolls, picture frames from the 1800s, and furniture from the 1700s to the present. Open: Mon. 3:30–7:30 P.M., Tues.–Sat. 10:00 A.M.–1:00 P.M. and 3:30–7:30 P.M.

THE QUIRINALE

BORSALINO

Via IV Novembre, 157B. Tel. 6/ 67 94 192.

This famous hat maker offers toppers for men and women. Choose a contemporary cap, or a style that dates to the 1930s. The store also sells trousers and suits. Open: Mon. 3:30–8:00 P.M., Tues.–Sat. 9:00 A.M.–1:00 P.M. and 3:30–8:00 P.M.

STAZIONE TERMINI

CESARE DIOMEDI LEATHER GOODS

Via Vittorio Emanuele Orlando, 96-97. Tel. 6/ 48 84 822.

The merchandise here is as charming as the store in

which it is sold. It offers a collection of leather goods, jeweled umbrellas, and gold cigarette cases in its quaint two-story space with a winding staircase. Open: Mon. 3:30–7:30 P.M., Tues.–Sat. 9:00 A.M.–1:00 P.M. and 3:30–7:30 P.M.

DISCOUNT SYSTEM

Via del Viminale, 35. Tel. 6/ 47 46 545.

Good quality Italian fashions for less are sold at this store. It's a good place to find famous-brand clothes at reasonable prices. All prices are one-half the original tag price. Open: Mon. 3:30–7:30 P.M., Tues.–Sat. 9:30 A.M.–1:00 P.M. and 3:30–7:30 P.M.

ECONOMY BOOK AND VIDEO CENTER

Via Torino, 136. Tel. 6/ 47 46 877.

Residents of Rome's English-speaking communities shop at this media center. It sells English-language books, greeting cards, and videos. Open: (summer) Mon.–Fri. 9:30 A.M.–7:30 P.M. and Sat. 9:30 A.M.–1:30 P.M.; (winter) Mon. 3:00–7:30 P.M., Tues.–Sat. 9:30 A.M.–7:30 P.M.

LEMBO

Via XX Settembre, 25A. Tel. 6/ 48 83 759.

It's easy to find a gift or something special for the home at this store, but deciding on just one thing may be a challenge. It has wonderful glassware, china, sterling silver, and crystal. Open: Mon.–Fri. 9:00 A.M.–7:30 P.M., Sat. 9:00 A.M.–2:00 P.M. and 3:30–7:30 P.M.

UPIM

Piazza Santa Maria Maggiore. Tel. 6/ 73 66 58.

This is a good place to buy anything that you forgot to pack for your trip. It's a department-type store filled with many essential items. Open: Mon. 1:00–7:30 P.M., Tues.–Sat. 9:00 A.M.–7:30 P.M.

THE VATICAN

BABY HOUSE

Via Cola di Rienzo, 117. Tel. 6/ 32 14 291.

You'll find children's and adolescents' togs by such famous designers as Bussardi, Laura Biagiotti, and Valentino here, as well as other famous brands. Open: Mon. 3:30–7:30 P.M., Tues.–Sat. 9:00 A.M.–1:00 P.M. and 3:30–7:30 P.M.

CASTRONI

Via Cola Di Rienzo, 196. Tel. 6/ 68 74 383.

Gourmets and foodies will enjoy browsing and/or buying in this exotic food store. Herbs from Apulia, peperoncino oil, cheese from Val d' Aosta, and an unusual brand of balsamic vinegar are among Castroni's offerings. Open: Mon.–Sat. 8:30 A.M.–2:00 P.M. and 3:30–8:00 P.M.

SAVELLI

Via Paola VI, 27. Tel. 6/ 68 30 7017.

Mosaics are in evidence at many historic sites throughout Rome, and this company offers some that you can take home. It also sells tabletops, boxes, and vases with mosaic patterns. Open: Mon.–Sat. 9:00 A.M.–6:30 P.M., Sun. 9:30 A.M.–1:30 P.M.

VIA VENETO

A. GRISPIGNI

Via Francesco Crispi, 59. Tel. 6/ 67 90 290.

Leather in Italy comes in many fine forms. Here, there's a beautiful collection of purses, desk sets, leather-covered boxes, and compacts. Some pieces have gold inlays. Open: Mon. 3:30–7:30 P.M., Tues.–Sat. 9:30 A.M.–1:00 P.M. and 3:30–7:30 P.M.

ANGELO

Via Bissolati, 34. Tel. 6/ 47 41 796.

The work of this custom tailor has been featured in *Esquire* and GQ. They tailor shirts, suits, dinner jackets, and casual wear. Order something that's made-to-order and have it sent home. Angelo ships anywhere around the world. Open: Mon.–Fri. 9:30 A.M.–1:00 P.M., 3:30–7:30 P.M.

LA BARBERA

Via Barbera, 74. Tel. 6/ 48 36 28.

This store specializes in optical supplies, and there's more here than you could guess. You'll find a selection of more than 5,000 sunglass frames, cameras, films, opera glasses, microscopes, and binoculars. Open: Tues.–Sat. 9:00 A.M.–1:00 P.M. and Mon.–Sat. 3:30–7:30 P.M.

BRUNO MAGLI

Via Veneto, 70A. Tel. 6/ 48 84 355.

This fashion-forward footwear designer was famous before his shoes made the news during the over-hyped trial of a U.S. celebrity. Dressy styles for men and women are his forte. Open: Mon. 3:30–7:30 P.M., Tues. –Sat. 9:30 A.M.–1:00 P.M. and 3:30–7:30 P.M.

E. FIORI

Via Ludovisi, 31. Tel. 6/ 48 19 296.

This jewelry store offers a good selection of watches, silverware, gold, bracelets, necklaces, and much more. Buy a loose gem and have it mounted in the setting of your choice. You also may have jewelry repaired here. Open: Mon. 3:30–7:30 P.M., Tues.–Sat. 9:00 A.M.–1:00 P.M. and 3:30–7:30 P.M.; closed in August.

ELENA

Via Sistina, 81. Tel. 67 81 500.

Prices on leather here are lower once in a while. Elena sells mostly wallets and bags, and you may find a bargain. Open: Mon. 3:30–7:30 P.M., Tues.–Sat. 10:30 A.M.–7:30 P.M.

GIOVANNI B. PANATTA FINE ART SHOP

Via Fransesco Crispi, 117. Tel. 6/ 67 95 948.

If sightseeing has put you in the mood to buy art,

visit this store. It sells medieval and Renaissance art reproductions, and artworks copied from a variety of eighteenth-century subjects. Prices are reasonable. Open: Mon. 3:30–7:30 P.M., Tues.–Sat. 9:15 A.M.–1:00 P.M. and 3:30–7:30 P.M.

LILY OF FLORENCE

Via Lombardia, 38. Tel. 6/ 47 40 262.

Find something in which to put your best foot forward. Visitors from the U.S. will feel at home here, because the store sells men's and women's shoes in American sizes. A wide range of colors, styles, and textures is offered. Open: Mon.–Sat. 9:30 A.M.–7:30 P.M.

PAPPAGALLO

Via Francesco Crispi, 115. Tel. 6/ 67 83 011.

Visit this suede and leather factory for its quality bags, wallets, and suede coats at reasonable prices. Everything sold here has been made on the premises. Open: Mon. 3:30–7:30 P.M., Tues.–Sat. 9:00 A.M.–1:00 P.M. and 3:30–7:30 P.M.

RAPHEAL SALATO

Via Veneto, 104. Tel. 6/ 48 46 77.

Women are sure to leave this store well-shod. It specializes in well-made shoes in a variety of colors and styles. Salato's also offers children's shoes and other leather goods. Open: Mon. 3:30–7:30 P.M., Tues.–Sat. 9:30 A.M.–1:30 P.M. and 3:30–7:30 P.M.

RIBOT

Via Veneto, 98A. Tel. 6/ 48 34 85.

Outfit yourself from head to toe at this store, which offers everything you could need in clothing, including neckties, suits, jackets, sportswear, and shoes. Open: Mon. 3:00–7:30 P.M., Tues.–Sat. 9:30 A.M.–1:30 P.M. and 3:30–7:30 P.M.

TOMASSINI DI LUISA ROMAGNOLI

Via Sistina, 119. Tel. 6/ 48 81 909.

Shoppers may select lingerie in Italian silks, cotton,

or nylon from this store. Items are sold ready to wear, or clients may order custom creations. Open: Mon. 3:30–7:30 P.M., Tues.–Sat. 9:00 A.M.–1:00 P.M. and 3:30–7:30 P.M.

OUTER ROME

ENOTECA ROCCHI

Via Alessandro Scarlatti, 7. Tel. 6/ 85 51 022.

Ask for help in choosing delicious liqueurs and wines at Enoteca Rocchi. The selection is huge, and the store can ship your purchase anywhere. Open: Mon.–Sat. 8:30 A.M.–2:00 P.M. and 4:30–8:00 P.M.; closed August.

STANDA

Corso Francia, 124. Tel. 6/ 33 38 719.

Baubles, bangles, and beads make it great for browsing here. This department store offers display after display of accessories for all occasions. Open: Mon. 3:30–7:30 P.M., Tues.–Sat. 9:00 A.M.–1:00 P.M. and 2:30–7:30 P.M.

FLEA MARKETS

Be prepared for big crowds at the many flea markets around Rome. Shop early to beat the masses and get the best picking, and remember to beware of pickpockets.

OPEN AIR FLEA MARKET

Trastevere Rail Station to Porta Portese.

This bustling center of commerce sells anything from bushels of rosaries to hairpins, to televisions. By 10:30 A.M. the crowd is as diverse as the market's wares. The unsuspecting make easy prey for pickpockets here, so beware. Open: Sun. 7:00 A.M.–1:00 P.M.

PIAZZA FONTANELLA BORGHESE

Two blocks from Via Condotti.

Considered one of Rome's best flea markets, this one

has just twenty-four stalls, with a varied inventory that includes antique prints, maps, and coins. Some items are brand new, and careful shoppers have been known to find a first-edition book. Open: Mon.–Sat. 9:00 A.M.–6:00 P.M.

VIA SANNIO

Via Sannio.

Shop during the week to avoid the high-crime times. Popular with the locals, this market has inexpensive but quality items, and everything is new. No antiques. Vendors who sell at Porta Portese on Sundays have booths here. There is a metro and bus stop here, too. Open: Mon.–Sat. 8:00 A.M.–1:00 P.M.

SPECIAL ADVENTURES

CANOEING

Via Marcantonio Colonna, 44, Prati. Tel. 6/ 32 16 804.
Admission: Course cost, L230,000; plus membership fee, L20,000.
Open: Mon.–Fri. 5:00–8:00 P.M.

This is a two-weekend river adventure for the outdoorsy type. The canoeing expedition travels the rivers of Lazio and Umbria.

SCUBA DIVING

Via Luigi Rizzo, 83. Tel. 6/ 39 72 2074.
Admission: Membership, L90,000 a year; courses, L250,000–L800,000.
Open: Mon.–Fri. 4:00–8:00 P.M.

Learn scuba diving in beautiful Rome, if you're going to be in the city for many months. This company offers diving lessons that begin in a pool and eventually move to the sea near Rome. Courses last from one to three months, and include insurance, and use of three pools and the gym.

WINDSURFING AND SAILING

Fregene at the Stabilimento La Baia (tel. 6/ 66 56 1647), Miraggio Sporting Club (tel. 6/ 66 56 1802), and Centro Surf Bracciano at Lago di Bracciano (no phone) offer windsurfing. Sailboats and sailing lessons at Castel Porziano (first gate) at Fregene are also available.

SPORTS

PARTICIPANT SPORTS

BICYCLING

The traffic in Rome is congested, and seldom seems to cease. But there are a few somewhat isolated places in Rome where a bike ride can be very enjoyable. There are the gardens at the Villa Borghese and the Velodromo Olimpico, which are for very serious cyclers. Also tempting is the Villa Circuit. For more information, contact the **Federazione Ciclista Italiana**, *Via Leopoldo Franchetti, 2. Tel. 6/ 36 85 7255.*

The following places rent bicycles:

I BIKE ROMA

Tel. 6/ 32 25 240.

Cost: Per hour, L5,000; all day, L13,000.

Open: Daily 9:00 A.M.–7:30 P.M.

This outfit rents bikes from its convenient locations in the Villa Borghese parking lot, Piazza San Silvestro, Piazza del Popolo, and Via di Porta Castello.

NINO COLLATI

Via del Pellegrino, 82. Tel. 6/ 88 01 084.

Cost/Open: Operating hours and costs vary. Call for opening times and rates.

Choose from an assortment of bicycles to rent for a leisurely day of taking in the sights of Rome.

BOATING

Boating on the Tiber is a special experience, or you may prefer sailing on the sea. Rome has all types of boating adventures for visitors, even luxury cruises. For general information on Tiber boat trips, contact **EPT**, *Via*

Parigi, 5. Tel. 6/ 48 81 851. For a list of boat rental outlets and their locations, contact the **Comitario Regionale**, *Via G G Belli, 27. Tel 6/ 32 12 992, fax 6/ 32 10 371.*

AQUARIUS

Via del Casale Santarelli, 41, Ciampino. Tel 6/ 75 84 7352.

Sail on the sea, or take a leisurely boat ride down the Italian coast. This boat-charter company in Ciampino can set you up with whatever you need for wherever you want to go. Call for rates and availability.

AXA-RIGA YACHTS

191 Via Eschillo, Room 51. Tel. 6/ 50 90 222, fax 6/ 50 91 7530.

Cost: One day, L34,000–L857,000 for up to eight people (includes yacht, insurance of yacht, etc.).

Open: Varies according to the season. Call for availability.

You can charter a boat for a day's outing or longer from this company. Call for rates and reservation requirements.

FEDERAZIONE ITALIANA CANOTTAGGIO

Viale Tiziano 70, 00196. Tel. 6/ 39 66 620.

This company has boats for rent at locations that include Villa Borghese and Lake Bracciano. At Lake Albano in the Castelli Romani Region, there are international sailing championships. Call for rates and availability.

MAL DE MARE

Vicolo del Clinque, 46. Tel. 6/ 58 09 668.

Cost: Call for rates and availability.

This Trastevere bar is a good place to charter boats, organize a cruise, and catch up on boating tips from the locals. Call for rates and availability.

LA MONTAGNA INIZIATIVA

Via Marcantonio Colonna, 44, Prati. Tel. 6/ 32 16 804.

Cost: Varies according to the season.

Open: Mon.–Fri. 5:00–8:00 P.M.

A weekend river trip is a wonderful retreat after sightseeing in the city. This company offers weekend trips at Umbria and Lazio. Call for rates.

BOWLING

BOWLING BRUNSWICK

Lungotevere Acqua Acetosa. Tel. 6/ 80 86 147.
Cost: One game, L7,800; shoes, L2,000.
Open: 10:00 A.M.–1:00 A.M.

The homesick and those concerned about their handicaps will enjoy a few games at Bowling Brunswick. This large, fun bowling alley will make you feel at home.

BOWLING ROMA

Viale Regina Margherita, 181. Tel. 6/ 85 51 184.
Open: Daily.
Cost: Call for rates.

Somewhat smaller than Bowling Brunswick, this alley is a great place for people-watching as well as bowling.

FITNESS CENTERS

Most fitness centers in Rome are private, so most visitors use their hotel facilities. Private clubs offer temporary memberships, but the fees are generally pretty substantial. These clubs also get crowded because there really aren't that many places to work out in Rome. Americans also might miss the air conditioning; most gyms here do not have it. Just like in many gyms in the United States, Roman gyms are social scenes, too. People-watching often takes precedence over serious workouts, so you'll feel most inconspicuous if you wear the latest workout attire.

CAVALIERI HILTON

Via Cadlolo, 101. Tel. 6/ 35 091.
Cost: Mon.–Fri., L40,000; Sat.–Sun., L50,000.
Open: Daily 9:00 A.M.–7:00 P.M.

This fitness center has extensive facilities, including a sauna, exercise room, steam room, two clay tennis courts, an outdoor swimming pool, and a six-hundred-meter jogging path on the hotel grounds.

CENTRO INTERNAZIONALE DI DANZA

Via Francesco di Sales, 14. Tel. 6/ 68 68 138.
Open: Daily 9:00 A.M.–5:30 P.M.
Cost: Call for rates.

Aerobics and dancing enthusiasts can get their fitness fixes here. It has complete facilities, and classes are reasonably priced.

NAVONA HEALTH CENTER

Via dei Banchi Nuovi, 39. Tel. 6/ 68 96 104.
Cost: Members, L800,000 per year; daily rate for non-members, L15,000 (if presented by a member).
Open: Mon., Wed., Fri. 9:00 A.M.–9:00 P.M., Tues.–Thurs. 10:00 A.M.–9:00 P.M.

This gym is much more low key than the Roman Sports Center, but it doesn't have a pool or sauna. Instructors are friendly and actually will help you. Nonmembers are welcome in the three-room historical palazzo, but call for rates. Guests get a discount if presented by a member.

ROMAN SPORTS CENTER

Via Galoppatoio, 33. Tel. 6/ 32 01 667.
Cost: L25,000 per day.
Open: Daily 9:00 A.M.–10:00 P.M.

This air-conditioned club with an American owner is the gym of choice for the beautiful-body set. It has the most up-to-date equipment, but don't count on getting help from the instructors to use it. Visitors, however, are welcome. There is a pool, sauna, Jacuzzi, two gyms, aerobic classes, and a squash court available for visitors. The parade of people watchers may be distracting.

GOLF

The courses in Rome are generally private, but visitors may pay fees to play. If you would like to play golf while in Rome, make sure that you make reservations well in advance. Visitors will probably have trouble getting a tee time on short notice, any day of the week. For more information, contact the **Italian Golf Federation**, 388

Via Flaminia. Tel. 6/ 32 31 825 or 6/ 32 32 300, fax 6/ 78 34 6219.

Visitors are welcome if they can present a membership card from a golf club back home. You may have to pay a fee. Call the golf club of your choice for details.

CIRCOLO DEL GOLF ROMA

Via Acqua Santa, 3. Tel. 6/ 78 43 079.
Cost: L70,000; discount after 10:30 A.M., L50,000; holidays, L100,000 (very difficult to play during holidays because there are a lot of competitions booked).
Open: Tues.–Sun. 8:00 A.M.–the end of daylight.

Here you can play golf against a backdrop of ancient aqueduct ruins located about eight miles south of Rome. Though rough and windy, it is one of the oldest and best golf clubs in Rome. Visitors are welcome to play on the 18-hole course.

COUNTRY CLUB CASTEL GANDOLFO

Via di Santo Spirito, 13. Tel. 6/ 93 12 30 184.
Cost: Tues.–Fri., L60,000; Sat.–Sun. L100,000 per person.
Open: Tues.–Sun. 8:00 A.M.–5:30 P.M.

A volcano crater is at the center of this golf course with fairways designed by Robert Trent Jones. As one of the capital's most unique 18-hole courses, it features a clubhouse in a sixteenth-century structure with a view of the course. Visitors are welcome.

GOLF CLUB FIORANELLO

Viale della Repubblica. Tel. 6/ 71 38 213.
Cost: Weekdays, L60,000; weekends, L70,000; golf cart, L40,000.
Open: Thurs.–Sun. 8:00 A.M.–8:00 P.M.

One of Rome's newer courses, Club Fioranello offers another choice for golfers vacationing in Rome. Nonmembers are also welcome.

OLGIATA GOLF CLUB

Largo Olgiata, 15, on Via Cassia. Tel. 6/ 37 89 141.
Cost: Call for rates and opening times.

Located about twelve miles from the center of Rome, this club offers an 18-hole course. Visitors are welcome.

SHERATON GOLF

Viale Parco de Medici, 22. Tel. 6/ 65 53 477.

Cost: L80,000–L100,000.

Open: Wed.–Sun. 8:00 A.M.–until one-half hour past dark.

Visitors are welcome here as long as they can provide proof of membership from their golf or country club back home.

HORSEBACK RIDING

Rome offers many options for those who are interested in riding horses. You may rent a horse, take lessons to polish your riding skills, or even tour the countryside on horseback. Tack and equipment usually are English style. For more information, contact the **Italian Federation of Equestrian Sports**, *Viale Tiziano, 70. Tel. 6/ 71 83 143, or the* **National Association for Equestrian Tourism**, *Via A. Borelli, 5. Tel. 6/ 44 41 179.*

ASSOCIAZIONE SPORTIVA VILLA BORGHESE

Via del Galoppatoio, 23. Tel. 6/ 36 06 797.

This Rome riding club is one of the most convenient. The scenery is pleasant.

CENTRO IPPICO MONTE DEL PAVONE

Via di Baccano, Campagno. Tel. 6/ 90 41 378.

This is the club where you can enjoy a scenic nighttime ride around Lake Martignano. It also offers daytime riding.

TURISMO VERDE

Via Fortuny, 20. Tel. 6/ 32 03 464.

Take a vacation from your vacation at this club. It specializes in horseback excursions that last from a weekend to a week.

You'll find listed below a few of the more convenient equestrian centers in Rome:

CIRCOLO IPPICO OLIGIATA

Largo Oligiata, 15. Tel. 6/ 37 88 792.

SOCIETÀ IPPICA ROMANA

Via Monti della Farnesina, 18. Tel. 6/ 39 66 214.

JOGGING

There are many places to go jogging in Rome. Many of the fitness centers have tracks, as do several parks throughout the city. The Villas generally are considered safe for joggers, even at night, but remember your safety precautions if you like to run when it's dark.

CAVALIERI HILTON

Via Cadlolo 101, Monte Mario. Tel. 6/ 35 091.

Open to the public, this jogging path is a third of a mile long. It is nicely landscaped, with many trees, shrubs, and flowers.

CIRCUS MAXIMUS

Along Via delle Terme di Caracalla

Don't jog here after dark, but do try to run through these fabulous ruins if you have the time. Circus Maximus was built by ancient Romans but now nothing more than just a shell remains, but it has a footpath inside. The scenery adds an archaeological flavor to the jogging experience.

PIAZZA DI SIENA

Located in the park of the Villa Borghese.

This grass horse track is open to joggers. The verdant setting makes for a beautiful jog.

VILLA ADA

Off Via Salaria, on the Janiculum.

Benito Mussolini used this area for his private park. It's a good place to go on a long run away from city noise and traffic.

VILLA BORGHESE

Enter at the top of Via Veneto or from Piazza del Popolo.

The beautiful scenery surrounding the network of paths and trails here offers a delightful respite from the city's traffic. One of the half-mile trails winds among the marble statuary.

VILLA DORIA PAMPHILI

On the Janiculum.

Joggers may choose from among three tracks here for a long, relaxing run. This area is well away from heavy traffic.

SWIMMING

You may be surprised at how few public swimming areas there are in a city that gets as hot as Rome does in the summer. Yes, Rome is famous for its baths, but it doesn't offer many swimming pools. If you're staying in one of the better hotels at the center of Rome, this won't be a problem. Those whose hotels don't have a swimming pool may still find a place to take a refreshing dip. Most swimming facilities charge a fee for entrance and the use of the changing rooms.

CAVALIERI HILTON

Via Cadlolo, 101. Tel. 6/ 35 091.

Cost: Mon.–Fri., L40,000/day; children 6–12 yrs., L30,000, under 6, free. Sat.–Sun., L50,000; children 6–12 yrs., L40,000, under 6, free.

Luckily, non-guests are allowed to use the outdoor pool here for a fee. The lush landscaping and peaceful atmosphere make a visit to this swimming pool worth the fee. It's probably one of the quietest pools that you will find in Rome.

HOTEL ALDOVRANDI

Via Ulisse Aldovrandi, 15. Tel. 6/ 86 21 2411.

Cost: Call for rates and opening times.

For a fee, this hotel opens its beautifully landscaped outdoor pool to non-guests.

PISCINA DELLE ROSE

Viale America, 20, EUR. Tel. 6/ 59 26 717.

Cost: Mon.–Fri. 9:00 A.M.–2:00 P.M., L10,000; 2:00–7:00 P.M., L12,000; full day, L15,000; Sat.–Sun., extra L1,000.
Open: May–Sept. 9:00 A.M.–7:00 P.M.

This Olympic-size pool is open to the public between June and September.

PISCINA OLIMPICA

Foro Italico. Tel 6/ 32 36 076.
Cost: Call for rates and opening times.

The general public is welcome to use this swimming pool during summer months.

ROMAN SPORT CENTER

Via del Galoppatoio, 33. Tel. 6/ 32 01 667.

There are two large swimming pools and saunas available here, but you'd better be confident about your body. As mentioned earlier, this club is a venue for the beautiful crowd and they like to display their beautiful bodies. If you don't like to do the same, you may feel a little uncomfortable.

TENNIS

Tennis is a popular sport in Rome, and it's played under precise protocols. The dress code is strictly tennis whites only. Your court manners should be up to speed. Most of the better courts belong to private clubs, so you might have to pay a fee to play. Reserve courts way in advance, because the more popular clubs can be booked solid for days. For more information, contact the **Italian Tennis Federation**, *Viale Tiziano, 70. Tel. 6/ 32 83 807 or 6/ 32 40 578.*

Here's a list of public courts in Rome (membership still required, call for visitor rates):

EUR

Viale dellArtigianato, 2. Tel. 6/ 59 24 693.

FORO ITALICO

Via Gladiatori, 31. Tel. 6/ 32 19 021.

TENNIS BELLE ARTI
Via Flaminia, 158. Tel. 6/ 36 00 602.

TRE FONTANE
Via della Tre Fontane. Tel 6/ 59 26 386.

The following clubs require no membership:

CENTRO SPORTIVO ITALIANO
Lungotevere Flaminio, 55. Tel 6/ 32 24 842.

OASI DI PACE
Via delgi Eugenii, 2. Tel. 6/ 71 84 550.

Swim or swing your racquet here. This club offers a swimming pool and four tennis courts.

Others open to the public:

GINNASTICA ROMA
Via del Muro Torto, 5. Tel. 6/ 48 85 566.

Try getting a game going at this venue. It has five courts available for play.

TENNIS CLUB PARIOLI
Largo de Morpurgo, 2, Via Salaria.
Tel. 6/ 86 20 0883.
Cost: Membership, L13,000; non-members, L15,000 (if accompanied by a member).
Open: Daily 7:00 A.M.–2:00 A.M.

Tennis for the fashionable set is the main attraction at this prestigious club.

SPECTATOR SPORTS

AUTO RACING

Valle Lunga racetrack, Campagnano di Roma, Via Cassia, KM 34. Tel. 6/ 90 41 027.
Admission: Entrance, L5,000; car practice, L50,000; motorcycle practice, L30,000.

Open: Sun.–Sat. 9:30 A.M.–6:30 P.M.

Those with sensitive hearing should bring ear plugs to enjoy one of the world's most popular events. This is an excellent venue in which to see some top-flight racing.

BASKETBALL

Though still second to football, basketball is so quickly becoming a favorite in Italy, Italian teams are attracting many U.S. professionals to play for them.

PALAZZO DELLO SPORT

Viale dell'Umaneismo. Tel. 6/ 59 25 107.

Major basketball games of Rome are played here, but, depending on the season in which you visit, you may be able to see a boxing match or other indoor sporting event.

GREYHOUND RACING

Via della Vasca Navale, 6. Tel 6/ 55 66 258.

Admission: Ticket for men, L2,000; women free.

Open: Wed. and Thurs. evenings and on Sun. mornings.

Women enjoy watching the dogs race free here. Come see greyhound racing at its best at this track.

HORSE RACING

Via Appia Nuova, 1255. Tel. 6/ 71 83 143.

Open: Call for opening hours and rates.

This well-maintained track hosts Europe's elite on the days of big feature races. Flat racing is the main event at this century-old Capannelle track.

HORSE RACING

Via del Mare, Km 9.3. Tel. 6/ 52 90 269.

Admission: Call for rates.

Open: Mon.–Sat. 2:00–6:00 P.M.

The very popular trotting races are held here. Call for a schedule of upcoming races.

SOCCER

Sunday afternoons are game time for Italy's favorite sport of soccer. Without a doubt, it's the leading spectator sport in this country. Its fans take the game very seriously, displaying a passion that few other soccer fans on earth could match. The season runs from fall to spring.

FORO ITALICO

Tel. 6/ 33 36 316.

Mussolini built this Olympic Stadium, which is now the site of home games for the two Roman teams, Roma and Lazio.

TENNIS

Although there are several courts in Rome, there's really only one tennis tournament of any importance.

CAMPIONATO INTERNAZIONALE DE TENNIS

Played at the Foro Italico, Via Gladiatori, 31.
Tel. 6/ 32 19 021.

The Italian Open is held each May. If you'd like to attend any of the semifinal or final games, be prepared to reserve your tickets at least four months in advance. Contact the **Federazione Italiana Tennis**, *70 Viale Tiziano. Tel. 6/ 32 33 807 or 6/ 32 40 578.* If you'd like to see one of the other games, however, tickets for same-day events are not difficult to get. Contact the **Foro Italico Box Office**, *tel. 6/ 36 851.*

OTHER

INTERNATIONAL RIDING SHOW

Piazza di Siena in Villa Borghese.

This equestrian show is held in late April and early May. It's a very stylish event, attracting the privileged set. Competition among riders can be intense. For more information, call the **Italian Federation of Equestrian Sports**, *Viale Tiziano, 70. Tel. 6/32 33 806.*

Notes

PART 6

Out of Town

DAY TRIPS AND EXCURSIONS

Although the city of Rome is packed full of wonderful sights and things to do, it's nice to travel beyond the walls into the Italian countryside where the lifestyle and scenery is very different. Try to schedule your excursions during the week if possible. Traveling on the weekends is not a good idea because the locals travel at this time, resulting in many crowded areas. To the north of Rome you'll see dramatic hills spotted with high lakes. As you travel south of Rome the terrain softens with gentle rolling hills, and the overall landscape becomes green and lush in comparison to the northern areas.

Just after you leave Rome's southern perimeter city walls, you'll find the Old Appian Way. Today many of Rome's wealthy make their homes here. In 312 B.C., the road was paved with hand-laid stones and considered to be one of the most impressive roads in the world. Today you can still see part of the original paving stones that once provided firm footing for the Roman troops as they forged their way to Brindisi seaport.

On the following pages I've listed a few side-trip destinations you may like to visit. I've included sights to see, as well as places to stay and eat in most of the towns. There are several towns that are interesting and not far from Rome. The Castelli Romani area has a hilly terrain covered in wine producing grapes. In fact, this area of Italy has become famous for its wines. Here, you can view the necropolises in Cerveteri and the Etruscan tomb paintings in Tarquinia. Another destination is Rome's ancient seaport of Ostia Antica which still has extensive Roman ruins for public viewing. If you enjoy the scenery of grand villas and lush landscapes, then head for Tivoli.

EXCURSIONS OUTSIDE OF ROME:

SUGGESTED ITINERARY

DAY TRIP ONE:

Morning: Visit Tivoli, about 20 miles east of Rome. See Villa Adriana (Hadrian's Villa) and Villa Gregoriana.

Afternoon: Lunch at Albergo Ristorante Adriano and visit Villa d'Este in the afternoon.

Evening: Dinner in Rome.

DAY TRIP TWO:

Morning: Visit Ostia Antica in the morning, the port of ancient Rome.

Afternoon: Lunch at La Posta Vecchia, about ten miles north of the airport. This was J. Paul Getty's private villa on the ocean, now a luxury hotel. (I recommend checking in to spend the night on your last day in Rome, leaving from the airport the following day.) If you don't plan on spending the night there, head back to Rome for last minute shopping, and remember to toss a coin in the Trevi Fountain, insuring that you'll soon return.

EXPENSE CHART

ACCOMMODATIONS

CATEGORY	COST*
Expensive	L250,000 and over
Moderate	L120,000-L250,000
Inexpensive	L120,000 and under

*for a standard double room

EXPENSE CHART

MEALS CATEGORY	COST*
$$$$	L120,000 and over
$$$	L65,000-L120,000
$$	L40,000-L65,000
$	L40,000 and under

*per person for a three-course meal

ANZIO & NETTUNO

The serene seaside resorts of Anzio and Nettuno are about forty-four miles south of Rome. During World War II many lives were lost at both places. Nettuno has a cemetery granted by the Italian government for American soldiers, and there is a British cemetery in Anzio.

Caligula and Nero were among the wealthy Romans who built villas at Anzio. Much of the port city suffered major damage during World War II, and has been rebuilt. Nettuno is a medieval walled town surrounding a castle that was built for Alexander VI. This city has a rapidly developing modern district.

The ruins of an Imperial Villa, also known as Nero's Villa, dating back to somewhere between the second century B.C. and the third century A.D., is in the vicinity, near Arco Muto. This is the probable site of the Temple of Fortune that numerous pilgrims once visited.

To visit, take one of the COTRAL buses, which leave from the EUR-Fermini Station. Buses depart from 5:30 A.M. to 10:00 P.M. daily. The cost is L4,300, and the ride takes about thirty minutes. If you are traveling by car, you can visit Ostia Antica and then drive on to Anzio and Nettuno.

ACCOMMODATIONS

MODERATE

L145,000–L220,000 HOTEL DEI CESARI
Via Mantova 3, 0042, Anzio. Tel. 6/ 98 79 01, fax 6/ 98 79 0835.

This hotel is located right at the beach. Some of the rooms are on the beach; others that are located in the main part of the hotel, are not. Each room has a private bath with tub or shower, direct-dial telephone with 24-hour switchboard service, and mini-bar. Rooms in the main part of the hotel have air conditioning, and color TV with CNN and the Sky Channel. The annex by the beach has no air conditioning or TV. This hotel, which closes fifteen days in August, has seventy-one rooms, a gym with spa and therapy, and a restaurant. AE, DC, MC, V.

THE APPIAN WAY

The Appian Way, or Via Appia Antica, was built around 312 B.C. It can be reached by Bus 118 from the Colosseum. This runs by Via San Gregorio, Via delle Terme di Caracalla, Via di Porta San Sebastiano, Porta San Sebastiano, and Via Appia Antica, and as far as the Tomb of Cecilia Metalla. Though unattractive and heavily traveled, it was the leader among all roads leading into Rome. It extended from Rome to Capua, and parts are still paved with the stones the Romans laid. Since Roman law forbade burial inside the walls of the city, the Appian Way became the area for cemeteries, mausoleums, and the first catacombs built by early Christians. Romans built great monuments above the ground, while Christians met in the catacombs beneath. There are many sights to see along this ancient road. Buses pass by the Colosseum and out to the Baths of Caracalla, through Porta San Sebastiano, a fortified gateway which now contains the Museum of the Walls. Upon leaving the city, remember to watch for the impressive view of the old walls that surround the city of Rome.

Another stopping point is the Catacombs of San Sebastiano, which date back to the third century A.D., and are built near caves or catacombs, which extend for miles and are in several levels. The catacombs were usually built on land belonging to newly converted, wealthy Christians who wanted to bury their dead rather than cremate them, which was the Roman tradition. San Sebastiano, one of the seven pilgrimage churches, was built here in the fourth century. It is the place where the bodies of St. Peter and St. Paul were kept temporarily after their deaths. The church was rebuilt in the seventeenth century.

The next point of interest is the ruins of the Circus of Maxentius. The Emperor Maxentius built the racetrack in 309 A.D. His son is entombed in the Mausoleum of Romulus there. The marble-lined Tomb of Cecilia Metella, where the daughter of a Roman general is buried, is just beyond. Built around 50 B.C., the tomb and the Circus Maxentius are among the most interesting and impressive sights on the road. From here, you take the bus back to the city center of Rome. The Appian Way eventually turns into Via Cecilia Metella.

CASTELLI ROMANI, FRASCATI

Known collectively as Castelli Romani, or Roman castles, there are thirteen ancient towns where popes and mighty families built fortifications, palaces, and other retreats. Famous for their white wines, these scenic little towns are in the lovely Alban Hills just south of Rome. Many Romans like to have lunch there or visit during the weekend. In the summer, the traffic can get pretty heavy, especially between towns. Visit the Castelli by car and meander along the country roads. You can also take the COTRAL buses, which leave the Anagnina Station at the end of Metro Linea A.

DINING OUT

$ LA TAVERNA

Via Nemorense 13, Nemi, Castelli Romani.
Tel. 06/ 93 68 135.
Price/Entree: L16,000–L21,000.
Open: Thurs.–Tues. lunch 12:30–2:00 P.M., dinner 9:00–10:00 P.M.
Credit Cards: AE, DC, MC, V.

This tavern has a rustic setting and offers a large variety of dishes. Specialties include fettucine with mushrooms and dishes of pork chop and grilled lamb. Seasonal items include wild strawberries or a dish made with large noodles and hare sauce.

FRASCATI

Frascati is a charming little town in the Castelli Romani. Approximately thirteen miles from Rome, it is known for its villas, parks, and white wine. Many historic buildings here were destroyed or badly damaged during the war in 1943-1944, but were rebuilt after the war. Visit the gardens of the Villas Aldobrandini and Torlonia. Frascati is reached by car on Via Tuscolana. After leaving Rome by Porta San Giovanni, Via Appia Nuova continues a short distance to Piazza Sulmona where Via Tuscolana begins.

DINING OUT

✓ $ CACCIANI RESTAURANT

Via Armando Diaz 13, Frascati. Tel. 6/ 94 20 378.
Price/Entree: Appetizers, L12,000 - L20,000; main courses, L18,000–L28,000.
Open: Tues.–Sun. lunch 12:30–3:00 P.M., dinner 7:30–10:30 P.M.
Credit Cards: AE, DC, MC, V.

The best and most beautiful restaurant in Frascati, Cacciani has a terrace that extends over the valley, offering guests a spectacular view. The restaurant is large but it fills up fast, so plan to arrive at an off-peak time. Pasta specialties include fettucine and *rigatoni alla vaccinara.* I suggest the main course of baby lamb with white wine and vinegar sauce. Cacciani, as you might have guessed, has a large selection of famous wines also available.

CERVETERI, TARQUINIA, TUSCANIA, VITERBO

CERVETERI

Cerveteri is about forty-five minutes from Rome by car. It is twenty-eight miles northwest of Rome Via Aurelia or you can take Metro Linea A in Rome to the Lepanto stop. From Via Lepanto, take an COTRAL bus to Cerveteri (a forty-minute ride). It is best to drive to Cerveteri, because the sightseeing is great. There are the beautiful hills of the countryside, medieval walls, and modern towers to see. This city itself is laid out much like a regular city, but its streets are lined with tombs instead of shops, and offer accommodations for mourners. The whispering of the pine trees is about all you hear in this quiet place.

TARQUINIA

Tarquinia is sixty miles northwest of Rome. Take Metro Linea A in Rome to the Lepanto stop. From Via Lepanto there are eight COTRAL buses leaving daily for Barriera San Guisto, a neighboring town to Tarquinia. Visiting Tarquinia can be difficult. Groups, rather than individuals, must be accompanied by a guide to go on the tour. No more than five of the 5,000 tombs are open for visitors per day, because the tombs need to be protected and preserved. You may visit the Tarquinia National Museum and the Etruscan Necropolis on your trip. A ticket for one of the museums admits the bearer to the other.

TUSCANIA

Tuscania is approximately forty-four miles from Rome and fifteen miles west of Viterbo. During the summer take the COTRAL bus from Saxa Rubra. During the winter take the bus to Viterbo, then change buses to Tuscania. This is an experience to see; each part of it has an interesting history. The eighth-century basilicas of Santa Maria Maggiore and San Pietro, rebuilt in the eleventh, twelfth, and thirteenth centuries, offer a glimpse of the very heart of the Etruscan civilization. An earthquake nearly destroyed this area in 1971.

VITERBO

Viterbo is a sixty minute ride. You can take the Ferrovia Roma Nord train to the Saxa Rubra stop where you can catch the COTRAL bus to Viterbo. A walking tour is the best way to see all of Viterbo, among the most interesting of Rome's day trip destinations. It has winding, narrow, cobblestone streets, with ritzy, antique buildings. The fountain and courtyard is a favorite meeting place for visitors and townspeople. Some of the most popular sites are the Piazza San Lorenzo, the cathedral, the Gothic bell tower, and the Convent of Santa Maria della Verità, a church.

DINING OUT

$ AQUILANTI

Via del Santuario, 4. Tel. 6/ 34 19 11.
Price/Entree: Appetizers, L12,000–L25,000; main courses, L18,000–L30,000.
Open: Wed.–Mon. lunch 12:00 noon–3:00 P.M., dinner 7:30–10:00 P.M.
Credit Cards: AE, DC, MC, V.

Italian fare is the specialty and the wine list is fantastic. Enjoy such offerings as *fettuccine allo stennarello*, *ravioli de ricotta e spinaci all etrusca*, and *vitella* (veal) *alla montanera*.

FREGENE

This area is famous for its resorts, with thirteen clubs. All of them are fairly similar. These resorts are not as exclusive as higher-priced locales, but they're a fun and relaxing place to visit. Attire is dressy casual, but bring your swimming suit for a day around the pool or at the seaside. Sogno del Mare features live bands and swimming pools. Gilda on the Beach, Tattou, and Miraggio are popular for the younger crowd. From Via Lepanto, take the COTRAL bus to Fregene.

ACCOMMODATIONS

MODERATE

L140,000–L160,000 LA CONCHIGLIA
Lungomare di Ponente, 4. Tel. and fax 6/ 66 85 385.

Set right on the beach, this hotel offers spectacular views of the water and the pine trees. The guest rooms have air conditioning, telephone, television, and some have a mini-bar. There's a highly rated restaurant in the hotel. Shaded by bamboo, the restaurant sits in the breezy garden. Try the spaghetti with lobster and grilled fish. Meals start at L45,000. AE, MC, V.

OSTIA ANTICA

The ancient port city of Ostia Antica dates back to the fourth century B.C., and is fourteen miles from Rome. Mussolini's government initiated extensive excavations from 1938 until 1942, and new treasures are still being discovered today. The atmosphere is one of historical features in a park setting. Remains of warehouses, shops, baths and barracks, temples, and theaters are something to see. Among the sights are the Baths of Neptune, the mosaic pavement at Piazza delle Corporazione, temples and basilicas at the Forum, Museo Ostiense, and the mosaics and paintings at the Baths of Sette Sepienti. To reach the Ostia Antica, take the Metro Linea B, and change at the Magliana stop, where a train will take you to your final destination. By car, take Via del Mare just south of San Paolo fuori le Mura.

PALESTRINA, SUBIACO, TIVOLI

PALESTRINA

Set on the slopes of Mount Ginestro, Palestrina once was known as a prime holiday spot. About twenty-three miles outside of Rome, it offers a panoramic view of the emerald plains and mountains in the distance. Bombs in World War II exposed the ancient foundations of the Temple of Fortuna Primigenia, which extends far into the plain below. You can take a forty-minute train ride from Termini Station, or catch the COTRAL bus from Via Gaeta to reach Palestrina.

ACCOMMODATIONS

INEXPENSIVE

L50,000–L100,000 ALBERGO STELLA
Piazza della Liberazione, 3. Tel. 6/ 95 38 172.

This casual hotel has whispering trees with a fountain outside, and warm colors, leather furnishings, and autographed celebrity photos inside. The restaurant on the premises has the same relaxing ambiance. AE, MC, V.

DINING OUT

$ RESTAURANT COCCIA
Piazza della Liberazione, 3. Tel. 6/ 95 38 172.
Price/Entree: Meals, L35,000.
Open: Daily 12:00 noon–3:00 P.M. and 7:00–9:00 P.M.
Credit Cards: AE, DC, V.

Interesting accessories make this restaurant visually appealing. There's a small bar where you might enjoy an apéritif before dinner. Roman cuisine is the specialty.

SUBIACO

Catch the COTRAL bus from the Rebibbia Station, and you will get to Subiaco in a little more than an hour. Buses leave every forty minutes, and Subiaco is about forty miles away from Rome. It's better, however, to take a car there, because after the bus drops you off at Santa Scolastica, a convent, you will have to walk to the other attractions. The convent has a library that holds volumes from the first print shop in Italy. Don't miss visiting the monastery of St. Benedict with its nine imposing arches. It has been perched on a cliff for eight hundred years.

TIVOLI

Tivoli is famous for its beautiful location, villas, gardens, clean air, and cascading waters. It is a charming hilltop town on the Aniene, about twenty miles northeast of Rome. Known as a resort for wealthy Roman citizens throughout the ages, it is still a popular summer place. The thermal waters here were considered to be therapeutic. Tivoli's main attractions are the beautiful architecture of the Villa Adriana, the gardens of the sixteenth-century Villa d'Este, and the park-like Villa Gregoriana. The vast and luxurious remains of the Villa Adriana are almost a city in itself, with many buildings, two swimming pools, a gymnasium, two libraries, thermal baths, and more. The luxurious lifestyle was revived in Renaissance times by the owner of the Villa d'Este, the town's most famous site. It is an old monastery enlarged and decorated with frescoes. From the Rebibbia Station, stop on Metro Linea B to Tivoli. Those buses leave every fifteen minutes.

DINING OUT

$–$$ ALBERGO RISTORANTE ADRIANO

Via di Villa Adriana, 194. Tel. 7/ 74 53 5028.

Price/Entree: Main courses, L16,000–L25,000; fixed-price lunch, L30,000; fixed-price dinner, L50,000–L60,000.

Open: Daily, lunch 12:30–2:30 P.M., dinner Mon.–Sat. 8:00–10:00 P.M.
Credit Cards: AE, DC, MC, V.

Dine on the terrace in the summer, or enjoy a meal indoors in a room beautifully decorated with high ceilings, terra cotta walls, and classical moldings. Offerings include such items as homemade pastas, roast lamb, deviled chicken, veal, and a variety of salads and cheeses.

$ LE CINQUE STATUE
Via Quintilio Varo 1, Tivoli. Tel. 7/ 74 20 366.
Price/Entree: Main courses, L16,000–L25,000.
Open: Lunch Sat.–Thurs. 12:30–3:00 P.M., dinner Sat.–Thurs. 7:30–10:00 P.M.
Closed Fridays and Aug. 15–Sept. 7.
Credit Cards: DC, MC, V.

Just across from the entrance to the Villa Gregoriana, this cozy restaurant serves dishes with the wines of the Castelli Romani. Meat antipasto, crespelle, lamb, rigatoni, and tripe are among the flavorful menu items. Try an assortment of fruits and ice creams for dessert.

PALO LAZIALE

The Romans colonized this little fishing village by the sea in 247 B.C. Visit the Oasi Naturale di Palo Laziale, a reserve owned by the Wildlife Fund. It is lush with myrtle and laurel bushes, cyclamens, orchids, and violets, and has hordes of marine birds frequenting the grounds. Mosaics were discovered in 1974 in a Roman villa here, and there's a museum being constructed. Take the COTRAL bus from Via Lepanto to Palo Laziale (23 miles).

ACCOMMODATIONS

EXPENSIVE

✓ ❤ **L640,000–L2,140,000 LA POSTA VECCHIA** *00055 Palo Laziale, Ladispoli. Tel. 6/ 99 49 501, fax 6/ 99 49 507.*

This former private residence of John Paul Getty offers a glimpse into the lifestyle of one of the richest men in the world. Now a private luxury five-star hotel, it is very exclusive and extravagantly restored. La Posta Vecchia, twenty minutes north of the Rome airport, still appears to be a private villa. There is always someone waiting to welcome you to this magnificent, seventeenth-century villa that was built amid archeological ruins in a stunning parkland estate by the sea. After driving down a winding road, you'll arrive at huge closed gates that swing slowly open. The public rooms have priceless antiques, paintings, and carpets from John Paul Getty's collection. There is a library, dining room, living room, and bar. A sweeping terrace overlooks the Mediterranean; it's the perfect place for evening cocktails. Getty added a solarium and an indoor pool before he died, and his Roman archeological museum is set in a private cellar, filled with artifacts discovered during renovation of the property. Getty's old bedroom, now the John Paul Getty Suite, or the Medici Suite, with a sunken bathroom and pink marble tub, are among the best rooms. There are nine double rooms and eight suites with air conditioning. Limousine service is provided to and from the airport. All major credit cards accepted.

PORTO ERCOLE

Porto Ercole, a lovely village on the Mediterranean coast, is a pleasant two-hour drive along the shore north past Tarquinia. It is on the Argentario peninsula, between two medieval castles. The Spanish occupied Porto Ercole for 150 years. Il Pellicano, an exclusive getaway resort, is set there on a cliff. There is a beautiful, long, sandy beach to the south on the causeway.

ACCOMMODATIONS

L42,600–L1,947,000 IL PELLICANO HOTEL

Localita Cala dei Santi, 58018 Porto Ercole. Tel. 5/64 83 38 01, fax 5/64 83 34 18.

An American woman and Italian pilot built this casually sophisticated manor house as their love nest. The Il Pellicano resort, with 34 rooms, is a great place to relax. There's a heated cliffside saltwater pool, or a tiny terrace overlooking the rocky beach that's perfect for sunbathing. Two- and three-bedroom cottages, many with fireplaces, have whitewashed walls, tile floors, beamed ceilings, country antiques, and private baths. They are nestled within the olive trees and gardens surrounding the main house. Ask for full sea-view accommodations if you're indulging yourself. Garden view units are just as nice inside and are more economical. The resort is relaxing and casual, but you'll need to wear a jacket at night if you go to the restaurant for dinner. Activities at the resort include golf, skeet shooting, water-skiing, sailing, barbecues, and tennis. AE, MC, V.

CONVERSION CHART

SYSTEM OF MEASUREMENT

LENGTH

1 inch (in.)	= 2.54 cm		
1 foot (ft.)	= 12 in.	= 30.48 cm	= .305 m
1 yard	= 3 ft.	= .915 m	
1 mile (mi.)	= 5,280 ft.	= 1.609 km	

To convert miles to kilometers, multiply the number of miles by 1.61 (for example, 100 mi. x 1.61 = 161 km). This conversion can be used to convert speeds from miles per hour to kilometers per hour.

To convert kilometers to miles, multiply the number of kilometers by .62 (for example, 50 km x .62 = 31 mi.). This conversion can also be used to convert speeds from kilometers per hour to miles per hour.

WEIGHT

1 ounce (oz.)	= 28.35 grams	
1 pound (lb.)	= 16 oz.	= 453.6 grams = .45 kg
1 ton= 2,000 lb.	= 907 kg	= .91 metric ton

To convert pounds to kilograms, multiply the number of pounds by .45 (for example, 50 lb. x .45 = 22.5 kg).

To convert kilograms to pounds, multiply the number of kilos by 2.2 (for example, 25 kg x 2.2 = 55 lb.).

Travel Diary

Index

B

C